my quest for FREEDOM

My Quest for FREEDOM

George J. Knava

Rutledge Books, Inc.

Danbury, CT

Rutledge Books, Inc.
107 Mill Plain Road, Danbury, CT 06811
1-800-278-8533
www.rutledgebooks.com

Manufactured in the United States of America

Cataloging in Publication Data
Knava, George J.
My quest for freedom

ISBN: 1-58244-051-4

1. Czechoslovakia -- Biography.
2. Refuges -- United States -- Biography.
3. United States -- Biography.
929.2 / 0973

Library of Congress Card Number: 99-067091

Dedication

For my wonderful wife, Madeline,
to whom I am indebted for her help and patience.

CONTENTS

Acknowledgements

Thanks to Mrs. Edith Zeldes for her encouragement and gentle criticism. I am grateful to my dear friends, Mrs. Ora Dennis and Mrs. Geraldine B. Hugg for giving me enthusiastic inspiration to put my life story on paper.

I would like to thank Mr. William B. Tobey and Mr. George B. Cannon, both attorneys, former English Instructors, and avid literary critics, for their insight, comments, and advice for copyediting the manuscript.

I would like to thank Ms. Joanne H. McGrath and Mr. Mike Mills, my helpful and friendly typists, and Judie Mills for all of her editing expertise.

I would also like to thank Mr. John Laub for his artistic contributions throughout the book.

PREFACE

THERE WERE SEVERAL REASONS THAT PROMPTED ME TO WRITE THE STORY OF my life. One of them was my decision to put down on paper how I actually left my homeland—and thus let my sisters, brothers, and their families know what had happened to me so many years ago.

Another reason was that several people I met listened to some short episodes and encouraged me to write my story. I talked about it at parties, in the office where I worked, in a drugstore where I waited for prescriptions, and at club meetings. The people who heard it would say to me, "My goodness, George, this is so interesting, you should write a book!" Other people to whom I talked about my past experiences would say, "George, this could be a movie. Why don't you do something about it?" After all these remarks, as my retirement approached, I finally started to gather notes, having in mind that someday I would really write a book.

Human nature varies. Some people like to read novels, others enjoy mysteries, detective stories, or fiction, while still others prefer biographies, novels based on true stories, or autobiographies. I felt that my story would be interesting for those who like autobiographies, since it would first cover events during my youth in the country of my birth, Czechoslovakia. I lived there under six years of Nazi occupation during World War II, and later escaped into the American zone of Germany when the Communists seized power.

Later, as part of my emigration process, I traveled most of the way around the world: from Nordenham, Germany, to Africa, Australia, New Zealand, the Fiji Islands, Hawaii, Vancouver, San Francisco, and finally, to New York City.

INTRODUCTION

COME TAKE A TRIP AROUND THE WORLD WITH ME—BY LAND AND BY OCEAN liners, across five seas in fifty-five days. It will be a long, long trip, but I will try to be good company to those who join me by reading this book. It should be interesting for the reader who likes true stories, because I will talk about many fascinating events. It will also be geographically educational as we visit many exotic places.

But first let me, your traveling companion, make a confession: I have never written a book before, so I have to beg your indulgence and ask for your patience. However, my English will be easy to read, and I promise to explain everything clearly and carefully. Also, it might be useful to have a map of the world or a globe available so that you can see the location of those places that we will visit. Well, let's get started.

PART I

EUROPE

CHAPTER 1

BIRTHPLACE

I WAS BORN IN MARCH 1923 IN THE BOHEMIAN PROVINCE OF CZECHOSLOVAKIA, that picturesque country in the heart of Europe. It is approximately nine and half times larger than the state of Connecticut. Visitors admire its high mountains, deep valleys, numerous forests, underground caves, rivers and brooks—rich in fish—and lakes full of carp. Thousands of tourists visit the health spas, mineral springs, and the 2,500 castles and other historic buildings. Czechoslovakian handicrafts such as crystal and jewelry are known throughout the world for their beauty and exceptional artistic designs.

I was the youngest of seven children in our family of four girls and three boys. The first child was my brother, Frantisek, born in 1903. Then came my four sisters—Marie in 1905, Frantiska in 1907, Ludmila in 1909, Anna in 1911—and my brother Vincenc in 1914. I arrived in 1923. My father was not too happy when I was born, as he was already fifty-one and my mother was forty-six. Frantisek, who was then twenty, had been out on a date with his girlfriend when he returned home to see a baby brother. When I was older, he told me that I welcomed him with my eyes wide open. I weighed 11 pounds, 2 ounces. A midwife, my father's unmarried sister, delivered us all in our farmhouse. Since there was no doctor in our village of eight hundred, my aunt delivered just about all the babies born there for many years.

In our rural area, there were only 7 farmhouses; three-quarters of a mile away was the main village, which then had 120 houses. We had a very small farm consisting of a few acres of land, with three cows, two goats, two pigs, thirty-five geese, twenty-two ducks, forty hens, one rooster, sixty rabbits, a dog, and three cats. There was no electricity or running water. There was an outhouse across the yard. When we wanted to take a bath, we had to heat water in pots on the coal stove and combine the hot and cold water in a big trough. For privacy, we put chairs around the trough and three blankets over the top of the chairs. For light, we used kerosene lamps and candles. But in 1933 an electric line was brought in from the main village. This was very welcome, and made a tremendous difference in our life-style.

When I was four years old my mother died, at the age of fifty, from a strep throat infection. There were no antibiotics then, or any other medicine to save her life. It was a big loss for our family. I remember only two occasions of being with my mother: the first time she was sitting in the kitchen grinding coffee, with me on her lap, and the second time she was ill with the strep throat, lying in a bed, and she asked me to bring her a mug of milk. I remember the mug was white with a painted cluster of purple plums. Milk was the only nourishment because of her swollen throat. Soon after, in October 1927, she died. My sisters did not allow me to see her. They never discussed the loss of our mother, nor did they talk about her.

As I reminisce, I feel sad that I do not have more memories of my mother. I had no idea what a mother's love represented-a touch, a caress, or any other expression of love. I never remember a word from her, nor do I remember what my father called her. Perhaps he called her Mom or Loisy, as her name was Aloisie. I knew that all my sisters loved me, but they did not show their affection with hugs and kisses.

When I was only five years old, I played the harmonium at my sister's wedding. The title of the song was "Our True Love," which I played by ear. They had to give me a special stool so I could reach the foot pedals. I learned the song after hearing my brother Frantisek play it. He was a musician and played the harmonium, the violin, and the trumpet in the Czech military band. My own musical ability was obvious to all. At the age of five, my father taught me to play the violin.

Even before I was old enough to go to school, the music teacher asked my father if he could borrow me to sing, "Tece voda tece" ("Run Water Run"), a favorite of our president, Thomas Garrigue Masaryk. I sang it at a local restaurant when the town celebrated the president's birthday on March 7. Because my mother had died only months before, most of the women in the audience wept while I was singing.

When I was eight years old, the teacher presented a Mother's Day program in which I sang a song called, "A Child Becomes an Orphan." He also asked my brother Vincenc to play my father during the performance. On stage, I knelt beside Vincenc, who was seated in a chair. In the song I asked, "Father, what did you do with my mother?" My brother answered, "Your mother is dead. She lies in the cemetery near the door, and nobody can awaken her."

While we sang, the teacher accompanied us very softly on his violin. I looked down from the stage at the audience, and I saw women wiping their eyes because they knew we had both lost our own mother a few years ago. I will never forget that program.

Another time the teacher directed a children's show. I wore a clown's costume, full of jingle bells. Just before the intermission, the teacher had me run on stage and say a rhyme in Czech, "Ahoj, ahoj, ahoj, I am a small clown." Then I paused and said loudly, "Intermission." I ran off stage with the jingle bells rattling, and the curtain closed. I could hear loud applause as the teacher tapped me on my shoulder and complimented me on a job well done.

As I was walking home from school, I would sometimes see women working in the fields, either planting or harvesting their crops. I would greet them by calling, "May God Help You!" They would answer, "May God Do So!" They also added, "That's a good boy." Their praise always made me look forward to seeing them.

I was motherless but not unhappy, since I was busy with farm chores, or performing in the music teacher's programs, or fishing. Our rural farm life had its own charm because we knew nothing of the luxuries elsewhere. A luxury for me was a delicious bundt cake that my sister baked on my nameday, April 24.

By this time, my oldest brother, Frantisek, and my two oldest sisters, Marie and Frantiska, had left home to be employed elsewhere. My sister Ludmila took over raising me, while my sister Anna became a seamstress and made many of my clothes. My brother, Vincenc, had turned thirteen and was going to school in a nearby larger town, Chrudim. Life was not easy then. There were not enough hands to work the farm, and everyone had to help. Fortunately, my father was not only a farmer but a skilled musician. He played several instruments and was quite in demand locally and by a bandleader in Chrudim. He played at concerts, funerals, dances, and large weddings, making much needed extra income.

For all five years of grammar school I was a straight A student. I was especially good in art class. One day while walking to school I picked up a leaf that had fallen from a chestnut tree. I took it to class, put it on a sheet of watercolor paper, and traced its outline in pencil. Then I dipped a "foot" pen in India ink and went over the outline. The foot pen made thick lines, which formed borders for the watercolor paint. Next I painted the leaf with neutral colors. It came out so well that I used this method again and again for other subjects. During a school year, we would make sixty to sixty-five paintings, about half of which I took home. The rest were framed and displayed at the school. They all bore my name, which made me very proud. Who knows, maybe they're still there.

As I was the best student in school, there was a certain amount of envy-not only by my classmates, but also by their parents. Some boys challenged me in math or in games, and when they couldn't win, they tried to beat me up because I was very small. When we had exercises on the playground, we had to stand in formation according to height. I was always the last because I was so short.

I was nine or ten years old when my brother's friend gave me a pair of skates. These skates were not like the ones you see now on hockey players. They weren't mounted on boots, but had to be mounted by a crank on regular high topped shoes. The jaws had points that dug into the heel, and the front jaws tightened by a crank at the side of the thick leather sole. In order not to keep falling while learning how to skate, I pushed my toboggan in front of me until I succeeded in staying upright. We had a river behind our garden, so I was on the ice as often as the weather permitted. Soon I was progressing very well with skating.

There were twelve children in our section of seven houses. I was the only one who had skates, so again there was much envy. My father's brother, a manufacturer of winter sports equipment, gave me a hockey stick, and my brother gave me a puck. This was great for me. I chased the puck on the river ice as often as I could, and later I played for the village hockey team.

My sister Ludmila was very good to me, but she also was very strict. When I did something wrong, she would warn me not to do it again, but she never hit me. My father was always in the field or performing as a musician, so he couldn't watch over me or supervise everything in the household. I was later told that he sometimes thought about finding a spouse. Because he played at concerts and dances, he certainly had opportunities to meet eligible widows. However, when he mentioned them at home, Ludmila, Anna, and Vincenc would not hear of it. They didn't want any stepmother in the house. It was naturally very hard for him to accept his children's objections. Nevertheless he did, and consequently he never remarried.

As years went by, Ludmila took care of the farm with my father with occasional help from Anna, Vincenc, and me. My main tasks were to gather greens for the rabbits and to take care of the geese—heading them out from the fenced garden to a harvested field where they would pick up grain that had dropped from the cut wheat stems. Since every farm in the area had so many geese, all the children had the same chore. Usually we were all in the same field with a hundred or more geese. At first the geese would intermingle, but at the end of the day they separated again into individual groups belonging to each farm. Then, with their pouches full of wheat, they would slowly leave the field without any command and march off in one long row. The reason for this was that they knew water was waiting for them in a huge trough at home. Sometimes one or two of them would jump in to bathe in the trough.

I often also took them out to the river behind our garden to take a bath. It was necessary to keep them as clean as possible, because in the summertime their feathers and goosedown had to be plucked to make them feel cooler. This was my sister Ludmila's job and she knew exactly what to do. The geese didn't mind, since it was very uncomfortable for them to have all their feathers in warm weather. In the winter, we ripped off the stems of the feathers individually, creating 100% goosedown. This expensive material went into quilted comforters, pillows, and bedding.

I was rewarded for duties well carried out. Ludmila went to the Chrudim market on Wednesdays and Saturdays. She would usually go by train on the way to market because of the heavy basket full of produce she took to sell: butter, chickens, rabbits, ducklings, white cheese, eggs, and other farm products. Then she would go to the greengrocer to buy me the largest orange available, which the grocer always reserved for me. Ludmila did this faithfully every time she went to the marketplace, so I couldn't wait to see her walking back from the nearby train stop.

About once a year, my father would buy me a pair of new shoes. These were to be worn only to school and church. The old pair would be almost falling apart, and I would finish them off while playing soccer or other games.

Money was very scarce during the Depression. I remember I had only three toys: tennis balls (not for playing tennis, but just for throwing around or hitting with a piece of wood against our big barn gate); a box of square blocks which, after the correct setting, showed a certain picture; and a toy consisting of two wooden blacksmiths holding hammers and striking an anvil. The latter was mounted on wheels and could be pulled by a string. It was a great thrill for me to have such a unique toy, which no other boy in the village possessed. My oldest sister Marie had given it to me, when she came home from her job as a servant for a wealthy mining family in northern Bohemia. Soon after that visit, Marie married and moved some fifteen miles from our farm.

Our family was Roman Catholic. When I was about 9 years old, I had my First Communion. The day before, I went to confession to tell the priest the sins I had committed, such as throwing stones and picking fruit from a neighbor's trees. We were told at school to write down our sins so that we would not forget them at the time of confession. We were also told that we must ask our parents for forgiveness if we had caused them any sadness, or lied to them, etc. I approached my father and he put his hand on my head and said, "May God forgive you." After that I went on foot three-quarters of a mile to church for the confession.

When I arrived, my school classmates were all lined up, holding their lists of sins. Well, now was the time for me to reach into my pocket for my own list. But when I did so, there was no paper. I had lost it! That meant I didn't have any sins to read to the priest. I was frantic, frightened, and didn't know what to do. Then I had an idea. I knew that my friend, a classmate named Jan Kurc, had a bicycle-and he lived near the church. I went to his house and asked Jan if he would lend me the bike. He did, and I was soon on my way home to search for my lost paper with the sins.

Jan's bike had only one good pedal, so it was a very worrisome trip. Still everything went well until I suddenly hit an uneven part of the dirt road and landed in the river. Oh, boy! What to do now? Well, there was no other way than to just get back on the bike and proceed home. Luckily nobody was in the yard, and I retraced my every step until I found the piece of paper. I jumped on the bike and rushed to the church. I left the bike behind a bush and walked in for confession.

There were only two classmates standing before the booth. It was a warm day; I wore navy shorts and a jacket. Of course, the shorts were still a little wet but being navy, they didn't show the dampness. After about ten minutes, my turn came and I recited my sins. Then I immediately went to get the bicycle and returned it to Jan. I didn't tell him why I'd needed the bike. And fortunately, he didn't ask—so I didn't have to lie and commit another sin. By the time I arrived home, the shorts were dry and nobody knew what had happened. The next day I went to church to receive my communion.

A year later, I became an altar boy. We had mass in our church only every fourth Sunday because there were not enough priests in the area, and one priest had to come from the distant parish of Mikulovice. It was a new experience for me to be an altar boy. We were paid only when there was a wedding. The bride, groom, and bridal party went around the altar and dropped money into a designated tray. Because there were two altar boys, we divided the money. It was very welcome, every koruna (about 10 cents) was needed since money was scarce.

In 1933, when I was ten, the time had come for my confirmation. I asked my uncle, Josef Knava—my father's brother—who was custodian and rang the church bells, to be my patron. He willingly accepted. The ceremony took place when the bishop from a large city arrived to say mass. We formed a line, the patrons standing in back of us, and when my turn came, my patron put his hand on top of my head to witness my confirmation. At this time I acquired my middle name, Josef, after my uncle. My uncle gave me a gift, a round pocket watch with a leather strap for fastening to my vest's buttonhole.

I didn't have any picture books, storybooks, or animal books during my childhood. The only picture book I saw was one that we read during the religious hour at school when the priest came every week to teach catechism. I liked the holy pictures and articles in this book, and I almost knew them by heart. I also knew several phrases in Latin, which I had learned from serving as an altar boy during masses. Our priest noticed this and pointed it out to our regular teacher, Mrs. Chalupova,. One day, Mrs. Chalupova happened to meet my father and told him about my interest in the religious book. She recommended that I become a priest, because I knew how to sing and was always a straight A student.

CHAPTER 2

SCHOOL YEARS: THE EARLY GRADES

MY FATHER WASN'T SURE WHAT TO DO WITH ME WHEN I WAS ELEVEN, BUT eventually he arranged for me to go to a school in Chrudim called the "Gymnasium," or secondary school. Attendance there was for eight years. The first-year curriculum included German and in the third year, Latin—which I didn't like, despite already knowing several phrases of the language.

I was the only student from our village to study at the Gymnasium, and somehow the people in the village started to think that one day I might become a priest. They liked and respected me, even after I left grammar school in our village and stopped being an altar boy. I did go to church every fourth Sunday to sing with the choir. When my brother Frantisek played the organ, I stood next to him and sang the hymns. Whenever my brother Vincenc was home he also attended church and sang with us. People were impressed that three brothers all had such musical ability.

Just before the end of my second year at the Gymnasium, I decided not to continue the next year because I would have to study Latin. I told my father about my decision, and explained that I didn't want to become a priest. He accepted my choice without anger. After the summer vacation he arranged for me to go to secondary school, equivalent to eighth grade elsewhere. This change was good for me because there I studied math, which was not a strong subject at the Gymnasium. German was to be taught in the following year. I was at the head of the class again.

One day my teacher, Mr. Hahn, decided to teach French. I thought I would try it. The first word he taught was "garçon" ("boy" in English). He made us pronounce it about fifteen times, telling us to make the sound nasal. I didn't like it and never went to the next lesson.

Vincenc studied English at college, which I heard him reciting while doing his homework. My father had given him money to buy an English-Czech/Czech-English dictionary and out of curiosity, I looked up some words. I used it later when I went to the same college. Before my escape, I packed only a few things in my briefcase, but one item was my dictionary—which traveled with me around the world. I still have it and occasionally use it.

The years 1931, 1932, and 1933 were very hard because of the Depression. Money was scarce. We were lucky that we could live off our farm products, and that our dad was a musician and made some extra income from time to time. Money was needed for the necessities of everyday life; for example, shoes and boots had to be repaired. I remember that the shoemaker came after the grain harvest and brought a bill for shoe repairs he had made during the year. My father offered to pay him with a bag of wheat, which was worth the equivalent amount of the bill. The shoemaker accepted the trade as it had been agreed upon ahead of time. He took the wheat to the flourmill and received flour for it.

One day four musicians appeared in our yard and played a couple of tunes. They didn't know that my father was a musician. My father gave them a big wedge of homemade bread my sister had baked. Ludmila baked six huge loaves of pure rye bread at a time, each weighing ten to eleven pounds. To keep it from hardening, she put in a helping of mashed potatoes. The bread lasted for many weeks because it was kept in the coldest room in the house. Naturally, the last loaf was hardest of all. But even it was put to use by cutting the crust into pieces, which were dropped into boiling water with eggs, salt and pepper. A little garlic was added along with marjoram for aroma. The result was delicious; we loved it. It was called "the beggar's soup" because farmers would frequently give beggars a piece of the last loaf of bread. Traditionally, it was understood that these poor people would make soup out of it.

The musicians and beggars, however, would also take their collected bread to a large farm in a burlap bag. The farmer would pay them and use the bread as fodder for feeding animals.

Vincenc graduated from college, in 1933—the worst of times. At first he couldn't find employment anywhere in the neighboring towns. He continued looking and finally got a job in the Agricultural Corporation in Chrudim. However, the condition was that he must work the first two months without a salary. He accepted, living at home and using my father's bicycle for transportation.

As for myself, my sister Anna made clothes for me, including an overcoat. Somehow my father managed to find the money to buy the material. In turn, I helped Anna by bringing her necessary accessories from Chrudim where I was going to school. She wrote what she needed, and I brought it home so that she didn't have to waste time shopping. My assignment eventually ended when Anna married. But this was not at all bad for me, since she moved to Chrudim and lived a few houses away from my school. When we had afternoon sessions, I was invited to her home for lunch. She was not only an accomplished dressmaker, but an excellent cook. I greatly enjoyed her good meals.

Every winter we would have a pig-slaughtering day on our farm. We would hire the butcher to come and kill a big pig, usually weighing about five hundred pounds. It was an all-day affair, starting very early in the morning. By noon there was food galore. Fresh meat was pulled out from a huge pot and eaten with horseradish on rye bread. Naturally, there was beer to drink. By the end of the day, there were sausages made and excellent headcheese spiced and cooked to perfection. The carcass of the pig was kept in a very cold place overnight before cutting it up, separating the fat, and preparing the meat. The pieces intended for roasting were square; the ones that would be smoked were long and narrow. These narrow pieces were seasoned and hung in a special chamber of the chimney; then a fire was burned for several days to smoke the meat. Only cherry or hickory wood was used to give the meat a wonderful aroma and taste. This was a very big help for our food supply, because it made dozens of excellent meals.

CHAPTER 3

TEENAGE ERA

IT WAS VERY HARD FOR A TEENAGER TO BE WITHOUT MONEY. OVER THE COURSE of the year there were festivals, sport events, the ice-cream man with his tricycle, a thanksgiving feast, an amusement park, and more. Of course I knew when these events were scheduled, and I tried to save money for them. I polished shoes for Vincenc, Anna, and Ludmila, so that their shoes would be shiny when they went to dances. During vacation time I picked hops for making beer.

One farmer had huge hops growing on his vines, and he paid a set fee for every bushel picked. By the end of the season it amounted to a good sum of money for a youngster like myself. During a festival there was a merry-go-round in the village. I used to work as one of several boys up on a platform from which we pushed the merry-go-round. After so many stop-and-go rounds, one of us would get a free ride.

My brother Frantisek, the musician, often played at these festivals. He typically made twenty crowns a day, so I would ask him to give me a crown or two. When my sister Anna had a date with her boyfriend, she would tell me to watch for him. When he arrived on his bicycle I would say that Anna was getting ready. Her boyfriend was quite generous. He usually gave me five crowns, possibly because he thought that I would someday become his brother-in-law. He was also a musician and a cabinetmaker, so he had money.

Since we had a river by our garden I knew how to fish, but it was allowed only for people who had a fishing license. There were supposedly only twelve licenses allocated by the District Office for our village area. The man in charge was Mr. Kurc. But when I asked him to sell me a license, he refused, claiming there were already twelve people who bought licenses every year. I knew who they were. The teacher, the manager of the Agricultural Corporation, the mill owner, and other prominent personalities. So I didn't have a chance. Yet because I had asked for a license, I somehow felt covered in case he should catch me fishing. I fished for three reasons: first, I liked the fish pan-fried in lard with the aroma of caraway seeds and rye bread. Second, I gave some to my brother's family, because he also couldn't get a license. Third, I had a customer in Chrudim, Mrs. Brunclik, who waited for me at the railroad station. When the train arrived, I gave her a little parcel of fish, and she gave me a good amount of money.

Not many people can catch a fish using a noose instead of a hook. I knew exactly where the large fish were sunning themselves: by a willow tree which leaned over the edge of the river. I took very fine steel wire, made a noose out of it, tied it on a strong fishing line, and fastened to a short fishing pole. I sat in the willow's branches until the fish came along, waiting patiently until the biggest fish swam very close to my submerged noose. Then I would guide the noose just behind the gills and swiftly pull up the line. The fish always gave a big fight, but my gear was so strong that it couldn't get away. All I needed was just one nice one for Mrs. Brunclik, once or twice a week, per our agreement. For us at home, or for my brother, smaller pan fish were acceptable, and I caught those easily on a hook.

In the fall, when it was cooler, I caught larger fish using frogs as bait. Sometimes the mill owner let the water drain almost completely out, and there was a muddy spot in the river where I found large carp. The water formed a V in that area where it ran into the main stream, and the carp had to swim into this V to reach the main stream. As soon as I saw the mill's water going down, I took a big basket-woven by my father out of willow sprouts-and placed it in the bottom of the V. Sooner or later, at least one carp would land in the basket. This had to be done quickly, since I didn't want anyone to get the same idea and be ahead of me next time. The carp were a special treat just for Mrs. Brunclik, because she loved fish.

One of my classmates was the son of the school principal. He always had money and sometimes I went with him to the ice cream parlor-where he would devour one cone after another. Naturally, I had to make money so I could buy some ice cream, or at least a piece of chocolate.

Life on the farm was difficult. There was always work to be done from dawn to dark, and when I came home from school I had to perform my chores. As soon as the snow disappeared, the spinach picking started. Every farmer had received an order to pick so many burlap bags of spinach, which had to be delivered to the railroad station for loading onto a freight train.

After the ground warmed up and became workable, the potato planting began. Our village always tried to be among the first to produce and deliver early potatoes to the markets, hoping to beat our competitors in Italy.

Orders came in for 50-kilogram (100-pound) burlap bags of potatoes to be delivered to the railroad station. The same process went on later with other vegetables. Then came grain harvesting, threshing, and delivery. There was practically no time off except when it rained; then there was other work to be done inside the house.

Every year I was allowed a vacation during the first two weeks of July so I could visit my sisters Marie and Frantiska, who lived about fifteen miles from our farm. Marie had married a widower with a six-year-old daughter. He owned a restaurant and needed a wife who not only knew how to take care of a household and child, but was also a good cook. My brother-in-law was lucky, because those were exactly the skills Marie had learned when she'd worked for the wealthy family in northern Bohemia.

Guests came to their restaurant from as far off as Prague, seventy-five miles away. The area was beautiful. Its woods were filled with blueberry bushes, wild raspberries, and mushrooms. There were lovely hiking paths, and the river was good for fishing. I couldn't wait to go there every July, just as I had done since I was six years old. My sister Ludmila would put me on the bus in Chrudim, and my sister Frantiska would pick me up. I didn't like to stay with Frantiska, who lived on a farm similar to ours. I wanted to be with Marie, who had a grocery store with all kinds of household supplies, candy, and lemonade. As soon as I was old enough to ride a bicycle, my brother-in-law sent me to a neighboring butcher shop where I picked up meat products. He also sent me to the small town of Trhova Kamenice—where Frantiska's farm was—to purchase cognac and liqueurs. I would stop by Frantiska's, but only to pay a quick visit. I loved her, but Svobodne Hamry, where Marie lived, was the place that I preferred. When the two weeks passed and the time came to say good-bye, I hated to leave, knowing I would have to wait another year for my next vacation.

School started in the fall, and after classes I helped harvest the winter potatoes and cabbage. Sugar beets—which produced sugar, one of Czechoslovakia's most important exports—were harvested in October. The weather was cold at that time of the year, and it was always a race to get in the crop. Several tons of sugar beets were pulled out of the ground, trimmed of green, and delivered by cows and carriages to either the railroad station or a sugar mill in Chrudim. Sometimes we even worked by moonlight when the weather was good. The season ended after the sugar beet harvest, but my father had more work—plowing the fields for the next round of planting. The cycle repeated itself.

One of Ludmila's most difficult chores was to launder clothes in winter. She had to be very meticulous, because our water came from a shallow well and was rather hard. Ludmila liked to rinse the wash inside the house and then again in the river next to our garden. When the river froze, I had to take an axe and cut a hole in the ice so she could rinse our clothes in the soft river water.

For years and years my poor sister knelt on a burlap bag, rinsing the laundry in that icy water. I would bring her a pot of hot water to warm her hands, but eventually she developed severe arthritis in her fingers. Now 86 years old, Ludmila has a daughter who does her laundry in a washing machine.

Time was marching on. In 1938, changes were coming to our family. I was approaching my fifteenth birthday in March. My sister Anna was out of the house; so was my brother Vincenc, who had succeeded in getting a job in Prague with a large insurance company. Now there were just the three of us left in the farmhouse: my father, Ludmila, and myself. There were not enough hands for farming. My father was sixty-six, still active as a musician; but when he was away playing, the farm work was at a standstill. Ludmila, twenty-nine, didn't have a steady boyfriend, and seemed destined not to marry.

There were different people coming to our farm on bicycles, purchasing fresh vegetables and fruit from our large garden. One of them often talked about his single brother, three years older than my sister, who lived in a small village quite a distance from ours. Then one day when he came for vegetables, he brought this brother along and introduced him to Ludmila. After a few more such visits, the brother started coming by himself.

My father must have noticed there was now a possibility that Ludmila would get married. One day he asked both my sister and myself to sit down at the kitchen table for a talk. He asked us what our plans were. Did I want to take over the farm, or did my sister want it? Because my marks at school were very good, I told my father that I would rather go to college—and that the farm should be given to Ludmila.

My sister's steady boyfriend brought his father for a visit. Obviously, the father wanted to see both Ludmila and the farm. He must have approved of my sister—who was an excellent housewife and quite good looking—because he told my father, "I am bringing you a very honest man, my son Vaclav, and, if you wish, you can give him your daughter." In those days parents had much to say on behalf of their children's futures, so it was agreed that my sister would marry Vaclav Kovanda. But there was one important condition connected with that marriage: Both my sister and my future brother-in-law would have to sign a contract that they would provide all the necessary funds, food, and living quarters for me while attending college. In return, I would, time permitting after my homework, help as much as possible on the farm. Both sides agreed to the condition.

At the end of the 1938 school year we took our written and oral entrance exams for admission to college. The problem was that while 213 students applied, the college accepted only 93. I was at both an advantage and disadvantage. I had excellent grades, I was good at math, and I was fluent in German. But many students who hadn't passed their exams the previous year had in the meantime attended a business school-which had a curriculum similar to the first year of college-and thus were better prepared.

I was very nervous awaiting the test results, but several days later a letter arrived stating that I had passed the exam and was one of the 93 students who had been accepted. When I received the confirmation, I had to let the college know which language other than German I would study. I chose English.

A couple of weeks later I went to visit my sister Marie for a two-week vacation. She was very proud of me, and told many customers in her restaurant that the young man they'd seen there every summer now was going to be a college student.

CHAPTER 4

COLLEGE YEARS AND WORLD WAR II

IN EARLY SEPTEMBER 1938, I STARTED MY STUDIES AT THE STATE COMMERCIAL Academy in Chrudim, one of the leading academic towns in Czechoslovakia. The ninety-three new students were divided into two groups: classroom "A" for those who were taking English as a compulsory language, and classroom "B" for those who were taking French, Croatian, or Spanish.

In our classroom were forty-eight students, twelve girls and thirty-six boys. We had nineteen subjects in our curriculum, including languages, shorthand, calligraphy, international shipping, commercial science, double-entry bookkeeping, typing, geography, and history. The government subsided tuition, but parents had to provide books, school supplies, and transportation. There was only one building housing classrooms "A" and "B" for all four years. Each classroom had its own study room, so that a student's exposure was limited to the same people for their entire college experience. With a daily fare of nothing but hot dogs for lunch, you can imagine why none of us could ever look at one again. If we wanted some different kind of food, we had to go outside to buy it.

On the morning of March 15, 1939, I was walking with a group of my schoolmates down Main Street toward the center of Chrudim. It was our usual route to school—but this morning was a different. It was 7:30 A.M. and a light snow was falling when suddenly we heard an unfamiliar muffled roar. Curious, we turned and saw Nazi forces. Thus began the occupation of Czechoslovakia: with a procession of a dozen armored vehicles, mounted by German soldiers holding rifles, some facing left, some right, ready for possible resistance. We stopped in our tracks and stared in shock; some of the girls started to cry. In a few minutes it was over, the town was taken, and in two days the whole country was under Nazi power without a shot having been fired.

After the vehicles passed us, we proceeded on to school. Some of the students didn't realize what was going on, since they had arrived from a different direction. When I told them what we'd seen, they were stunned. After the opening bell, our professor entered the classroom. He formally announced that the country was occupied, and that everyone must accept it, and that we should avoid any contact with the Nazis. He allowed us a few minutes to calm down, then proceeded with his lecture and the usual daily schedule. But sadness pervaded the school.

It didn't take long for the curriculum to be adjusted. Instead of the usual four hours of German a week scheduled, there would now be seven. And of course, a large portrait of Adolph Hitler soon appeared on our classroom wall.

Because of the extra added hours of German, a new professor was hired who was supposed to be a specialist in the language. His name was Snasel, and he replaced our regular professor. I remember that when he entered the classroom and introduced himself, he said in German: "Von heute ab ihr seid unter meinem Komando, ja?" (In English that means: "From today on, you are under my command, yes?") Soon there was a rumor that he was pro-Nazi. We didn't like him, and we were frightened, but nobody dared show it.

There was constant tension and fear, the constant risk of being arrested for no reason. If someone said something against the Nazis, they were shipped off to a concentration camp and not seen again. Almost all Czechoslovakians were against the Germans, but there were a few collaborators who were pro-Nazi and who often remained incognito. That's why the situation was so dangerous, and why people avoided discussions about the Nazis unless they knew each other very well.

Everyone dreaded the words "concentration camp," but we actually didn't know much of what went on there. Concentration camps were never shown on the newsreels, after the war broke out in 1939, all we saw were German victories. I received some information from a neighboring farmer, who had a very powerful radio. On his short wave, we would tune into the BBC (British Broadcasting Company) when the nightly London broadcast came on every night.

Gradually, shortages increased and people developed methods for bartering and smuggling. Bicycle tires were very difficult to obtain, and everybody used a bicycle. Each village annually received only so many certificates for tires, and the mayor's office had a difficult time deciding who should receive them. The same occurred for shoes and gasoline. But at least in our village there was no problem with gasoline certificates, since only two farmers owned cars. These cars were supposed to be reported to the Nazis, but instead they were dismantled and concealed underneath haystacks. Everyone in our village knew about the hidden cars, but no one told the Nazis about them.

Probably the biggest problem for people in the cities was a shortage of food. Rationing coupons, distributed on a monthly basis, ran out very quickly-and city dwellers practically invaded the farms in nearby villages, begging for anything edible that they could buy. The problem was that the farmers had been ordered to produce certain quantities-known as "contingents"-that had to be sold at a price regulated by acreage, and filed in town records. Some inefficient farmers had a difficult time meeting the Nazis' requirements, while every farmer's yields were at the mercy of the weather.

My brother Frantisek was an excellent farmer, and he had no problem fulfilling the contingent. He calculated how much fodder (ground soybeans) should daily be fed to his cows so that they would yield milk containing the best fat content-an important factor for producing heavier cream and consequently more butter. With his surplus, Frantisek could sell dairy products for slightly higher prices, and use the extra money to make improvements on his farm.

One day Frantisek announced his latest plan: to accelerate production of early potatoes. If he was first with them on the market, he could command the highest price. He built a greenhouse the size of a car garage, where he sprouted potatoes by controlled heating and exposure to the sun. He made up about one hundred wooden trays, placed the potatoes in the trays one by one, and let the sun do the rest. Frantisek's idea worked, and the potatoes began to sprout. Then he hired several women to plant the sprouted potatoes in the field. The results were terrific. He beat the other farmers to market by three weeks and received a better price.

I usually reserved Sunday afternoons for visiting Frantisek, always eager to learn something new. He excelled at pruning and grafting fruit trees, and had become a consultant to other farmers in methods of growing fruits and vegetables. One Sunday he was not at home, and my sister-in-law told me he'd gone to visit the Novak farm. This was fine with me, since the Novaks had a very pretty daughter, Millie. When I arrived, my brother was cutting off the tops of "meruzalkas"-the base stalks for grafting on tree-type gooseberries, or red, black and white currants. That afternoon Frantisek was grafting gooseberries, and he greeted me with, "Why don't you try it, George?" He handed me a few grafts in damp sand, some raffia, and grafting wax that he used for waxing the tree wounds. He also gave me his spare sharp grafting knife to keep. (I still have it and still use it, all these decades years later). Unfortunately, I didn't see Millie that day because she'd gone out visiting.

I brought home everything my brother had given me, changed my clothes, and went right to work. By evening I had made twenty-eight graftings. It took several days to see if the grafts took. I must have had beginner's luck, since all of them succeeded. This meant that instead of having just plain bush stock, I had twenty-eight fruit trees, which in three years would produce plentiful gooseberries. My brother was very pleased with my results and told me that from then on, I could graft anything! He also taught me how to prune fruit trees. I acquired even more in that regard from Mr. Praizler and his book, *"Praizlerova citanka": Praizler's Book of Pruning Fruit Trees*. I met the author when he was invited to the Agricultural College in Chrudim to teach a two-day course on orchards. Although the other students were much older, I had the advantage of being asked by Mr. Praizler to climb up into the crown of the tree, and to cut in places that he pointed out to me. I learned more by doing that than by just watching or listening-and after fifty-seven years, I still cherish his autographed book.

More and more city people were desperately looking for farm products. My brother specialized in potatoes, and he had a good crop every year. One Sunday, many people came to his farm on bicycles with large handbags and metal baskets, mounted above the rear wheel. Frantisek hadn't picked enough potatoes to satisfy so many customers so he made a daring move. He put a harness on his ox, and hooked the harness to the "Devil": a machine with a blade on the bottom that dug into the ground under the potato bushes. While the ox pulled this machine, its rotary steel fingers threw the potatoes up onto the surface of the field. People would rush to pick them up, fill their containers with as much as they could carry, place these on the scale, pay my sister-in-law, and take off for home. There were no informers, nor-even if someone had wanted to snitch to the Nazis-were there any phones. In about two hours, half of the field behind my brother's barn was cleaned out. What an advantage! His customers did the picking for him, and he made money at the same time. Everyone was happy, even though what they'd done was forbidden under Nazi regulations.

But our motive was to aid Czech citizens first, rather than sending railroad cars of potatoes to Germany. Everyone in Czechoslovakia shared this anti-Nazi sentiment. We helped our own first. The feeling of being occupied by an enemy hung over us and dominated our thoughts.

In the early stages of the war, when Hitler was winning, economic conditions deteriorated and it became more and more impossible to obtain food, clothing, or even fabric for women who sewed for their families. Unless one knew of a source, it was difficult to find these basic necessities. I did have a source with whom I exchanged food for supplies. My brother Vincenc's mother-in-law had a business selling clothing, cloth, and thread in northern Bohemia. Many of our local farmers needed these items, so we worked out a system. I would buy their wheat and exchange it at the local flour mill for flour, onions, poppy seed, and smoked pork. It was a barter system that was necessary as money was short and I was still a dependent.

Although Ludmila and her husband had agreed to put me through college, spending extra money was not part of the bargain. While they were good to me, I never took advantage of their generosity. When I was home from school, I tried to help on the farm. I often found a note on the kitchen table telling me where I would be needed that day.

Sometimes I helped even when I hadn't been told. One of our cows was expected to calve any day, and we checked on her frequently. When I looked in on her that afternoon, I saw the calf's nose and eyes peeking out from the mother's body. No one was home, so I had to do this by myself. I rushed to the kitchen to wash my hands and rushed back to the barn. I had to carefully and gently free the calf's ears because they were obstructing the birth. The calf then came out quite easily and fell into my arms. I remembered to place the newborn calf underneath the mother's head so that she could clean it by licking its body. It was a great experience for me, and I felt very proud. The next day the calf stood on its feet, and looked so beautiful with curly hairs all over its body.

Even for farmers it was difficult to obtain butter, lard, and salt pork. We did not really know much about cooking oil, although we had heard of it. My brother-in-law decided to plant a large block of land poppies for the seed. It turned out to be a very good year for the crop, and we had many pounds of poppy seed. The idea was to roast the seeds, press them, and squeeze out the oil. We collected empty beer bottles and washed them. We knew a reliable man, Mr. Gylik, who either had the proper equipment or knew where to borrow it to help us. The date of production was set, and we worked all night extracting oil and bottling it. Naturally, this was not allowed by the Nazi authorities, so we took a big chance. But fortunately, no one knew anything about it except Mr. Gylik and us. The room where the processing took place had only one window that was covered by a blanket. The roasting aroma from the hot poppy seed was ventilated through an open staircase and up into the barn attic. By morning we had made thirty-five liters of poppy seed oil, very clear and very tasty for frying. It was a total success. We paid Mr. Gylik and gave him some of the oil.

One year we had a very good crop of Karlata blumy (Charles plums). The history behind these plums supposedly goes back to the year 1348, when the reigning king, Charles IV, ordered plum trees to be planted in Bohemia. We had plenty of them, but what to do with them? My brother-in-law, who was a very handy and inventive man, did some reading about how to make an alcoholic drink out of plums. Then he constructed a large wooden keg.

We picked as many plums as necessary to fill this large keg, and placed a heavy stone on the lid to weigh it down. In a few days the fermentation started.

After some time, Mr. Gylik arrived with another piece of equipment—a still—and we made thirty bottles of a very strong alcoholic drink, slivovitz. It tasted much like good vodka, so our efforts were a great success.

People living in the cities had a difficult time trying to buy food, other than that which was obtainable with rationing coupons. The coupons were insufficient and what was budgeted for a month was used up much too quickly. Therefore, people had to try to buy food elsewhere. But, food was hard to find and very expensive.

It was common practice on farms that after the geese laid eggs in the early spring the gander was no longer needed. First it would be fattened up, then slaughtered, then consumed at home or it was sold to someone living in a city. Ludmila decided to sell our gander because we needed the money. I was elected to deliver it to a cousin in Prague, who would share it with my brother.

So one spring weekend I boarded the train, carrying the carcass of a monster gander that weighed more than the largest turkey one can buy in an American supermarket. Four hours later, the train pulled into Masaryk Railroad Station and the passengers began to disembark. As we approached the exit gate, I could see that there were a couple of inspectors standing next to the ticket taker.

I paused behind a steel column, which was just wide enough to conceal me. There was no other way out but through the little narrow gate, past the inspectors. I had to make a quick decision. Rather than being caught, I could have sacrificed the gander by leaving it behind the column and just stroll through the gate. But luck was with me. There were about forty German soldiers walking by me carrying all kinds of military equipment. Because they were heavily laden, a wider gate was opened to let them out. I did a daring thing: I mingled with the soldiers and went through the gate as part of their group. The inspectors didn't pay any attention to the soldiers, and the soldiers didn't pay any attention to me. After I was on the other side of that gate, I got out of there as fast as possible and went to my cousin's apartment. It was a close call. Had I been caught, I could have been sent away.

My brother-in-law, Oldrich, sold a piece of pork to a person he knew, not realizing he was a Nazi sympathizer and informer. This man turned him in, the Nazis picked up Oldrich, and he spent more than two years in a concentration camp. When the war was over, Oldrich returned home, but he was a changed man.

In 1941, I was in my third year at the Commercial Academy. I was eighteen and active in many ways. I played hockey on our town's team, H. C. Tunechody. We were quite a successful team for a small village, which had a population of about eight hundred. I remember one game against Skutec, a much larger town. The score was tied, and there were only a few minutes left in the match, when I shot the winning goal.

The fans carried me off the field and gave me a drink of "punch"-which turned out to be cognac. Obviously I didn't have much food in my stomach after just finishing the game, and I immediately felt the impact of the alcohol.

It was the first time in my life I was actually drunk. I slept on the train coming home, but the day was not over for me or for the team. We had a dance that night to celebrate the victory, but this time I didn't indulge.

Soccer always was and still is the most popular sport in the Czech Republic, followed by hockey and tennis. But in my youth, tennis was only for the wealthy and there were very few tennis courts. During the winter these courts were sprayed with water and turned into skating rinks.

For the teenagers in our village, the German order prohibiting dancing was very stifling. We had to have some entertainment, so a local teacher, Mr. Sterba, tried to form a singing group. We got together once a week in a hall that was part shop, part restaurant, and part gymnasium, and which contained the same stage on which I used to sing while attending grammar school. I also joined a gymnastics group, which was part of a nationwide calisthenics organization, and which met every Tuesday and Friday.

The organization was called "Sokol," meaning "falcon," although it had nothing to do with the bird. Male members wore an embossed bronze insignia inscribed with the words "Na straz," which means "Beware of the enemy." I still have that insignia in my collection of mementos. At one point during my journey through Germany, it almost cost me my life.

The singing group wasn't entirely successful. There weren't enough good voices, so it was finally discontinued. Instead, we decided to meet every Saturday evening in a room next to the stage. Although at first we had no phonograph or trained musicians, I brought my harmonica and played most of the tunes to which we danced and sang along.

We were not sure if the Nazis forbade even this, but we continued these meetings. Later we all contributed and bought a phonograph and records. We had some good evenings there. It didn't cost us much money, and there was no age restriction for alcohol consumption. Oldrich, the son of the flour mill owner, often brought a bottle of wine and shared it with some of us—including Jirina, the girlfriend of my dreams, and her best friend, Millie. We kept the group together for some time, since there was no other entertainment except for sports and an occasional movie.

My main focus was on my studies, to ensure that I passed each of the four years of college. I liked to take my books out in the fields during the warmer months: walking between rows of crops and reciting out loud my pronunciation of German or English. My photographic memory also enabled me to learn all sorts of subjects, even when I didn't immediately fully understand the material.

The most difficult subjects for me were commercial science and double entry bookkeeping. We also had to memorize stories about German heroes and quite a number of selections in English. Consequently I spent a lot of time walking and studying in the fields.

Because Frantisek had taught me how to graft various types of trees, these walks became quite beneficial. Along the way I often saw wild fruit trees, and jotted down their locations in a little notebook I carried. In the fall, I took a hoe, dug up these wild saplings, and set them in our garden. By the next spring they were ready for grafting. In two or three years I was selling these cultivated fruit trees to farmers and small garden owners in our village.

Frantisek was surprised and happy that I learned a new hobby, and since he pruned and grafted for farmers in several dozen orchards, he even helped me with the sale of my fruit trees. It worked out very well. Obtaining food was becoming increasingly difficult. Although the last year of college was extremely demanding on my time, I continued helping to find food for Vincenc in Prague, for his wife's family in northern Bohemia, and for my cousin, Frantisek Kmonicek, who also lived in Prague. By now the Nazis were getting desperate, and ordered larger towns to use lawns and parks for planting vegetables rather than flowers.

We still managed to go to our neighbor's house to listen to the BBC for accurate news about the war. All we saw in newsreels were German victories—which we watched at the nearest movie theater in a village about two miles away. We would form a group of boys and girls and walked there as I played marches on my harmonica.

I had my eyes on Jirina Saravcova-the prettiest girl in the vicinity-but she was just fifteen years old, and was allowed to go out only in a group. Whenever I saw Jirina walking home from school, I would jump on my bicycle and meet up with her, offering to hang her book bag on my bike so she didn't have to carry it. I sensed that Jirina liked me, but we were not dating, since she was so young.

After vacation, she was admitted to the school of economics in Chrudim, where she had to stay in a dormitory all week. I knew for sure that Jirina was fond of me when she began to send me fragrant letters if she couldn't come home for a weekend. My father and my sister Ludmila naturally knew about it. They didn't say anything, probably because they looked at all this as puppy love.

One day I finally asked my father what he thought about my "dream girl." He said that Jirina's mother would eventually like me to become serious, but that her father was looking for a rich suitor since the Saravcovas were a wealthy family. I understood and accepted my father's opinion; after all, it was too early to think about marriage. But something happened during vacation when Jirina was home for two months.

The flour mill owner's son, Oldrich Hendrych, began to show a great interest in Jirina. He was a year older than I and had graduated from the same college I attended. Just as my father predicted, Jirina now had a rich suitor-and this created a big problem for me. I was dealing with Oldrich's brother, Vaclav, exchanging wheat for flour from their mill-an act forbidden by the Nazis.

It would be very dangerous if we were caught or if someone informed on us. Everybody was involved in the "black market" and no one we knew had ever been found out. But because I needed his brother to help me, I couldn't very well compete with Oldrich for Jirina.

The war conditions were in Oldrich's favor. During the summer I often saw Jirina and Oldrich together, and gradually I started to realize that he would win her. Oldrich had all the advantages: He was finished with college, he was the mill owner's son, and-in the opinion of her father-a better candidate.

That fall I returned to the Academy for my last year of college. The atmosphere at school was different now. Although the newsreels continued to show only German victories, Hitler had started losing ground. I remember the day the Nazis issued an order prohibiting dancing throughout the whole of Czechoslovakia. It didn't take us long to see why. They had taken over the dance halls for storage purposes, filling the halls with grain.

Time was marching on. The Nazi war campaign was becoming increasingly difficult; the Allies were bombing industrial plants, large cities, airports, railroad stations, train tracks, bridges, and, anything that would weaken Germany. On the front, Hitler was losing so many troops that he had to begin drafting teenagers. German factories were drained of workers because all the men were at the front. Now desperate, Hitler ordered all Czech males born in 1924 from Czechoslovakia to replace the losses from the German work force. This was terrifying for many Czechoslovakian families, since there was a very good possibility that their young men would be victims of Allied air attacks while working in German plants. I was lucky; I had been born in 1923 so I could continue with school.

During the war, spring was the most difficult time to obtain food. Winter reserves had dwindled, rationing coupons were quickly exhausted, and the black market was strong. City people were destitute; some even offered to exchange their wedding bands for food.

Once we ran out of rationing coupons and couldn't even buy a hot dog. There was a butcher not too far from the college who made meatloaf out of horsemeat. We didn't particularly like its appearance or its taste, but horsemeat didn't require coupons, so it had to do.

The butcher sold a lot of it. We called the meatloaf, "better-than-nothing," and ate it with bread or on a hard roll.

With the arrival of June came final exams, which were both oral and written. Each student had to choose five subjects. Three-languages-were compulsory: Czech, German, and English. The fourth subject was commercial science, international shipping, or double entry bookkeeping. The fifth subject was either geography or history. For my elective courses, I chose double entry bookkeeping and geography. As I was a stamp collector, I had a good overall knowledge of countries around the world, and I liked geography.

The date for my oral exams came on June 26, 1942. Every student was given a certain number of days to prepare. The first letter of the student's last name governed the date of the exam. My letter was "K" for Knava, which meant I had eight days to get ready. Some students received fewer days and some as many as twelve. Three weeks before the oral exams were to take place, we had to go through written exams.

To be honest, I was frightened and worried because I didn't think eight days was enough time to study for five subjects. We received a list of almost two hundred questions, thirty-three of which were in English. I had to divide the time according to how many questions were allocated to each subject. I decided to start with English, then give two days to geography, two days to German, and three days to the remaining subjects.

I was determined to study each day from five o'clock in the morning until midnight. I set the alarm clock for the first day and started with the English questions. I finished all but two by midnight. One of those last two questions was the "Bill of Exchange." But I let it go. I had to go to bed and so I'd be rested to start geography in the morning.

Again, I set the alarm clock for five o'clock and studied geography the next two days. The problem was that during the third day, I was getting sleepy early in the evening, and I still had much to study. Another student advised me to have cigarettes on hand and to light one in case I became sleepy. I did just that. (I remember the cigarette brand was "Egypt"). This was a great surprise to my sister, Ludmila, who looked at me rather curiously and asked me why I was smoking. When I told her, she wasn't very pleased but said nothing.

On the eighth day, June 25, I went to bed around midnight, exhausted and worried. I went over all the subjects and tried to think of something that I might have forgotten to review. Sure enough, I remembered that I hadn't studied numbers thirty-two and thirty three of the English questions. I got up, darkened the windows with blankets, and went through all the English lectures—but this time in opposite order, from thirty-three to one. It was three o'clock in the morning when I finished, but now I was satisfied. I was ready for the exams the next day.

There was a lot at stake. I had to pass the exams in order to fulfill my contract to my brother-in-law, and I couldn't afford to repeat a year. I set the alarm clock for six A.M. The train was due at the railroad stop at twenty minutes past seven. My father and my sister wished me good luck and I left, accompanied by my dog, Bonzo. Approximately two hundred feet from the train stop I sent him home. Bonzo was well trained and he knew he had to leave.

On June 26, 1942, at 2:30 P.M., my turn came for the oral exams in English, German, and geography.

I was called by our principal, Professor Vasina, who asked me to sit on a chair across from Professor Ruzicka, the geography teacher. At the end of the wide, long, green table was the director of another college, who was there as a witness, along with other professors, also serving as witnesses. Professor Ruzicka handed me a small box, containing all the geography questions that I had to answer. I pulled out the first question and had to talk about Erzgebirge, (in Czech, Krusne hory, the mountain in northern Bohemia near the German border). Every student was required to talk about the subject for several minutes. The professor was satisfied with my response.

The next subject was German. Professor Zeifart handed me a box and I pulled out the question, "Friedrich der Grosse"—the German hero, Friedrich the Great. Fortunately I knew the story well, and I still remember part of it today after fifty-seven years. I passed.

The last subject was English, for whom we also had Professor Zeifart. He handed me a box with thirty-three English questions and asked me to take one out. Guess which question I pulled out? Question number thirty-two. I was to talk about the "Bill of Exchange," the question I had gone over so late the previous night. I couldn't believe my eyes. I passed, but what a coincidence! I felt lucky and happy!

Professor Vasina told me that I had passed my final exams. He congratulated me on behalf of all the professors and the director, and said that my diploma would arrive later by mail. And, because I had nice handwriting, I was asked to write the names of all forty-eight students on their diplomas.

Outside this room were several other classmates waiting for their turn after me. They asked me how it was going and whether I had passed. When I answered that I had, they congratulated me on my success. That was my last day of school. I returned home.

When I got off the train near our farm, I could see my father in front of the house. I could also see our neighbor, Mr. Sulc, an unfriendly fellow who probably would hope that I had not passed my finals. He was a spiteful man, perhaps because his son, Josef, was not college material.

I was whistling a happy tune. That gave my father the idea that I must have passed. My dog Bonzo ran to welcome me, excited as usual. I told everyone the good news. With my wet eyes, I thanked them for letting me attend college. I had fulfilled my contract; my goal was achieved. The next day, my sister baked me a very nice cake in celebration. When I saw my brother, Frantisek, he also heartily congratulated me.

Before starting my first job, I spent my usual two weeks of vacation with my sister, Marie. This time I went on bicycle. On the way I stopped to visit Anna in Chrudim, and Frantiska in Trhova Kamenice. They were happy too.

During that two-week vacation, my diploma arrived in the mail.

CHAPTER 5

MY FIRST EMPLOYMENT

AFTER RETURNING FROM VACATION, I DECIDED IT WAS TIME TO START working. My employer was the Agricultural Corporation in Pardubice, a town with a population of about 150,000, that was six miles from my village. My friend, Josef Kaplan, a teammate from our hockey team, had already started to work there, and on his recommendation the company gave me a job. There was no transportation except by bicycle to my new place of work. Josef lived a mile away at the other end of our village, and he waited for me every morning so we could travel together.

The company dealt mostly with agricultural products: potatoes, wheat, fodder for animals, but primarily oats for Nazi military horses. Potatoes and fodder for the public were sold and distributed from a warehouse adjacent to the corporate headquarters. The grain was stored in several dance halls that had been confiscated by the Nazis.

Josef was not from an agricultural family. His father was a mailman, and since they had no animals or fields to work, he was not familiar with agricultural products. He was also a graduate of the State Commercial Academy, but in Class "B" where they didn't teach English. Instead, Josef had studied French. He was working with the company's accountant. I was in sales as a buyer of grain and potatoes from farmers.

Because it was just after harvest time, the company sent me to farms in a wide circle around the town, with the task of buying grain, hay, and straw. This circle reached as far as where my sisters Marie and Frantiska lived, so I had a chance to see them when I was in their vicinity. On these occasions I would stay overnight. They couldn't understand why, after all my studies, I had to travel on bicycle from village to village to see farmers and buy their products. But, as I told them, a job was a job—and with the food shortages in cities, it was better for me to deal with farmers, who were the source of produce.

The job was not easy. During the day, farmers were mostly out in their fields, so I had to wait until evening to do business with them at home. Another problem was that our company was new and it was very hard to work against established competition. Consequently, results were not great, but the company understood. Soon, however, I was needed for other jobs within the corporate headquarters-mainly for periodic inspections of the grain stored in dance halls, and for the sale of fodder to the public.

In order to inspect the dance halls every ten days, I had the use of a motorcycle owned by the company. The halls were filled with oats, and it was important to watch the temperature of the grain. In every hall was a thermometer mounted on a long stick. It had a steel probe, with a housing behind, that contained the thermometer. My task was to insert this stick deep into the oats, wait a bit, then pull it out and read the temperature. Then the reading had to be entered into the hall's register. I went from one dance hall to another taking these readings. If my report showed the temperature was too high, the company sent several men to that particular hall to throw the grain and air it out-just like shoveling snow in winter.

There were tons and tons of oats stored in these halls, and occasionally people asked me if I would give them some grain for their rabbits. I couldn't do it, of course, since it was far too dangerous. So whenever they asked, I said "no," but I left the door open and walked away around the corner as if I was doing something else. In the meantime, they filled up their containers and quickly left. These were people who had rabbits but no fields, and since we had about sixty rabbits at home, I understood what they were up against trying to get fodder.

In one hall, I saw many rats as big as young woodchucks. When I reported it, they had to be poisoned. On top of the stored grain there were strings lined up lengthwise and widthwise creating a checkerboard with five-foot squares. On each intersection, there was a little bag with poison (about twice the size of a tea bag), and this was pushed down with the string about a yard deep into the grain. It had to be done quickly because there were many intersections on top of the stored grain. As soon as the little bags were inside, the heat of the grain started to change the poison powder into smoke. When the last bag was inserted, the hall was closed tight, marked with death placards on its windows, and for ten days no one was allowed to open the door. Soon the hall looked as if it were full of heavy fog.

After ten days, three of us came to inspect the result of the poison. We came with the company's small truck. Sure enough, there were dozens of dead rats around the walls and by the door. They had to be picked up, put in special bags, sealed, and put on the truck. We stayed there for two hours, leaving the door and all the windows open to air out the hall. Then, everything was closed; the mission was accomplished. I couldn't believe how effective those little poison bags were.

During the winter months, temperature measuring was not necessary. Instead, I worked in the office and waited on customers in the warehouse. The main business was the sale of grain combined with molasses. This fodder came ready-mixed in big bags, so handling was quite easy. The job was not hard, but sometimes I had to work overtime—without overtime pay—when the railroad car arrived with potatoes or fodder late in the afternoon and had to be unloaded right away.

The most difficult part was traveling to and from work in the fall when it rained. I only had one topcoat and it was not waterproof. When I came home at night there wasn't enough time to dry it, and if it rained the next morning, I just had to wear it wet. Sometimes it rained three days consecutively, which was not too pleasant.

Another problem for Josef and me was blown bicycle tires. Because he was larger than I was, he would put me on the handlebar, drive the bike with one hand, and hold the crippled bike with the other hand. If it was my bicycle with the flat, I had to guide it on foot all the way from

Josef's home to mine. After supper I had to repair the tube to have the bike ready for the next day. Because of constant usage, we blew out many tires. It became a problem getting new ones, since the mayor had only so many certificates that had to last the whole town for a year. To whom should he give them first? Everyone was using bicycles; our town only had two cars, and those had been hidden from the Nazis.

The next year, 1943, was even harder because of the killing of Reinhard Heydrich in Prague the previous summer. The Nazis considered him Hitler's right hand. Many people were murdered in retribution for his death, and the town of Lidice was completely destroyed: 289 people died and the village itself was leveled. The mood throughout the whole nation was tense, because the partisans were increasing their anti-Nazi activities. Once they drilled holes in the bottom of a railroad car full of grain. The storage car was almost empty by the time it arrived at its destination. When we reported this to the German authorities, the Oberstaabsintendant, Lieutenant Colonel Oswald Tobisch, came to our company very angry and distraught. We explained that our company had nothing to do with the partisans' sabotage. The birds on the track had a good meal.

In the spring of 1943, Mr. Mladek, our branch manager in the town of Holice v Cechach had an accident and broke his leg. He needed help because the farmers were coming for seed, fertilizer, and other products for spring planting. Our company transferred me to assist Mr. Mladek, who couldn't do any lifting and was active mostly in the office. This temporary transfer meant a longer commute for me: some eleven miles, one way, on my bicycle. The train went to Holice, but at the wrong time both morning and evening. In addition, it cost money which I didn't have. But the bicycle trip meant the loss of valuable time for me, since now I had fewer hours for my farm work. I was not too happy with the arrangement, and neither was Mr. Mladek, who didn't want anyone around to witness his smuggling deals. I overlooked it and just did my job, and hoped it wouldn't last too long. Fortunately, after several weeks Mr. Mladek's leg healed and I was sent back to headquarters.

The long duration of the war had a great impact on all the population. There were shortages of practically everything; a constant search for food, supplies and clothes. People were despondent; no one smiled. Jewish people, who wore yellow bands on their arms with the inscription "Jude," were seen less and less. We knew from the BBC that they were being collected and transferred into concentration camps in Poland and Germany.

The partisans were increasingly active, so the Nazis started using dogs to search for them in the woods. Anyone who helped the partisans was arrested-and vanished. It was very difficult for the partisans during the winter, because their footprints showed in the snow. Yet in spite of that danger, the partisans remained active and the sabotage continued.

Hitler had spread himself too thin all over Europe. We knew he could not ultimately win the war, but no one knew how long our hard life would continue. From the BBC we were informed about the movements on the front, and we knew about the Allied bombing of Axis industrial cities. But we also knew about Germany's battleship, the Bismarck, and how frequently it was sinking British ships. We didn't like to hear that. We preferred to hear the BBC when it broadcast Winston Churchill's order, "Sink the Bismarck!"

The Allies bombed a few places in Czechoslovakia. One night they tried to destroy a gunpowder plant at Semtin, near the town of Paradubice where I worked. They did not have much luck, as the guiding flares were mistakenly dropped into a populated area behind the Labe River. That night forty-three people were killed and many others injured. The gunpowder plant was not touched.

With the approach of fall, the trips on my bicycle back and forth to work were tiring me, especially on rainy days. I needed a raincoat, better clothes, and new shoes. But as the war dragged on, everything became increasingly expensive and hard to find. The black market was booming-but money was lacking. Luckily, Anna had material for a man's suit, which she had purchased before the war. When she saw how hard it was for me to find clothing, she gave it to me to have a suit made. My brother-in-law didn't like that, and they had quite an argument. But since it had been bought with my sister's money, there was really nothing he could do about it. My material was dark navy and of good quality. I had a very nice suit made from it by the local tailor, Mr. Kaplan.

One day I went for a walk during lunch, and not far from my office I saw a sign in the window of a house, ROOM FOR RENT. There was an elderly lady standing in front. I stopped out of curiosity and explained to her that I rode my bicycle quite a distance every day, which was very unpleasant in bad weather. She said her name was Mrs. Landa, told me her weekly and monthly rates, and mentioned that I could use the kitchen for very light cooking. I told her I would let her know. When I returned home, I had a discussion with Ludmila and my father about the possibility of renting the room. They thought it was a good idea with winter approaching, so I took it for a week just to try it. My brother-in-law's brother, Josef Kovanda, had a shop nearby in which he sold many items, including food. This was quite convenient for me and for them, because when I went home to the farm, I could bring back some produce for them. Although I was paying for the room by the week, I stayed there only when the weather was bad or when I had to work late.

After six weeks the rainy season eased off, and winter was around the corner. Cold weather I could tolerate, but riding my bike in the rain was unbearable. In my rented room I missed listening to the BBC at my neighbors, and the sessions with my friends at the gym. Also, the rent was a heavy drain on my monthly salary, so I decided to move out. Mrs. Landa was disappointed, but she understood. When I said good-bye, she told that if I decided to come back, I would be welcome.

In November it was not unusual to experience frosty nights, and it wasn't long before the ponds produced enough ice for skating and for starting our annual hockey matches. Our team was organized for the season again. Playing hockey, getting together with friends at the local restaurant, and attending gym during the week, the winter went by quite well-in spite of being reminded daily about the war.

The BBC informed us continuously about actions on the front and about Nazi losses. The Allies were bombing German cities and various plants, thus demoralizing the whole country. I remember one spring day in 1944; we were standing on the sidewalk in front of our company's building during our lunch hour. Suddenly twenty-seven silver bombers appeared in the sky, approaching our area. We got out of there in a hurry as air-raid sirens began to sound the alarm.

We rushed into the cellar. In a minute we could hear the whistling bombs falling near us. After a few minutes things quieted down, so we left our shelter. Outside the nearby railroad station was in flames.

We saw two women walking in the street, weeping and holding each other, their torn dresses covered with ashes. They had managed to escape from the ruins of the railroad station, with smoke and fire all around them. Once again, the gunpowder plant had not been hit, but the railroad station, some railroad cars and the maintenance depot were demolished.

It was obvious that the Allies were concentrating on the disruption of railroad services and systematically destroying locomotives. We heard of incidents when engineers stopped their freight trains and ran away. In only a few seconds, machine-gun fire from Allied planes could riddle a locomotive. Soon we knew of several "engine cemeteries" throughout Bohemia, and speculated there must have been an equal number in Moravia. Yet, the Nazi-controlled newspapers and newsreels never mentioned these losses.

After the Allies' invasion of France, we thought Hitler's end must be near. Unfortunately, it wasn't. The Allies had to endure intense fighting in Southern Europe, and met with heavy Nazi resistance. However, they kept crushing German forces day by day, week by week, and month by month. The most effective Allied unit apparently was U.S. General Patton's Third Army.

In the early spring of 1945, I decided to visit Mrs. Landa to inquire if she had a room available. The winter had taken a heavy toll on me and my bicycle, which deteriorated so much that I had to make one tire out of two by putting two halves on one wheel and tapering the edges to smooth the ride.

Tires were still a big problem. Because of my long daily commute, they just didn't last very long. And no matter how carefully I tried to piece together the halves of tires, riding my bike was extremely unpleasant. Luckily, Mrs. Landa had two rooms available and gladly offered one to me. She also told me she had to report vacant rooms to the town hall, because the constant bombing of their cities had led many Germans to relocate in Czechoslovakia.

Two weeks later, a young German girl knocked on Mrs. Landa's door. The town hall had sent her to Mrs. Landa, who had to rent her the other vacant room. The girl was pretty, blond, and about twenty-three years old. Mrs. Landa could speak very little German, just enough to settle the rent issue. After a few days, I talked to this girl, whose name was Gertrude. She told me she worked at some District German Headquarters. I wondered where she had her meals, as she never used the kitchen. Since she came home late in the evening, I assumed she belonged to some German club or organization.

One morning when I stepped out of my room, I noticed there were a couple of magazines on the floor near my door. When I picked them up, I knew they must have come from Gertrude because they were printed in German. I stepped back into my room to look at them, and to my great astonishment saw that they showed half-naked women. I had never seen this kind of magazine before and, as a young man, I admittedly appreciated the pictures of beautiful women's bodies. But I didn't have time for more than a quick glance, since I had to have breakfast and go to work. I put the magazines in my room, and when I came home that evening, looked through them more carefully. Well, what was I to do about this? It put me in a precarious situation: The whole country hated Germans, so to strike up a friendship with any German, even a pretty girl, wasn't very smart. Luckily, it was the beginning of the weekend, so I had some time to mull over my predicament.

I realized what could happen after the war if somebody remembered having seen me with a German girl; I could be accused of collaboration with the Nazis. By Monday I decided against any further association with Gertrude. I simply wrote Danke Schoen—Thank You—on a slip of paper, and placed the magazines in front of her room. If Gertrude were Czech, things would have been different, but I just didn't feel comfortable about the whole situation. Yet the evenings were lonely in a strange house, confined to one room. I passed the time making an album of my loose photos and organizing my stamp collection.

I didn't really feel comfortable or safe in Pardubice because of the Allied bombings. The spring was rainy, just like the fall; the nights were long and because of working late, it was unpleasant making those bicycle trips home, especially on bad tires. But I did go home as often as the weather permitted. Also, I missed hearing the news on the BBC at my neighbor's house.

Suddenly, in late April, 1945, we began hearing detonations from the northeast. They sounded like cannons rather than bombs. The BBC confirmed that Russian troops were advancing in the direction of Czechoslovakia, and that Patton's Third Army was advancing toward Austria. We felt that Hitler's days were numbered, but no one knew how much longer it would take to finish him off. And something else was going on: There was a great influx of German refugees into our country. In late April, we had to allow two German women-a mother and her grown daughter-to occupy a room on our farm for an indefinite time without any payment. We also had to give them wash-up privileges in our kitchen, the only warm room in the house. However, at least they went into the village for their meals and returned to the farm only to sleep.

Because of these new boarders, I came home more frequently to help with translation, since my sister and father knew very little German. Fortunately, the women moved on after several days. It was assumed such refugees were headed west to escape from the Russians. Soon the BBC broadcast that fierce battles were raging near Dukla, as Russian troops moved through the Ukraine. Thousands of men died there during the fighting.

One day after work, Mrs. Landa told me Gertrude had left. Even Oberstaabsintendant Tobisch, the German Lieutenant Colonel, became unavailable and couldn't be reached by our office. The rumor was that his son had been killed while serving in the German Army, but no one in the Company could verify it. He was never seen again.

After May 1, 1945, there were all kinds of German Army vehicles on the roads, mainly trucks with suspicious-looking canvas covers. We thought that the Germans were finally leaving. This was confirmed when the BBC broadcast that Russian forces had won the battle near Dukla, and that German troops were speeding toward Prague. In the meantime, Patton's Third Army was headed towards Pilsen in Bohemia. Without doubt, his Army could have liberated Prague before the Russians. We later learned that because of the Yalta Agreement between President Roosevelt, Prime Minister Winston Churchill, and Russia's Marshal Stalin, the USSR was chosen to liberate Prague. As a result, General Patton was ordered to pull back to the demarcation line near Pilsen.

On May 5, Prague's radio station desperately signaled, "Prague calling for help, Prague calling for help!" In the background we could hear shooting. Suddenly the broadcast was interrupted, and we assumed that Nazis had seized the radio station. But soon it was back on air and again calling for help.

Soviet tanks moved into the center of Prague, and there was a savage battle in the vicinity of the Old Townhall on Oldtown Square. This marked the end of Nazi rule-Czechoslovakia was reborn. However, there was still some fighting in Prague; civilians were searching for Nazis throughout the city, seeking to kill them. This finale went on for four days.

My thoughts were with my brother, Vincenc, who lived and worked in Prague, and with my cousin, Frantisek Kmonicek, and his family. The radio asked people outside of the city to bring in food, since Prague's infrastructure had all but collapsed. Streetcars were not operating because there was no electricity. I decided to go to Prague with supplies for my brother and cousin. Ludmila packed a suitcase with flour, smoked pork, and a couple of jars of lard. I took the local train to Chrudim. From there I planned to hitch a ride, because we had heard that many trucks were headed for Prague. I positioned myself in front of the Hotel Panyrek on Main Street, and was surprised to see my neighbor, Josef Dasek. Neither of us had realized that we were setting off for the same destination.

I was lucky; after a few minutes a large truck filled with British soldiers stopped in front of the hotel. I couldn't understand why and how British soldiers had come to this area. One officer stepped down and headed in my direction. Because I knew English, I decided to inquire if the truck was headed towards Prague. He was surprised to hear someone speak English, and asked me if I knew the way. I said I did, and asked him in turn if he would take my neighbor and me with him.

He agreed, but said he only had one seat in the front. Josef would have to ride with the men under the canvas. This was fine with us. He helped me load my suitcase in the back. I asked Josef to watch it for me, and I went with the officer into the front. He asked me to sit in the middle between the driver and him. We introduced ourselves: He was Howard Kent and Andrew was the driver. We addressed each as George and Andrew, but when I called Howard "Officer Kent," the driver corrected me and said he was "Major Kent." I gave Andrew directions, and we set off along a secondary road that would eventually hook up with the main route to Prague.

I was quiet at the beginning. But in a little while, having decided to show off my English, I asked the major why these thirty-five British soldiers were in our vicinity. He explained they had been prisoners of war at the POW camp in Breslau. After their release, they'd been given this rundown truck.

About an hour later we caught up with hundreds, perhaps thousands, of German soldiers walking in an uninterrupted line, five abreast as far as the eye could see. They didn't have any rifles on their backs, just rucksacks with rolled blankets on top. The road was narrow, and Andrew had to slow down.

After several minutes of driving past this long line of German soldiers, Major Kent surprised me; he pulled out a pack of cigarettes, rolled down the window, and started to throw cigarettes to the soldiers walking alongside the truck. When he finished one pack, he opened another. I didn't ask him why, but I imagined that since he was also a soldier, he felt sorry for them. Perhaps the Germans didn't treat them badly in the Breslau POW camp.

We were still passing the endless line of German troops when we approached the town of Zbraslavice. Suddenly, we heard an explosion. Andrew stomped on the brakes, and he and Major Kent jumped out. It was a catastrophe; the right rear tire had blown out, and they didn't have a spare.

What now? I asked Major Kent if he wanted me to go for help. He said, "Thank you for your kind offer, George, but really, this will take some time. We may even have to stay here overnight, who knows. But I can speak German, and I'm sure someone nearby can also speak German. It will be better for you and your friend to find some other way to Prague. I am sorry this happened."

I thanked Major Kent on behalf of both of us, shook hands with him and the driver, and went to the rear of the truck. I asked one of the British soldiers if he would be kind enough to hand me my suitcase. I thanked him, and Josef and I started off, on the opposite side of the road from the German troops. The Germans kept walking, not paying any attention to the British. Major Kent told me they were headed toward the German border in order to be captured by Americans. They wanted to get away from the Russians, who were somewhere in back of them.

We hadn't even reached the outskirts of Zbraslavice when we saw a wrecker hooking up a stranded Volkswagen on the side of the road. The mechanic was a Czech civilian, but I saw he had two pistols, one on each hip. I asked him how we could get to Prague, where I had a brother and a cousin who needed the food I was carrying.

He told us the best way to hitch a ride would be to get on the main road, where many vehicles were headed toward Prague. As a matter of fact, he was also going that way-to take the stranded Volkswagen to the "cemetery," as he jokingly called it. He also had a lot of rifles on the wrecker. He told us to hop in, sit on the big toolbox, and put a rifle upright between our legs, just as if we were guards traveling with him. He observed that we must have seen thousands of German soldiers walking alongside the road. Three men with guns would be safer than one, even though the Germans apparently wanted only to go west and be taken prisoners by the Americans.

In a very short while we were on top of the wrecker, and off we went. We were lucky to have met this man. Josef and I held the rifles as he directed, but neither of us knew how to operate them, and we didn't even have any ammunition.

After two or three miles, the mechanic suddenly stopped the wrecker, jumped out of his cabin, and stalked off toward the German troops. He almost threw himself at them, and even ripped open one soldier's rucksack. He began yelling furiously: "You swine, you killed my brother, I wish I could kill you all!" I was terrified; I could not believe what I was seeing. The soldiers, fortunately, didn't know the Czech language. Still he took a terrible chance with his outburst. These men were undoubtedly experienced soldiers. We were outnumbered, thousands to three. I had a terrible fright, and when the mechanic hopped back on the wrecker I thanked God we were moving again. I thought the man was crazy to do what he did, since there was no traffic, no one around-just German soldiers by the thousands and only the three of us.

After this incident, we went nonstop for quite a while until we arrived at Malin. The driver of the wrecker pulled over and gave us directions. He said to turn left when we reached a busy road, and go towards Kolin. We thanked him. We didn't even know his name nor did he know ours. I was still shaky from the dangerous action the mechanic had undertaken. But he'd gotten away with it, and we were lucky to have met him.

When we reached the main route, there was a lot of traffic. We could see many Russian trucks pulling cannons in the back. Josef and I stood on the side waiting for the convoy to slow down so we could jump on one of the moving trucks. Finally we saw our chance and hopped on a truck pulling a cannon. Inside, under the canvas, were three Russian soldiers. I knew some Russian, so I said to the soldiers, "Zdrav stujte." Zdrav means health, stujte means stand. This, of course, doesn't make literal sense, so one had to understand it as "Good day." They replied, and didn't seem to mind that we had joined them.

It was getting late in the day, when suddenly we slowed down, and another neighbor of mine, Jaromir Michalec, jumped on the truck.

Neither Josef nor I had known he was heading to Prague, and Jaromir had not known we were either. I was shocked at his appearance. When I asked what had happened to him, Jaromir explained. "I was run over by a wheel of a cannon. I was trying to get on a truck, but I slipped and the cannon's wheel ran over my stomach. After a few minutes another truck stopped, and the driver pulled me off the road, but he couldn't stay since he had to keep going with the rest of the convoy. I was a little dizzy for a while, but then I felt better, so I decided to continue my trip to Prague."

I asked him if his ribs were aching or cracked, or if he had any other pains. He said he didn't but of course Jaromir couldn't see what he looked like. I thought of his mother, a wonderful lady, and how dismayed she would be at his appearance. I recommended that he return home.

When the truck stopped the next time, Jaromir got off, saying he would hitchhike home. From this, I assumed he couldn't have been feeling as well as he claimed. When I got back to our village the next day, the first thing I did was to visit Jaromir. He was very pale, but he seemed to be all right.

While Josef and I were in the Russian truck, I noticed there were four plastic bags of cocoa scattered over the floor, each weighing at least four pounds. I wished I could take one-I hadn't tasted cocoa for the six years' duration of the war- but I didn't dare.

It was getting dark. About 8:00 P.M., the truck stopped in Planany. We were told the crew on the truck would spend the night there. When we looked around, we saw several trucks with cannons in the back on the side of the road. We couldn't go any further. Now there was a problem: where to spend the night. We were parked in front of a small, neat house. I introduced myself to the lady of the house, who appeared about to give birth. I asked her if she knew where we could stay overnight. She said, "You may stay here, but you have to share a bed in the kitchen since it's the only one we have. The main bedroom has been taken by the Russian commander of the convoy." We happily accepted the offer, and I put my suitcase under the bed. We were very tired from a long and eventful day that I would never forget.

The Russian commander had apparently decided he didn't want to be alone in the master bedroom, and had brought in a female Russian soldier. They were having something to eat. The two were not exactly silent behind the closed door, giggling, talking and probably drinking vodka. After a while, we stopped paying attention and fell asleep.

In the morning, Mrs. Tomanek, the lady of the house, managed to give us a breakfast of scrambled eggs, a piece of rye bread, a cup of coffee, and a hard roll. In Czechoslovakia, bakeries create very tasty rolls of many shapes and tastes, some with rock salt and caraway seed, some with poppy seed, and some with a soft buttery taste. We had no money to pay her, but she didn't expect any. Before we left, she said she was very glad to have helped us, and very thankful that the war was over. She praised us for having the courage to hitchhike, with a heavy suitcase, for the sixty-five miles from our hometown to Prague.

After saying good-bye to her and her husband, we continued our trip. We hopped on the same truck with the bags of cocoa. I felt like stealing one to give it to Mrs. Tomanek, but I didn't want to run the risk of losing our transportation. I did something else, however; I collected the cocoa bags and placed them all underneath the wooden bench next to my suitcase. Since no one had paid attention to them, I worked out a plan to take one when we arrived in Prague.

In about an hour, we approached the outskirts. Until now, I hadn't even asked Josef who he was going to visit. He said he was only going to Prague out of curiosity, but added that his family had friends with whom he would stay overnight.

Fifteen minutes later the trucks left the main road and parked in a large open lot near the railroad station. I asked one of the Russian soldiers if this was as far as they would go for the time being. He said, "Da," meaning yes. All three of them jumped out. Now I had the opportunity to take one of the bags of cocoa. I held it by my left arm underneath my jacket and carried my suitcase in my right arm as Josef and I walked out of the parking lot. We didn't look for the driver to thank him for the ride. They were accustomed to having people around because everyone considered the war was over. People waved to the Russian convoys to express their thanks for liberty.

We were approaching a bridge with low stone walls, when we suddenly heard shots. There were dozens of people leaning against the wall and looking in the direction where the shots were coming from. We joined this group and also looked over the wall. I saw the railroad station and asked someone what was going on. He said some SS Nazis were being hunted among the railroad cars. When I heard that, I thought the onlookers were very foolish. All it would take would be one SS man with a machine gun to shower the onlookers with bullets. I said to Josef, "Let's get out of here in a hurry."

Seeing the railline, however, was cheering, since I knew both of the main railroad stations were near to my cousin Frantisek Kmonicek's apartment. In a few minutes we were there and receiving a very warm welcome. I introduced Josef to them. They couldn't believe that we had carried the heavy luggage such a distance. My cousin's wife offered us soup, omelets, and a cup of coffee with homemade buns. We were extremely hungry and very appreciative. Then Josef left to join his friends, even though transportation was difficult since streetcars were still not operating in many parts of the city.

My cousin's wife, who I called in Czech "svagrova," (sister-in-law) was at least thirty years older than I was. But we got along very well. In the afternoon, she and I walked to the Oldtown Square to look at the damage that had been done during the fighting. The Old Townhall was a beautiful historic building, which I had seen before the war. Now it was completely different. I was told that the Russian tanks had shot one round at each window on the second floor, since Nazis were probably hiding in the building. There was other damage around the Square, but fortunately, the fountain in the center wasn't touched.

We took a different route back to the apartment. As we went by the church on Jindrich Street, Svagrova said that she heard something frightful had happened there. She asked me if we could go in to learn what it was all about. I would have liked to, but I had on a new pair of very squeaky shoes. Out of respect, I decided to wait for her outside.

After a few minutes Svagrova came back, wiping away tears. "George, I just saw something terrible," she said. "I don't know if I should tell you. There were forty-eight small children inside, lined up in rows on the floor. The little girls and the little boys were sexually mutilated." I couldn't believe it. I was tempted to go in to see for myself, but quickly decided against it. I knew the image of those little victims would stay with me for the rest of my life.

We returned to Kmoniceks' apartment, filled with hatred for the Nazis. I couldn't deliver the food to my brother, since he lived on the other side of Prague, and there was no crosstown transportation. I had to leave his food with the Kmoniceks until they could contact Vincenc by phone. Frantisek discussed payment for their portion of the food. I didn't want much, but I had to have some money for the train fare home, and something for Ludmila.

After we settled the money matters, I asked my cousin if he could arrange for me to get an interview at the company where he worked. Frantisek agreed, and said he would let me know the result by mail. After a short while, I left and walked to the Masaryk Railroad Station for my return trip. I arrived home at 7:45 P.M. It was still daylight, and I had enough time to look at my grafted fruit trees to see how they were progressing.

The next day I went to work. The mood at the office was very happy, because Russian soldiers had appeared in town looking for wristwatches-the bigger and louder, the better. Since I didn't have a watch, it didn't concern me.

After work, I stopped to tell Mrs. Landa I would be giving up my room. As I entered the house, to my great surprise, I saw a Russian soldier washing his face in the toilet bowl. And he had about four wristwatches on each arm!

I returned the key to Mrs. Landa and said good-bye. When I returned home and told my sister, brother-in-law, and father about the Russian soldier, they could hardly believe the story.

In a few days a letter came from Frantisek Kmonicek to tell me that Vincenc had received the food. Also, he had very good news for me. I should come to the Poldi Steel Company, where he worked, for an interview as soon as possible. Excited by the prospect of a job, I went there by train the next day.

My cousin and Svagrova were very happy to see me. Frantisek took me to the third floor where he introduced me to Mr. Hruska, my future boss. I had my college papers with me and handed them to Mr. Hruska. After looking them over, he told me I was hired. We went to the Personnel Department where I filled out an application. I was to start work on June 1, 1945.

I went to see Frantisek to tell him I would be a fellow employee. He congratulated me and immediately called Vincenc to tell him the good news. Vincenc was very happy, but we had a problem-finding living quarters for me, because rooms were very hard to find.

The streetcars were finally running, and I took one to visit Vincenc, who lived on the other side of Prague. He had lived alone in the city during the war. His wife and son George, my godchild, had stayed with my sister-in-law's mother in northeast Bohemia. There were several reasons for this arrangement: the food shortages, the impossibility of finding an apartment, and the danger of Allied air attacks.

My brother rented a sizable room from a music composer, Mr. Koutek, and his wife. He asked Mrs. Koutek if I could live there with him until a room became available, elsewhere, and she consented. My brother wrote me that I could move in on June 1. I was so excited because to live and work in Prague had always been my dream. It is one of the most beautiful cities in the world. I couldn't wait to go and started all kinds of preparations for this enormous change in my life. I looked forward to it, but I also knew I would miss my life on the farm.

Before my departure to Prague, I had a long discussion with Ludmila. We agreed that I would return home every other weekend: to get food to take back to Prague, and to pick up the laundry my sister would do for me. And in order to help pay my train fare, I would take some farm products with me to be sold in Prague, where-in spite of the end of the war-food shortages continued.

Chapter 6

COLLABORATOR'S EXECUTION STORY

Several days after the war ended, a wanted German collaborator by the name of Dr. Pfitzner was captured in Prague. He was responsible for the loss of many Czechoslovak lives and therefore was convicted to be publicly hanged. The execution took place on a square not far from the center of Prague where a scaffolding had been built.

My cousin, Frantisek Kmonicek, asked me to accompany him to witness the ceremony. Because we were early we were able to stand close to the podium with the scaffolding.

Soon two policemen brought in the prisoner with his hands tied behind his back. They made him stand on a stool, which was underneath the noose hanging from the scaffolding above his head. Without any delay, the noose was lowered and placed around Pfitzner's neck. The executioner was ready to perform his part. He wore a black outfit, complete with a top hat and white gloves.

The policemen moved aside, and the executioner, a very tall man, stepped close to Pfitzner. He asked the prisoner if he had anything to say. Pfitzner replied in German, "Ich sterbe fuer Deutschland," which means, "I am dying for Germany." After his statement, the stool was pulled away, and the noose tightened. The executioner took Pfitzner by his chin, sharply jerking his head to one side, thus breaking his neck.

After it was over, the executioner took off his gloves, dropped them on the podium, and walked away. The happy crowd of about thirty thousand people applauded and slowly started to disperse. The city even provided extra streetcars to accommodate the crowd's transportation.

I had seen similar executions in the movies, but I never expected to witness a real one that closely.

CHAPTER 7

JOB IN PRAGUE

ON JUNE 1, 1945, I STARTED MY JOB IN THE DEPARTMENT OF STATISTICS AT Poldi Steel Company in Prague. Mr. Hruska introduced me to twelve colleagues in the department-four women and eight men. My task was to convert foreign currencies to U. S. dollars for steel sold all over the world at Poldi's seventy-five branches. The conversion had to be done every month, with figures shown by curves on big diagrams. Because I had been a postage stamp collector since the age of eleven, I already knew the currencies of many countries. Our office was very large and two of my colleagues, Jan Kriz and Henry Moulis, came up with the idea that after work hours we could play table tennis in the vacant area of the office. We asked for permission and, to our great surprise, the company even furnished a table and supplies. We all had a great deal of fun and became close friends.

The job was not difficult, but it required accuracy to correctly show the quantities of steel sold monthly, and the corresponding dollar amounts. Sometimes I also helped out in section of our department where there were three friendly girls. One day I whistled my favorite tune, "The Merry Widow," for them. They liked it, and asked me to whistle other tunes while we worked. Nobody complained.

Now that the war was over, dancing had been reinstated. Whenever dances took place in our village, I made sure to be there.

I started paying more attention to Jirina, who was getting prettier and prettier. She was eighteen, we were good friends, and I enjoyed dancing with her tremendously. But Oldrich was still on the scene. Since I came home only every two weeks. He was able to see Jirina more often than I could. Oldrich was working in the nearby town of Pardubice, only six miles away. I was in Prague, sixty-five miles away. My "spies" told me that they were seeing a lot of each other, so I was losing ground.

On September 1, 1945, I was recruited into the newly-created Czechoslovak Army for twenty-one months. Oldrich was a year older, and had to go for only five months-so again he had the advantage.

Chapter 8

MILITARY SERVICE

I had to report for duty at the military camp in Caslav, about thirty miles from my village. After registration, about forty of us were transferred to a vacant school building in Havlickuv Brod. There was no heat in the building and the September nights were very cold. We had to sleep in our uniforms, which consequently looked dreadful. My uniform was comprised of German SS pants, left behind by the Nazis; a Hungarian jacket (I couldn't understand where it came from); a Czech cap; and a Czech overcoat. We each received a rifle (origin unknown), and a leather belt with a bayonet.

Our group was to be trained for handling horses. I hated the smell of horses, and was very unhappy about my assignment. Fortunately, the next day our commander announced that he needed two men to be transferred to an automobile group in Sobeslav, a town a long way from my home village, about thirty miles west of Prague. My hand popped up like lightning, and by sheer luck, I was selected to be one of the two. The next day we were on our way.

The building in Sobeslav was relatively new, with quarters for about 160 men. After a training period, we would be assigned as instructors for older recruits who had been studying to become doctors, lawyers, engineers, or other professionals at the time Hitler closed the universities.

On October 23, I received a telegram that my 73-year-old father had passed away after a heart attack. This date was an unlucky one for our family, since eighteen years before, my mother had died also on October 23. Both were buried on October 26.

When I asked for time off to go home for my father's funeral, my request was denied on the grounds that our group would be taking the formal military oath on October 28-the anniversary of the founding of the first Czechoslovak Republic in 1918.

But after I returned to my bunk, I was informed that Captain Novotny wanted to see me. When I entered his office, he asked me, "Do you remember me?" I answered, "You look familiar, but I cannot remember from where." He replied, "I was the umpire at the hockey game when you played against H. C. Chrudim. The match was in your village, at the ring called Sokol Garden."

He asked how I liked the service. I replied I liked it very much, especially since my transfer from Havlickuv Brod to Sobeslav. He smiled, expressed his sympathy at the loss of my father, and handed me a three-day pass to go home for the funeral. We shook hands, and I left, wiping tears from my eyes.

Our father's death was a sad event for the entire family, but it was fortunate I was able to be at the funeral. We all recalled how our dear father struggled, without our mother, to raise us. I was proud to be a soldier, but I was not happy at my appearance in that uniform. Unfortunately, nobody had a new one I could borrow, because it had not yet been decided what color, style, and material would be used for the uniforms of the Czechoslovakian army. A short time later the decision was made, and we received brand-new uniforms.

During the next several months, we learned all there was to know about cannons that were pulled by trucks. The Russians had left behind the equipment on which we trained. Seventy Russian divisions, however, stayed in Czechoslovakia, supposedly to confiscate the Nazi arsenal. But they didn't stop there. The Russians began to take away everything they could lay their hands on: machinery, cement, bricks, the contents of all the warehouses. Night after night, railroad cars covered with canvas could be seen heading toward the Russian border. Although the Russians were

Czechoslovakia's liberators, our "love" for them was fading quickly.

The Czechoslovak government-in-exile, headed by President Dr. Edward Benes, returned from England to start a new nation. Czechoslovakia had been formed in 1918; now, it was formed again in 1945.

On October 28, 1945—the twenty-seventh anniversary of the establishment of the first Czechoslovak Republic—all the soldiers from our school marched in formation to the town square in Sobeslav, where we took an oath to serve the new republic. I was twenty-two years old. What a proud moment for me! I felt very important to be part of the rebirth of our country.

Towards the end of our schooling—having finished much theory and practice about 76-cm and 122-cm cannons—we needed to see how these weapons functioned in action. We were sent to Cesky Krumlov, in southern Bohemia, for military maneuvers. After being in school for some seven months, we thought this trip was like going on vacation.

The thirty-two soldiers in our group were housed in a big barn full of hay. The owner had a large farm, restaurant, and food store on the outskirts of Cesky Krumlov. During supper we could see pretty girls, a combination of farm help and waitresses. One soldier, Robert arranged a date with one of the girls who showed him the room where she slept.

We had just a couple of blankets; we spread one on the hay and covered ourselves with the other. By ten o'clock at night all of us were supposed to be in "the sack." We were, except for Robert, who was out on his date.

Thirty minutes later, Robert showed up, rather disappointed. When the girl had showed Robert her sleeping quarters, he considered it an invitation. But his biggest mistake, he confessed, was that he had slipped into her bed naked before she came in. When the girl entered, astonished and angry, she ordered him to get out of her bed and out of her room.

We laughed, so Robert added to our entertainment by telling us one joke after another. In order to remember them all, he had memorized them in alphabetical order. We laughed until our stomachs hurt, and none of us fell asleep until very late. I shall never forget that night.

The next day we headed toward a wooded area and some large fields owned by the farmer. He had donated one small decrepit barn to be used as a target. Our group had four cannons, which formed in Czech a "batery" (one "t" in the word). Each cannon had eight men. The truck brought in ammunition. After proper preparation, we finally could start shooting. The method in artillery is to first shoot long, then shoot short, and then halve that distance until you hit the target. Each cannon was allowed three shots. I was the math man for cannon number two. Nobody else struck the barn. I was very lucky, because I made the only hit, which destroyed the target. Our Captain said "Congratulations, job well done."

A few weeks later, we finished our training in Sobeslav, and I became a sergeant. Now our group was supposed to return to our original headquarters, Caslav, where we would begin our military service.

But with summer approaching, there was a change in our schedule. We would be given a few days' leave, then be sent to harvest hay in an area near the Czech-German border in northern Bohemia. I used my leave to go home for a visit with my sisters. Of course, I also hoped to see Jirina. For this visit I was wearing my new uniform and looked quite presentable. And at the local dance that weekend, I had a chance to dance with Jirina. But her pretty face attracted other suitors-namely Oldrich, who was seeing her more and more often.

Later there was a rumor that Jirina had gone to Prague to stay with relatives for "delicate" reasons. Her family claimed she went there to learn about meat preparation. Whatever the reason was, it didn't matter anymore-because even during my leave, I realized she was lost to me. I still had thirteen months of military service, while Oldrich had only five months to go. I didn't have a chance. But despite that disappointment, I had a very pleasant visit with four of my sisters and their families before returning to camp in Caslav,

After being back at camp for only a few days, I was made assistant to the chief officer and given a detail of thirty men to harvest hay in the northern part of Bohemia: the Sudetenland. That region was occupied mostly by Czech-Germans-citizens who spoke both languages and who, in 1938, opted to be annexed to the Third Reich.

When we arrived in the Sudetenland, I realized that its place names were all German: Sangerberg, Ober Perlsberg and Unter Perlsberg. I had never heard of those villages, which were only partially inhabited. Many houses were completely unoccupied, but they contained furniture and other belongings. The reason was that the people who once lived there were the same people who had wanted to be annexed by Germany. After the war, the new Czechoslovak government ordered them to leave and allowed them to take only 198 pounds of personal belongings. The evacuation order caused bitter feelings among those who had to emigrate. They destroyed everything they could, leaving behind broken sewing machines, tools, porcelain dishes, and clocks.

Since I could speak German, the chief officer told me to inspect the houses and warn any remaining people to stop their destruction. He assigned two soldiers with rifles as my escort. Going from house to house, I pretended to make a list of what was to remain untouched.

I remember one home where a very old lady said in German, "Es lebe unsere schoene Tschechische Heimat!" which means, "Long live our beautiful Czech homeland!" Her feelings, of course, were an exception to most others in the area. Nevertheless, her family also had to pack and leave. In the eyes of the Czechoslovak government, these people were considered to be Nazi collaborators and possibly dangerous to the Czechs.

The next day a long two-horse carriage came to collect the old woman's family and their few packed belongings. It was not a pleasant sight. It created an ambivalent feeling among the soldiers, but the move had to be carried out per our orders. After this evacuation, the village was completely empty except for our group.

The next agenda was to harvest hay, which was not easy because the area was extremely hilly, and the grass had to be cut by hand-held scythes. Luckily, every house had a scythe, but many soldiers didn't know how to use one. Still, they had to try, even if the job was not done perfectly.

I knew how to use one since I was born on a farm. When the time came to harvest the hay, my father, brother-in-law, and I would get up at four A.M. and start work. By ten o'clock the whole meadow would be cut. I showed the soldiers how to do it, and eventually the hay had been harvested, picked up, and stored in barns.

It took a long time to do the three villages, which were approximately two miles apart. But the work was done cheerfully, because the war was over and we were doing everything for our new Czechoslovakia. And our spirits were also high because in the near future we would be transferred out of the Sudetenland.

After opening his orders one day, the chief officer told us to finalize our operations so that we could be ready to leave. A few days before the end of August we returned to our headquarters in Caslav. This gave me an opportunity to go home for a weekend to see my family and friends. Frantisek met me at the train stop. Since my other brother, Vincenc, lived in Prague, I wouldn't see him until Christmas. But we all remained in touch, and the family seemed even closer since our father's death.

I had no sooner returned to Caslav than I was transferred to Jindrichuv Hradec, to serve as an instructor to the recruits who would serve five months there. These were the former university students, who were now continuing their studies that had been interrupted when Hitler closed universities. Another sergeant, Josef Kafka, came with me. The two of us were to be instructors for forty men. The officer in charge was again to be Captain Novotny, who had been with us at Sobeslav. He would bring four soldiers from Caslav to handle the beds and other equipment for the recruits.

On September 1, 1946, the recruits arrived at the military school in Jindrichuv Hradec, a fairly large town located in southern Bohemia. They were "old men"-all over thirty!

There was one large room for twenty-six men under the charge of Sergeant Kafka, and one smaller room for fourteen men under my charge. But when I entered my room to give it a final check, I counted the bunk beds: fourteen. Where was one for me? I tried to locate the captain to find out if there was some last minute change, but he wasn't around. By 4:30 P.M., thirty-nine recruits were settled in. Now they were waiting for their first meal to be served around 6:00 o'clock.

I decided to take a walk before dinner to become acquainted with the facilities. But I hesitated when I saw one more recruit standing helplessly in the hallway, surrounded by bundles. When I asked him what he was doing, he said his name was Karel Rudolf, and that he was supposed to appear at Jindrichuv Hradec for five months of service. Then I asked him why he had so many things. He said his brother-in-law had served in the U.S. Army during World War II, and had given Karel all kinds of equipment he had used during the war. I was interested in him immediately because he had all that American equipment! I found two soldiers and had them install a bunk bed. After I helped Karel bring his bundles to our room, I took the bottom bunk and gave him half of the space underneath my bed. Everything was done just in time for supper; Karel even had his own dish and utensils.

After the meal, I had a long talk with Karel. He was thirty-two, single, and lived with his parents in the center of Prague. He knew the street where I worked very well, and I knew the building where he and his family lived.

The time for "lights out" was set at nine o'clock, since everybody had to get up at six the next morning for exercises. Even in the dark, there was quite a lot of talking until I told everybody to get some sleep; they had a long day ahead of them.

The curriculum consisted of theory in the morning and practice in the afternoon. The first few days were rather difficult for men in an entirely new environment. Many of them were married with families, and they were lonely because no one was allowed to leave the premises for the first month.

In the evenings after supper, there was a chance for everyone to get acquainted. I had long conversations with Karel, who was from a wealthy family. He had a very pretty girlfriend named Vlasta, a prima ballerina at the National Theater in Prague. We talked about Prague and our backgrounds.

Captain Novotny liked his men to sing military songs. Since I came from a musical family, he asked me to teach this group the same songs I had taught my fellow soldiers in Sobeslav. Some of the men didn't mind, but others were less enthusiastic about the military and seemed a little resentful.

One day the captain told me to take the men in a field to teach them how to crawl with a rifle in one hand. Because I had gone through this experience in my days as a recruit, I knew they wouldn't like it-especially at this time of the year, when the fields were rough from plowing. I had to teach them correctly, in case the captain came to watch. But I felt sorry for them, since they all were at least ten years older than I was. I decided to take them up to the nearby hilly area, hoping there would be a meadow there. Luckily, we found one. We did a few exercises, and then I gave them a rest.

It was a beautiful day, and I assigned one man to be on the lookout for a possible visit by the captain on his horse. After about an hour, the man on watch reported that Captain Novotny was approaching. I quickly asked the men to form a half-circle, and to sing the military songs they knew best. When the captain rode up, I pretended I didn't know he was near us. We continued to sing. When I was alerted by one man that the Captain Novotny was behind me, I turned around and yelled at the men, "Attention!" The captain dismounted, tied his horse to a nearby tree, and asked me how the men were progressing. I could tell he was pleased about the singing, but he said, "I don't see any mud on the men's elbows. How come?" Since I had to think up a quick reply, I told him I had decided to conduct the exercise on the meadow because I didn't know about facilities where we could wash off mud. He told me to take the men back to the school, hopped on his horse, and left as I saluted him.

After this encounter, the men were all smiles. I felt as if I won a medal. I sensed that I had gained their respect and admiration. That evening, I overheard a few favorable comments about "Sergeant Knava."

After several weeks of theory, the soldiers had to prepare for a written exam. Although they didn't seem to take it very seriously, I attempted to convince them they should-because based on these tests, some of them would be promoted at Christmas. And with a promotion came better pay that could be used to help their families.

One evening I took Karel's rifle and began to break it down. Each part had a different description, which I asked the soldiers to write on a sheet of paper. They were a bit reluctant at first, but nevertheless followed my instructions. The following evening I talked about some other subject, which was also in their curriculum. For several nights we continued this routine, up until the test day arrived.

After their written exam, when the men returned to their quarters, relaxed and happy because the test had been easy. Thanking me, they acknowledged that the nightly sessions had helped.

At Christmas, five of the fourteen men in my room were promoted to first rank. In Josef Kafka's room, only three out of twenty-six were promoted. Now my men were grateful that they hadn't wasted time playing cards or telling jokes. Those extra studies had resulted in giving them a feeling of pride—and they would now be allowed to visit their families for the holidays.

The promotion of these five men called for a celebration. Unfortunately, something had happened and soldiers without existing rank couldn't leave the base. Since I could, my men asked me to go downtown to buy a bottle of brandy.

I found a store, but it only had crëme de menthe. Because I didn't want to return empty-handed and disappoint the men, I bought two bottles. They expected something different, but I had no choice; everything else had been sold out.

After supper, I was offered the first drink by one of the promoted soldiers. I didn't care for crëme de menthe, but out of politeness I drank it. After a while, another promoted man wanted me to have a drink with him. Soon after, a third approached me, then a fourth, a fifth. At this point, I decided I had had enough! No more drinking!

I tried to find some way to keep myself occupied because I didn't want them to insist that I have more drinks. I had seen one of the men cleaning and polishing his clarinet one evening. Now I asked him if I could borrow it. He pulled it out of its case, assembled it, handed it to me, and asked me to try it. I didn't know how to play the instrument very well, but I was determined to keep busy.

For a time this worked, but as the mood in the room kept progressing, I was approached again to have more drinks, which I shouldn't have accepted—but did. Since I wasn't in the habit of drinking alcohol, I felt them strongly. Well, to be frank about it, I got very sick. Ever since that time,

I do not like or even want to see green candy, let alone crëme de menthe.

The next day, luckily, was Sunday, so we could nurse our hangovers. A couple of the men apologized to me and told me I was a good sport. We all got along well, even though I knew they didn't take the military very seriously. To them it was just a matter of serving out those five months, as ordered by the government.

And finally the time came to say good-bye. Of course the men were glad it was over since now they could go home to their families. But for me it was not over, because I still had four more months to go on my twenty-one months of service. I didn't like to see Karel Rudolf leaving for Prague. I was a sergeant, and he was a private; nevertheless, we had become good friends. When we said our farewells, he insisted that I come see him and his parents after I was discharged.

Captain Novotny called Kafka and me to his office, and informed us that we would be going back to headquarters in Caslav the next day. He thanked us for our patience with the older men, and said that all in all, it had been a success.

When we arrived in Caslav and reported in, the chief officer told me there was a good chance that Kafka and I would soon be promoted to the rank of lieutenant. I was certain it would come at the time of my discharge, but not before. Probably Captain Novotny had something to do with it, since he was so pleased with our work at the training school in Jindrichuv Hradec.

During my seventeen months of service, the highest-ranking officer I had seen was Captain Novotny, except for a Major I glimpsed once when we were parading in Sobeslav. But something interesting happened to me the day after we returned to headquarters. I went to the restroom, where there were usually several soldiers around. But this time it happened I was there alone. After a few seconds, someone entered to do the same thing I had to do. I glanced at the other man, and saw a beautiful uniform trimmed with gold. It was General Vydra, Commander-in-Chief of the entire area. The military rule was that in a latrine, men of lower rank didn't have to salute someone of higher rank. So I didn't, but for a moment I was in shock. Not too many ordinary soldiers get the opportunity to be that close to a General! It really was a big surprise that nature had given me that chance.

My next assignment was to take charge of cleaning the military vehicles in Caslav: trucks that were pulling cannons, Volkswagens, and several other kinds of vehicles scattered around the facility. There was a lot of work to be done, and several soldiers were assigned to assist me. One day I met the chief in the yard. Out of curiosity, I asked him why we were doing this job. He said the vehicles had to be prepared for a twelve-week military auto course that would take place. Since I wanted very badly to be in that course, I immediately applied.

But the chief told me that it would not be possible. My promotion to lieutenant had come through, and officers were not eligible for such a course. While we were talking about it, he mentioned that he would have to find a man of lower rank, probably a sergeant, to keep attendance, issue tools, and generally supervise. I told him that I would like to give up my promotion to be accepted in the course. The chief couldn't believe what I'd said. He asked if I was really serious about my decision, and I assured him that I was. He said it might not be possible, but promised to keep my suggestion in mind.

I wanted this course badly because I knew that after I got out of the army it would be almost impossible for me to obtain this knowledge and receive a license, which also would be very costly. I would gladly sacrifice the promotion, because I'd be eligible for it anyway at the time of my discharge. At the end of the course, graduates would be given a military driver's license, which would be valid in civilian life. This was now my goal.

Luck was with me. A few days later, the chief told me I was accepted, provided that I would sign a document declining the promotion. I gladly did, and soon started the course with about thirty other soldiers. We learned how to dismantle and reassemble engines-and, more important to me, how to drive. After twelve weeks, all of us were given a license, authorizing us to drive motorcycles, cars, trucks, and buses. I was very happy, because this license would be a very valuable document in civilian life.

There was now less than a month remaining of my military service. After the end of the auto course, I found out that maneuvers were being planned on the commander's order. The idea was to try out the vehicles we had repaired in the course, and to give the men a chance to drive them. The commander set a date for the near future, with the maneuvers taking place over several days.

But I had a problem, so I decided to consult a friend in the Medical Building, Dr. Hauser, to have him examine an ingrown toe nail that was causing me great discomfort. I told him I was supposed to take part in the upcoming maneuvers, but that it would be hard for me to be mobile when I was in so much pain. He told me to go with him to the next room, which contained all kinds of shining medical accessories. I sat in a chair and put my right foot on a cushioned stool. Dr. Hauser took a pair of scissors, poked underneath my toenail, and cut it in half. He ripped out the bad half and the operation was over-with no injection, no freezing, nothing. I saw stars for a few seconds, but my toe instantly felt better. The doctor used a liquid to clean off the blood, bandaged my foot, and gave me a slip of paper which ordered that I take two weeks off duty for healing. When he was finished, he smiled and said, "No maneuvers, Sarge." I thanked him and left with a bundled-up foot.

By the time my toe healed, I had just about finished my military service. I was discharged on June 30, 1947, and went home to the dear old farm to join Ludmila, my brother-in-law, and their six-year-old daughter, Marie. It was a happy day for me to be back in civilian life.

CHAPTER 9

NEW BEGINNING AFTER MILITARY SERVICE

IT WAS TIME TO GO BACK TO WORK, AND SOON I WAS IN PRAGUE—AT THE SAME company, Poldi Steel, which I had left at the end of August 1945. To my great surprise, almost all my former colleagues were still there. Mr. Hruska introduced me to some new staff and showed me my assigned desk. My job would be the same as it had been before I went into the service.

It was good to see my close friends, Henry Moulis and Jan Kriz, who had kept the table tennis alive in the vacant area of the office. They filled me in on news around Poldi Steel. The Communist Party was expanding, not only throughout the country, but also in the company. The three of us knew each other very well, and we were all unsympathetic with the communist doctrine. They warned me to avoid any political conversations with other people on staff. I was told that those who belonged to the Communist Party were having frequent meetings after work, which was not a good sign for us anti-communists. I concentrated on my work and let life go on, because I had other things to worry about.

During my military service many changes had occurred, including some that drastically affected my new civilian life. One of the most crucial was that all the money people held in bank accounts had been canceled nationwide, and a new monetary system created. Because I'd known I would be away in the service for twenty-one months, I hadn't bought many clothes, thinking I would get a wardrobe after my discharge. Therefore, I had built up my savings account in the state bank (Postovni Sporitelna). My account had a total of Kcs 56,000 (Kcs means Czechoslovak crowns), which would have given me enough money to buy the clothes I'd need after the service. But now all this money had been wiped out. I was allowed only Kcs 1,000, which was just enough to purchase one shirt and a tie.

This, of course, was a big blow to my new beginning. I needed all kinds of help: a room to live in somewhere in Prague, and money to buy a few more clothes.

Luckily, Vincenc came to my rescue. He loaned me Kcs 1,000, and I bought another shirt and tie. He also invited me to live temporarily with him and his family.

They had found a small apartment on the other side of Prague after the war. It was close to my brother's place of work, but it was forty minutes by streetcar to my office. It was very cramped quarters for three adults and their six-year-old son, George, my godchild. There was only space in the bedroom for a double bed and a crib. Therefore, the three grown-ups had to sleep in the same bed! This was a very awkward arrangement, and I knew I had to move out as soon as possible.

I told my brother and sister-in-law I'd be coming home later since I would be looking for a room nearer my office. I managed to get a map of the city and decided to do a street-by-street search every evening after work. It was summer, and many people were sitting on the steps of their apartment buildings, trying to catch a breath of fresh air. It was a hot, hard chore to keep asking these people if they knew of an available room. But I didn't give up, because I had to find something.

One evening, after about three weeks of frustration, I was lucky. One elderly lady was leaning out of her window, talking to another lady standing on the sidewalk. I greeted them, "Good evening," and asked them if they knew where I could find a room. The lady on the sidewalk asked the lady in the window, "Mrs. Blecha, why don't you help this young man? Don't you have an extra room you could rent?"

Mrs. Blecha, a lady in her seventies, looked at her, then looked at me. After a moment of hesitation, she invited me in to see her extra room. It was wonderfully cool, spacious, and clean. She said I would have to share the bathroom, but that I could use her kitchen, provided I would leave the utensils clean. I gladly agreed to all the rules. Cleanliness was a fundamental rule in my life, so I had no problem with that. I asked Mrs. Blecha if I could have the room at the end of the month, when I would be paid. Since she had to discuss this with her son, she told me to return the next evening.

Mrs. Blecha's son was waiting for me, and after he'd asked a few questions, I knew I'd passed the inspection. Mrs. Blecha then said the rent was Kcs 600 a month. Since I only earned Kcs 1,650 a month, this was quite a lot. But I accepted, because I had to move out of my brother and my sister-in-law's apartment to give them privacy.

Soon I had settled into my new room and become familiar with the stove, dishes, and utensils. I had also become better acquainted with Mrs. Blecha, who was a very pleasant lady. I saw little of her son, because he was a member of Prague's National Theater Symphony Orchestra, which performed in the evenings. Of course I was working during the day, and every other weekend I went home.

I lived in the section of Prague called Vinohrady, on a street named Kanalska. This new location was great for me, since I could walk to and from work. I was rather lonely, however, because up until now I had always been around people. I didn't have a radio, so I read and went sightseeing or visiting.

Toward the end of the year, the company arranged for its employees to attend an English course once a week. I welcomed this opportunity and signed up. Five years had elapsed since I'd finished school, and I was very rusty. However, the language came back to me quickly. I knew Mr. Stone, who was in charge of the English section of Poldi Steel, and I hoped to transfer into his section.

Luckily I met some young British men and women who were attending the "World Festival of Youth" in Prague. This friendship helped to further improve my English, because every day after work I showed them Prague's beautiful sights. I was very happy for the opportunity to be with these young people; it gave me a chance to practice my English, and their company was entertaining. Before they left Prague, we exchanged names and addresses.

In the office everything was basically the same, day after day. After work, I always reserved some time to join my friends Henry and Jan for a game of table tennis. This was cheap entertainment and a nice change from the daily routine. But I was worried about money. I needed so many things, and the train fare to go home every other weekend was quite expensive. With Christmas approaching, I had to purchase gifts for my family, but because of my low income, I couldn't buy much.

On Christmas Eve, I took a train home to join my sister Ludmila, my brother-in-law Vaclav, and their lovely little daughter, Marie. The company had given us our pay in advance rather than at the end of the month, and although I couldn't afford expensive gifts, I had managed to find something for everyone.

When I boarded the train, there was a vacant seat by the window. I decided to take a nap, since it was almost a four-hour trip. But I opened my eyes when I felt someone sitting down across from me. It was a very pretty girl in her early twenties. I tried to strike up a conversation by asking how far she was going. She gave an abrupt reply and did not encourage further discussion. I could take a hint, so I tried to look out the window instead of at her. But a few minutes later, the girl pulled a package from her handbag and opened it up to reveal a wristwatch. She kept staring at it, turning it back and forth with a great deal of curiosity. I thought she must have just bought it. I saw an opportunity to start a conversation again, observing that it had become very hard to find watches, since the war. She told me she had purchased it for her boyfriend, but that she had also bought him material for a new suit. Now she was undecided which of the two gifts to give him. I asked her how much the watch cost. She looked at the receipt and said the price was Kcs 1,340-almost eighty percent of my monthly pay. I asked for permission to look at it. She handed it to me, and said it was a German

Army watch that could run for forty-eight hours without rewinding. I told her that if she decided to give her boyfriend the material for the suit, I would be interested in purchasing the watch for cash. I knew I had just about enough money to buy it, and I needed a watch.

She thought it over, and finally said I could have the watch for the price shown on the slip. I gave her that amount, and I was left with Kcs 56 (about $5.00)—just enough to pay for my train fare on the local train. In a short while I had to get off, so I thanked her, and wished her a happy future with her boyfriend.

I still have that watch after fifty-two years, and it has traveled around the world with me. I just now wound it as I am typing, and it's running perfectly! Of course, back in the 1947 Christmas holidays, I had to borrow money from my sister to hold me through until the next pay-check. She gave it to me gladly, and was very happy that I was lucky enough to buy myself a much-wanted Christmas present. I will never forget that Kcs 56 I had left in my big wallet. I still have that wallet, also; and I had it in my jacket pocket when I left Czechoslovakia. It looks rather shabby, and it's oversized for American money, but I have kept it as a memento of that long-ago time.

I returned to Prague and Poldi Steel after the New Year. Early in 1948, the Communists started their activities in earnest. They asked people to join the Communist Party and to come to their meetings-to prepare for the country's takeover. They asked me, too, by placing a form on my desk. This I discarded, and they knew it. But our bosses at Poldi joined the Party, and they were kept aware of who was with them because they received membership lists from communist organizers. Naturally, some employees started getting better jobs and raises in pay.

Across from my desk was the desk of a man named Karel Velk. When I came back to work after my discharge from the military, he was a fervent anti-communist. But now I couldn't be sure. I didn't know if he attended the Party's frequent meetings, and I didn't ask since I tried to avoid any political discussions.

Occasionally, I mentioned to Karel Velk that I wondered how far I could progress at the company, since my current job did not pay very well. Unlike me, Karel didn't have much education, and the only reason he was at Poldi Steel was that he had been a close friend of Mr. Hruska for many years.

During our conversations, Karel told me that he had a part-time business selling hot dogs in different locations around Prague, but that it didn't bring much money because he couldn't get a stand in the huge stadium at Strahov where soccer games were played before as many as 90,000 fans.

Some time later we returned to the same subject, and Karel confided that he had finally received a permit to sell hot dogs at Strahov. I asked him how he'd managed that. Karel replied that he had joined the Communist Party. He also told me that he'd been summoned to a party meeting at Poldi, where the chief comrade asked him why he had switched from anti-communism. Karel said he replied, "I was always with the strongest political party, so I switched to the strong Communist Party."

Because the comrades had known him for many years, he succeeded with his maneuver, but I was surprised that he told me the story. From that day on, I refrained from any further political conversations with Karel Velk, because I didn't trust him. I knew that anything I said would be reported to his buddy, Mr. Hruska.

During a visit with my cousin Frantisek Kmonicek, he suggested that I try to get into the English Section, where he knew Mr. Stone, the manager. He said I should ask Mr. Stone for a position, and tell him that I was Frantisek's cousin.

Eventually I did as Frantisek had suggested, and the meeting seemed to go well. Mr. Stone asked me if I knew English, and when I said I did, he told his secretary to give me some dictation.

The secretary picked up a typed sheet of paper, gave me a blank sheet, and started to dictate in English. When we finished, she read my lines and I noticed that she made very few corrections. Then she gave Mr. Stone the sheet I had written. He looked at it, said he could use me, and promised to be in touch. I thanked him and left.

After my interview I waited a long time, but in vain. Mr. Stone never called. When Frantisek saw him and asked why, his answer was, "My hands are tied." When my cousin told me what Mr. Stone said, I felt disgusted. Since I wasn't a member of the Communist Party, my every effort was a waste of time. I couldn't understand how the other personnel remained in the English Section if they weren't party members. Or were they? One had no way of knowing.

I foresaw that my prospects with Poldi Steel were dim. I continued to go once a week to the free courses given by the company. But the way things were now, I was surprised that they had even accepted me for enrollment.

CHAPTER 10

COMMUNIST TAKEOVER

ON FEBRUARY 25, 1948, SOMETHING UNUSUAL HAPPENED. WE WERE NOTIFIED that at 1:00 P.M. there would be a general strike, and that all employees of Poldi Steel had to report to Venceslav Square. We were ordered to meet in front of the building, where Communist organizers told us to form a line and march to Venceslav Square.

When we arrived, the square was filled with people, all waiting and watching a podium that had apparently been built specifically for this occasion. Soon after one o'clock, Klement Gottwald—head of the Communist Party of Czechoslovakia—stepped onto the podium, approached the microphone, and said, "I have just arrived from President Dr. Edward Benes, who signed a proclamation that, of this moment, Czechoslovakia will be governed by the Communist Party."

At least 100,000 demonstrators, who had obviously been organized ahead of time, began to yell, "Long live Klement Gottwald!" He then gave a speech, which we heard from loudspeakers mounted on the buildings and trees around the square. After Gottwald finished, we had to return to the office so no counter-demonstrations would be possible.

It was a day of glory for Czechoslovakia's Communists, but not, of course, for me, Henry, Jan, and a few others in our section. Still, the next day, there was hardly any noticeable change in our office, except that Karel Velk now frequently went to visit his long time friend and our boss, Mr. Hruska. I felt rather uneasy sitting at my desk and facing

Karel, knowing that he had become a "comrade." From then on, I avoided any discussions with him and concentrated only on my job.

The Communists reorganized Parliament, and there, as elsewhere, it was very hard for anti-communists. One well-known and well-liked member of Parliament was Jan Masaryk, son of the late president of Czechoslovakia, Thomas Garrigue Masaryk. Now there were rumors that he was facing dangerous opposition from the Communists. Masaryk told a friend-the famous writer Marcia Davenport-that he feared for his life.

On March 10, 1948, a tragic thing happened: The Communists shot Jan Masaryk in the head and threw him out of a window in Cerninsky Palace. They claimed that he had committed suicide.

I joined thousands of shocked and saddened people to bid farewell to this great man, who had been First Secretary of the United Nations. I saw Masaryk in his casket, and noticed a bruise on his face. I will never forget that occasion.

Now the Communists started to flex their muscles in rural areas. Fields were taken from farmers, borderlines between individual farms were eliminated, and the Czechoslovakian countryside changed to one huge field as far as the eye could see. My sisters and my brother, Frantisek, lost their land and all their equipment. Several large farmers in my village were asked to join the Communist Party, and told that if they agreed, they could stay on their farms as managers-but never again as owners. None of them accepted, so the Communists relocated them to the uninhabited Sudetenland.

The Communists seized the restaurant of my sister, Marie. But because they couldn't find a replacement who could match her excellent cooking, they let her manage the restaurant with her stepdaughter. They also confiscated Ludmila's land, and every morning at 3:15, she had to go heat water for 275 calves in the village stables. Frantisek lost his farm, but because of his special skills, he was allowed to stay on to work as a planting organizer. My sister, Anna, lived in Chrudim, where her husband, a cabinetmaker, worked for a business that was taken over by the Communists. Vincenc was employed by an insurance company, as an inspector of payments for retired people. When I saw him in 1990-after forty-one years in 1990-Vincenc told me that one day his boss advised him to sign a party membership card or risk losing his apartment.

I could go on and on about what happened after the Communist takeover. People whose businesses had been in their families for generations were relocated if they didn't join the Communist Party, while unskilled "comrades" took over managerial positions.

One year after my return to Poldi Steel, I thought I was due for an increase in salary. Mr. Hruska had told me that he was very pleased with my work, so I asked him for a raise. He didn't say yes or no, but told me he would bring up my request at the next meeting.

Some time went by, but Mr. Hruska never gave me a favorable answer. Of course, I knew why: I wasn't a member of the Communist Party.

I talked to my friends, Henry and Jan, and asked if either of them had received a raise. They both gave me the same answer. There had been no pay increases since the Communists assumed power.

I'd hoped that Vincenc might get me a job where he worked. But he pointed out that I'd be even worse off there. I would be starting on the bottom rung at his company, I would be asked to join the Party, I would be on the other side of Prague, I would have to go through the agony of looking for a new room. We discarded the idea, so I had to stay put and hope that something would change for the better. Instead things got much worse-especially for my sister, Frantiska.

The confiscation of farms had taken place most slowly in the mountainous regions, where the parcels of land were small. Frantiska and her family lived in just such an area, so their farm hadn't been seized immediately after the Communist takeover. But even there, confiscation was inevitable.

My brother-in-law, Oldrich Nemec, Frantiska's husband, possessed numerous small blocks of farmland, as well as large areas of forest. He bitterly-and openly-opposed the Communists' appropriation of privately-owned land. This infuriated local party members who, despite the fact that they had known Oldrich since childhood, threatened him with prosecution if he resisted their orders.

The pressure on my brother-in-law continued to mount. After the Communists confiscated his land and farm equipment, Oldrich lived in fear, certain that next they would put him in jail or send him to the Sudetenland. And so he made a calamitous decision: on February 12, 1952, Oldrich hung himself in the attic. He was forty-six years old. Later my sister found a note he had left in his desk:

Part I

Addressed to Town Police:

This note is about a signed promise to the Town Authorities as follows:

"I didn't cancel the written promise, but I cannot convince the farmers alone—and I will not turn in Czech people. I know that I would be sentenced for that kind of act for a long time—possibly for my whole life. I didn't do anything wrong."

Part II

Addressed to local farmers:

"I am sacrificing my life for you—for your better future—be true to your Czech heritage—and live in harmony. My life was ruined by comrade Bohac and by several other comrades belonging to the Local National Committee, mainly comrade Dusanek and others."

Part III

Addressed to the family:

"To all dear ones!"

"I do not like to leave you—we lived well and in harmony—stay calm and strong about my passing. Hopefully you will find some nice people who will help you,—my nerves are totally ruined—it is impossible for me to live like this—perhaps God and you all will forgive me for this action."

Your Dad

But in 1948, Frantiska's tragedy was still in the future, and I was preoccupied with my own problems. Christmas was approaching but I was not in the mood to welcome it. I still needed many things-and I still didn't have much money. In fact, I just barely got by month to month.

One day I happened to see Mr. Blecha, who was visiting his mother. I asked him how things were with the National Symphony and he replied that it was going very well indeed. After he left, I had an idea. I came from a musical family, and I knew how to read music. I decided to contact the Prague Conservatory of Music, to find out about learning an instrument. They said it was possible, but it would be very expensive. As a less costly alternative, they suggested that I rent an instrument and practice at home. I would be assigned a professor, who would help me with weekly lessons. That sounded fine, so I rented a trumpet, and I started practicing. Mrs. Blecha didn't mind, she said it was just like the old days when her son used to practice.

I liked the trumpet, and I was doing quite well. I thought that eventually I could join a small band and make extra money like my father and Frantisek once had.

Meanwhile, the mood in the office was very unpleasant. Gradually there were alterations in personnel at every level. Even top executives were replaced by hard-line Communists, whether or not they were qualified for the positions. Every time I heard someone calling another man "Comrade," I felt as if I was being stabbed by a long needle. Henry, Jan and I continued to resist joining the party, so we knew that our futures with Poldi Steel didn't look very bright.

After the Communist takeover, Prague-and all other cities and towns throughout the entire nation-were subject to the party's whims. Streets designations were changed from heroic Czech and Slovak names to Lenin Street, Stalin Street, Red Army Street, and so forth. Venceslav Square was full of large pictures of Lenin and Stalin, and festooned with Soviet flags bearing the insignia of the sickle and hammer. For me, and millions of other anti-communists, all this was just heart-breaking.

Sometimes during my train trips home, I saw people from towns near my home village. There was still a shortage of food in cities, so they went to their relatives for supplies. On one trip early in 1949, I sat across from Millie Kovarova, whom I had known since our school days. I also knew Millie's sister Vera and her brother Ervin, who had gone to school on the same local train that I had always taken.

I asked Millie about her family, and we covered a wide range of conversation. But I didn't talk about politics, because I had heard a rumor that Millie's father was Chief of Police in her hometown, Hrochuv Tynec, only three stops away from mine.

Gradually, other passengers got off the train, and there were just the two of us left in our car. When Millie asked what my job was, I told her about Poldi Steel, and the difficulties in being given a raise or promotion because I was not a member of the Communist Party.

Then, without stopping to think, I suddenly remarked, "I wish I could get out of this country to stop this miserable hard life." Millie looked at me, and after a short hesitation, asked: "Do you mean it?" I replied, "Certainly, I mean it." She stared at me. Now I was frightened, because I didn't know anything about her politics. Perhaps I had made a serious mistake. But after a few seconds, Millie said, "Maybe I can help you, if you wish."

Now I was the one staring. She smiled at my look of surprise, and continued. "I can introduce you to underground people who can get you out of the country, if that's what you want." I was weak with relief and I couldn't believe what had just happened. But what would happen next? Millie told me the plan.

She set a date for me to meet at a house in Prague, not far from my living quarters. There were about ten people there, men and women, young and middle-aged. Everyone used an alias. My name wasn't George, Millie's name wasn't Millie. We were all scared but united. The idea of this underground group was to help those who were in trouble with or being hunted by the Communists.

One of the people, a sixty-four-year-old architect, was ill. His right breast was swollen, oozing puss and blood. His fictitious name was Mr. Barta. The Communists had taken his business, and then expected him to give up his other assets. Because he was on the "black list" (wanted by the Communists), he couldn't go to any hospital for treatment. He was hiding in different places, moving from friend to friend, but mainly staying in the Ambassador Hotel on Venceslav Square, under a fictitious name. But as soon as the weather was suitable, Mr. Barta would

George at age 12

Built in 1637, St. John's Church in my birthplace Tunechody near Chrudim. George served as an altar boy in 1934 and 1935.

George studied in Chrudim for eight years.

Our family's farmhouse built in Tunechody by my parents in 1912.

My sister Ludmila and her prized product, a 400-pound pig.

Left: George's sister Marie's wedding photo in 1929.

Below: Marie's restaurant built out of logs and clay in 1637, and refurbished in 1794. It is famous for excellent cooking and baking and is preserved by the Historical Society.

Above: My brother Vincenc (left), and George in his SOKOL uniform. They were walking in Prague attending the festival in 1938.

Right: George at 15.

Above: Professor Vasina among his students in 1938-1942. (George is in the front row.)

Right: George's graduation photo taken in 1942 at the end of my studies at the College of Commercial Academy in Chrudim.

George on a Jawa 250 ccm during my first job.

The company truck George used to transport grain from farmers to the warehouse.

Above: Prague, Czechoslovakia

Right: Three silver buttons on George's military uniform represent the rank of a sergeant while the silver bordering stripes indicate a college graduate.

The oldtown square in Prague where the Nazis were defeated in May 1945.

The entrance into D.P. Camp Zoo in Hamburg, Germany in the British Zone. George is standing in front of the camp police guardhouse.

George reading the office closing sign at Easter at D.P. Camp Zoo. George always carried his most important papers and possessions with him.

Left to right: Ray Maidment, George's boss, his wife, Betty, and George in their flat (apartment) in Hamburg. They are still great friends to this day.

The interior of the British High Court, where George worked as an interpreter.

Above: Fairsea

Right: On the deck of the ship, Fairsea. George was headed for Aden as the weather was suddenly getting very warm.

have to be smuggled out of the country into the U.S. zone of Germany. A detailed plan would be worked out in the near future.

No one in my office, not even Henry and Jan, would be told that I had joined the Underground. Millie and I agreed we wouldn't even telephone each other. I also didn't want any mail or any visitors coming to my living quarters, because I was afraid Mrs. Blecha would notice the unusual activity. Millie told me she intended to go home the last weekend of February, so I also made plans to go home that weekend.

I decided to pay a visit to Karel Rudolf and his parents in downtown Prague. He was very glad to see me, as were his parents. We had a nice reunion. I hadn't seen him since his military discharge, and by now he had finished his studies and become a lawyer. I was offered very pleasant hospitality in their luxurious apartment. After a long while, Karel's father excused himself to take care of some business, and Mrs. Rudolf went off to discuss some domestic work with a maid. I was alone with Karel.

I knew I could trust him, so I explained about the situation at Poldi Steel and about my possible chance to get out of Czechoslovakia. He understood, and said that his oldest brother, Jan, had left the country and was temporarily living in Sweden, hoping to go from there to the United States. Karel told me to let him know if and when I was leaving, so that he could give me the name of a friend who ran a refugee camp near Munich. We had one more drink and said good-bye.

On the last weekend in February, I met Millie at a designated place in the railroad station, and we took the train together. She told me Mr. Barta's health was getting worse and that he might have to leave soon. She also told me they were looking for someone to take Mr. Barta across the Czech-German border.

When I arrived home everything was as usual. My little niece, Marie, had all kinds of reports to give me about her neighbor, her friend Vera, her school, and my dog Bonzo. I always brought her and Ludmila chocolate wafers or some kind of candy.

After supper, my brother-in-law and I went to the village restaurant. I knew that Frantisek would be there to have his usual two beers. It was still wintertime, but not too severe. The restaurant was nice and warm, which went well with the excellent cold Czech beer. One room was occupied with card players, and in the next room I played pool with some of my friends.

The next day, Sunday, I tried to surreptitiously locate some things: my harmonica, grafting knife, briefcase, and papers. Ludmila didn't know, of course, that I was collecting my belongings to take with me to Prague. The only question that she raised was about the briefcase, so I told her I needed it to carry sheet music. Later in the afternoon, my good sister had my wash and food ready, and the time came to leave for the train. I bade good-bye to all, as usual, and said I would be back in two weeks.

Millie boarded the local train at her town's stop, and we were on our way to Prague. There was a long train ride ahead so we had an opportunity to discuss some details she would have to take care of after my departure from the country. I gave her Vincenc's telephone number, and Millie would notify him where to pick up my belongings. He had no idea that I was in the Underground.

When I returned to my living quarters, Mrs. Blecha was not at home. I wanted to make myself a cup of coffee, but in the kitchen I found a note from her son saying that Mrs. Blecha had been admitted to the hospital. I worried about her. She was such a nice lady, and her declining health made me very uneasy.

About a week later, Millie notified me that Mr. Barta wanted to meet me in the lobby of the Ambassador Hotel. I went there, and he told me we would need money for the train fare to the Black Forest in Southern Bohemia, where we were supposed to cross the Czech-German border. He also told me our departure was set for late March, and that the exact date would depend on the weather and availability of a guide to take us to the border.

Our conversation was as brief and quiet as possible. I told Mr. Barta that I would do my best to get some money, and let him know through Millie. I didn't even understand how he could manage to stay in that nice hotel, which was very expensive. He must have had extra income, because his business had been seized by the Communists.

Now that I had the departure dates, I had a lot to think about and a lot to plan. How could I raise some money? I couldn't ask my brothers or sisters or cousin, since nobody was supposed to know about my leaving.

I decided to start at work. I approached Mr. Hruska and asked if I could get an advance payment of Kcs 2,000 for my vacation, which I would be taking in the winter this year. I explained that I had been invited to visit my cousin's son, who lived near the Tatra Mountains in Slovakia. It was a long distance away, so the train fare would be expensive. I also needed spending money for my two weeks there. I offered to repay Kcs 400 from my salary over five months. Mr. Hruska was a little hesitant, but he had been very pleased with my work, and he had never personally asked me to join the party-although I had found the form on my desk a few times.

Because almost everyone wanted to have a summer vacation, Mr. Hruska finally decided it was advantageous that I'd planned to take mine in winter. He asked me to give him the dates, and I told him March 15 to March 26, 1949. Mr. Hruska told his secretary to prepare one memo that would show my vacation schedule and another memo that would cover my request for an advance on my salary. Both memos were done in triplicate: one each for Mr. Hruska, the Personnel Department, and me. However, the memo about my repayment plan had to be signed by a higher executive, Mr. Liska, and Mr. Hruska sent me to him for his signature.

I went to Mr. Liska's office and explained why I was there. He read the memo and said, "You will make four payments, each Kcs 500, in the next four months." Mr. Liska was new—a comrade of course—and he had replaced a very nice man who was obviously not a party member. Apparently just to show that he was the boss, he ordered this change. He corrected the repayment figures, signed the memo, and gave it to me. I thanked him and left.

When I returned to Mr. Hruska's office and handed him the corrected memo, he looked a little surprised. But the change had come from a boss, so it had to be all right. He gave me one copy of each memo, and told me to take the others to his secretary. The secretary asked me to wait a moment while she went somewhere. In a few minutes she came back and said I would get the money on the Friday before my vacation. This was fine with me.

I was surprised that I had succeeded with my plan; I hadn't really thought it would work because I wasn't a comrade. However, I was relieved because now I would have money in time for my escape.

As agreed, I wanted to inform my friend, Karel Rudolf, about my plans. When we met at his home, I told him everything. He was happy for me and said that he had prepared something for me to take.

Karel brought in a large brown bag from the next room, and started to take things from it: ski boots, shorts for warmer weather, two boxes of beautiful pink pearl necklaces, twelve in each box. He explained, "You will not have any DM [Deutsche Marks] right away, but in a pinch you could get some money for these necklaces." I couldn't believe his generosity. And that wasn't all. He opened the drawer of his desk and handed me a brass compass, saying, "You were an artillery man, you never know when you might need this."

After Karel put those things in the bag, we had a drink together, and during our conversation he mentioned that one of these days he, too, might escape. The main reason he couldn't leave now was that his parents were elderly, and his older brother was in Sweden, his younger brother was incapable of caring for the parents. Karel's girlfriend, Vlasta, also had parents and a brother to worry about. All of this played a major role in his staying, at least for the time being.

Now the time had come for our farewells. Karel asked me to write him. We gave each other a friendly hug, and with my eyes full of tears, I left. It was a very emotional moment.

The time had also come for a farewell visit to my brother, Vincenc, and his family-even if they wouldn't realize I was there to say good-bye. I went to see them on March 12, just before making my last weekend trip home. George, my godchild, was eight years old and growing into a big boy. My sister-in-law, Jirina, was a very good baker, and she served some pastries to go with a cup of coffee. Vincenc told me that conditions at his office were not pleasant. The Communists were demanding attendance at their meetings and trying to brainwash people with their doctrine. We talked until the wee hours, but I finally had to say good-bye-trying not to show any emotion. After that night I didn't see Vincenc for forty-one years.

I encountered a similar situation two days later, when I went home for the weekend. By now I knew from Millie that the date for my escape was set for either March 26 or 27, depending on the weather.

After I arrived home on Saturday, March 13, I told Ludmila that I needed some exercise, and would take my bicycle to go visit our other three sisters: Marie, Frantiska, and Anna. It was late in the afternoon, but I didn't mind riding fifteen miles on my bike; I knew I wouldn't see them for a long time.

It was a very difficult evening for me: trying to be like an actor, pretending nothing unusual was going to happen two weeks later. I dared not tell my sisters and brothers about my decision to leave Czechoslovakia. After I was gone, they would undoubtedly be questioned by the police and asked why they hadn't reported my intentions. It would be hard for them to lie convincingly, but this way they could honestly say that none of them had known what I planned to do.

It was around 10:30 P.M. when I arrived back at Ludmila's. As usual, she was getting my laundry ready for my next day's trip to Prague. I sat with her for quite a while, telling her news about the other sisters. My brother-in-law and little Marie were already in bed. Finally, I also had to call it a day because I was exhausted and emotionally wrung out.

The next day I had one more visit to make: with my brother, Frantisek, and his family. Again I pretended to be an actor, and I managed to get through the afternoon without giving anything away.

After Sunday dinner, while my Ludmila washed dishes, I looked in a cabinet drawer where I kept various small things. There was the insignia of my gymnastic group, the bronze "Sokol" pin, which I'd had since the early days of the Nazi occupation. I pinned it on the lapel of my suit. Another thing I came across was the fountain pen. I had used during my military service. I filled it with ink, and tucked it in my pocket.

As usual, Ludmila had my small suitcase ready, left open in case I wanted to add something at the last moment. I looked inside to check the contents. Since I wouldn't be able to take much with me, I removed a few things: some small towels, handkerchiefs, a couple pairs of socks, and a tablecloth. So that my sister wouldn't wonder about what I was doing, I told her that I was running out of drawer space in my room.

It was time to go to the train stop just as I always did. I thanked my sister, and gave her my usual hug and kiss on her cheek. I asked little Marie to find my dog, so that she and Bonzo could accompany me to the end of the garden. The next time I saw Ludmila, she was 81 years old, and Marie had recently celebrated her fiftieth birthday.

I tried not to cry after I got on the train. I wished that Millie had been traveling with me for this last painful trip. She was the only one who could know what I was feeling that night. And of course, Millie had become very important to me. Without her, I would never have had the chance to escape to freedom.

When I entered my room in Prague, I knew that the next two weeks would be quite different than when I was routinely going to work. Millie and I had made arrangements to meet at a nearby house, because I had to stick close to home in case there was a sudden change of plans.

It was very hard to pass the time in one small room. I tried to be busy myself with decisions about what to pack and what to leave behind.

I still had something important to take care of: writing letters to my brothers and sisters that I would mail on the last day before leaving. This was very important, because if any of them were questioned by the police, the letters would be proof that they didn't know I had planned to escape. Because I had no typewriter, I had to write six identical letters by hand. I thought long and hard about what to say, and after a couple of false starts, decided on a very brief note:

I will not be seeing you for some time in the near future. I am going on a business trip to do some research with regard to ore for the steel production. I will contact you or see you when I return to Prague.

Your brother,

George

I placed all six letters inside my briefcase. I also packed the two boxes of pearl necklaces and the shorts from my dear friend, Karel Rudolf. Next I put in a kitchen knife, a dish cloth, a pair of clean socks, and an English-Czech/Czech-English dictionary. The harmonica, compass, and papers I planned to carry in my pockets. I had a new pair of shoes, made by the local shoemaker in our village, but there was no room for them because I had to have some space for food. I would wear the ski boots that Karel had given me.

On Wednesday, March 24, Millie told me the departure day was definite: Saturday, March 27. Mr. Barta would come by taxi to pick me up around noon. She delivered a message from him to take very few things with me; he had money in Germany, and when we arrived there, he would dress me from head to toe. Millie also told me she would come to help me pack on Friday evening.

Well, the schedule was set. I now had only to count the hours. I wrote a note to Mrs. Blecha's son, asking him to be kind enough to return my trumpet to the Conservatory of Music. The rent had been paid. I would leave the note and the key on the kitchen table.

Millie arrived right on time Friday evening. I told her I had taken care of the last-minute errands. But I hadn't packed, because I wanted her to know what was in the two suitcases that Vincenc would pick up after Millie notified him.

I started to take some items out of the chest of drawers: clothes, linen, a few books, glasses, dishes, utensils, towels, and other various items. I offered Millie a few things while we packed, but she only took a few coat hangers and some sugar, coffee and tea.

It was after 10:00 P.M. when we finished, and we still had to take suitcases to the Underground building. The last thing I packed was a sheet of one hundred mint postage stamps, issued in 1948 to commemorate the six-hundredth anniversary of Charles University.

Just before we left, Millie handed me Kcs 4,000 and said, "George, take this money. I want you to have some extra hard currency. I know you need it. Who knows, maybe someday you can help my father."

I was astonished. I hesitated to take the money, but she insisted. I thanked her, and promised I would eventually return it. I didn't ask Millie why she mentioned her father, but I thought his being a police chief under the Communist regime might have something to do with it.

It was time to go. I picked up the heavy suitcase, and Millie took the lighter one, and we walked a couple of blocks to the underground building. I told the people there my brother would collect the suitcases after Millie called him. They asked me to take care of Mr. Barta, and wished me good luck. Millie and I both thanked them, said good night, and left.

I accompanied Millie to the nearest streetcar stop. She said, "I hope you will make it safely, and that Mr. Barta will get some medical help. He is really very ill. I wish you both good luck." The streetcar was just arriving. I gave Millie a big hug and kiss, and with my eyes full of tears, waved good-bye. I walked home with churning emotions, and felt frightened.

*My wife and I saw Millie after forty-one years in her Prague apartment. When I rang the bell she opened the door, but didn't recognize me and asked to see my identification card. When I did, she began to cry. I wouldn't have recognized her in the street either.

Millie told us she had almost lost her 19-year-old son when the Communists beat him up and several others who were in an anti-government demonstration on Venceslav Square. She said it was a miracle he had survived, but that he had suffered some permanent damage.

Millie went on to say that she'd had a nervous breakdown after her son's disaster. Her husband couldn't cope with the situation, and they divorced.

I asked her if she received the Kcs 4,000 that I sent her from Hamburg in 1950. Millie said she did, and that I shouldn't have done it.

She opened a jar of home-canned wild blueberries and offered us some in small dishes. Millie said she found them in the woods near Prague and told us that since President Vaclav Havel's wife, Olga, loves blueberries, Millie always shares them with her.

Then she showed us a basket of walnuts and said, "These walnuts are also for Olga. I pick them on the outskirts of Prague when I go on my bicycle rides."

I was very much surprised that Millie was so close to President Havel and his wife, and I asked her how it came about. She explained that the President had wanted to know the names of all victims of communist oppression. He then visited with them and their families, and that's how she became friends with the President and his wife.

Before I left, I gave Millie a $20 bill and thanked her again for all she had done for me. Later I sent her a package from the United States with two beautiful blouses chosen by my wife.

On my next trip to the Czech Republic in 1993, I saw Millie again. This time our meeting was easier. I asked her how she was, and she said she had completely recovered from her breakdown. We had a nice talk, and before I left I gave her $50. But I could never repay Millie for the kindness she had shown me in 1949.

CHAPTER 11

ESCAPE ANXIETY

AT NOON ON MARCH 27, 1949, THERE WAS A KNOCK AT THE DOOR OF MY rooming house. It was the architect, Mr. Barta, who had arrived in a taxi. To my great astonishment, I realized he was drunk.

For a second, I thought something must be wrong, and that the plan had gone awry. But Mr. Barta seemed happy and excited as he hustled me out to the waiting taxi, whispering instructions that I should keep quiet during the ride.

At Smichov Railroad Station. Mr. Barta paid the driver and we walked inside. We were met by a young Underground member who called himself Robert. The three of us boarded the train and sat quietly. I was extremely nervous, but I tried not to fidget. I kept telling myself that this was the first step in my quest for freedom.

At 1:30 P.M., the train pulled out of the station. We were on our way toward the Czech-German border, somewhere in the Black Forest. There was still no talking. Robert looked very serious, Mr. Barta looked very ill, and I probably looked very frightened. The hours dragged by slowly.

Finally, at about 9:30 P.M., we got off at the small village of Lenora. The area was uninhabited, because most of the population had been evacuated into Germany two years earlier, by the order of the Czech government.

Robert told us that his brother lived in Lenora, and had been one of the evacuees. But Robert had a key to his brother's house, and he quietly slipped us inside. Mr. Barta was still quite sick, so we put him to bed and covered him with our coats. Luckily, he soon stopped coughing and fell asleep. Now we had to wait until our designated departure time at 1:30 A.M.

I took out some bread and hard salami and shared the food with Robert. Even though I was warmly dressed I found myself shivering in this unheated house. Maybe it was nerves.

At 1:15, we awakened Mr. Barta and got ready for our three-and-a-half mile walk through the woods toward the border. I offered Mr. Barta some food, but he declined. We were relieved that his coughing had subsided, because in the silence of the night every little noise carried.

We left Robert's brother's house on schedule. After walking for a bit, we passed a frozen pond on the side of the road. Robert thought we could take a shortcut across the pond. He gestured for us to stay put while he tested the ice to determine if it was thick enough to cross. It wasn't, so we had to walk around it.

It was a clear night, very cold, with a fairly bright moon and a slight breeze. Robert had told us before we started that the first quarter-mile would be the most dangerous stretch, because we had to pass a police station, where there were dogs. Fortunately, the breeze was blowing from the direction of the station, which apparently deflected our scent.

The police station was surrounded by a solid wooden fence, which enclosed the dogs. As we passed the station, a car suddenly drove by, illuminating the area with its high beams and awakened a dog. Robert quickly motioned us into a ditch alongside the road until the dog stopped barking and the car passed.

We thought things had calmed down when another car appeared. Fortunately its passengers didn't notice us lying flat in the ditch.

I had all but stopped breathing, certain we would be caught. But everything was fine. After the second car passed, Robert gestured for us to leave the road, and walk toward the dense woods. He led us to a lonely path between trees that was covered with snow and fallen twigs. Every time I stepped on a twig in my heavy ski boots, there was a loud cracking sound. I decided to take off my boots and walk the remainder of the way in my socks.

I didn't realize how far it was, or that we would be walking through deep snow until 6 A.M. in the morning. But I managed, and we finally reached the border area. We stood on the edge of a dense forest, looking out at a meadow. Robert pointed to where the border was: a brook about five or six feet wide.

I tried to put on my ski boots, which was difficult to do over my soaking-wet socks. I dug out a dry pair of socks and pulled on the boots.

Now it was time to say good-bye. I gave Robert a hug and thanked him, as did Mr. Barta. As we walked towards the border, I looked behind and waved. When I looked back again, he was gone.

When we reached the narrow brook, I thought I could jump across it. But what about Mr. Barta? He was exhausted, ill, weak, hungry, and he'd begun to cough again. I looked around and saw a railed fence. One of the rails was hanging so I wrenched it off to use as a plank across the brook.

I walked over the plank first and stepped onto a snowbank, then watched as Mr. Barta unsteadily started across. At the last moment he slipped on the icy plank and fell into the brook.

Luckily, he was close enough for me to grab his arms and I pulled him up onto the snow bank. I knew we couldn't stay there while Mr. Barta recovered, and dragged him along hurrying as fast as possible away from the border. Although we were in Germany and on our way to freedom, this was a dangerous area. The Communists shot people even after they had crossed the border, and then pulled them back into Czechoslovakia. Since dawn was breaking, we were quite visible against the snow.

Finally I dragged Mr. Barta who revived and seemed able to walk. But by now we both were absolutely exhausted and needed to rest. I was a healthy twenty-six year old, so I couldn't imagine how Mr. Barta-who was over sixty and quite ill-must be feeling. We sat down behind a large boulder, where we shared some bread and salami. We allowed ourselves a short rest, then started off again. After a few hundred feet, we arrived at the same brook. But here it was on our left and here it was very shallow, with roots of trees making a bridge over it.

We stepped across on the roots and walked further along. But suddenly we found ourselves staring at the brook-this time on our right. Somehow we had wandered back into Czechoslovakia. What should we do now? I remembered Karel's compass that I had put in my pocket before leaving Prague. Using it, I determined which way to go. Once more, we crossed the brook back into Germany.

After walking several hundred feet in a new and hopefully correct direction, we saw white smoke rising from the chimney of a log cabin. Mr. Barta, who had built sugar mills in Bavaria and was familiar with its countryside, was smiling. He confidently announced that we had reached Bavaria.

In order to be sure, I decided to crawl toward the house to get a better look at some white lettering on the front door. Slowly and quietly, I crept under a window to the door, and saw three nameplates. I will never forget that moment as long as I live. The names were Ritter, Schneider, and Schueller-typical German names.

I slowly crawled back and told Mr. Barta what I'd seen. He said that settled it: we were in Germany. This time we walked normally towards the house. I knocked at the door and in a few moments, a very old woman opened it. She said in German, in a Schwabish accent, "Was wuenschen Sie" ("What do you wish?"). I asked Mr. Barta to speak to her, as he knew the Schwabish dialect very well.

Mr. Barta asked the lady how to get inland to the nearest railroad station or town. She said the road through a nearby field would take us to a town called Heidmuehle, which was the last stop on the railroad before the Czech border. We thanked her and walked on. It was now eight o'clock.

Suddenly we heard a swishing sound coming from a nearby hill. In a few seconds, a German policeman on skis stopped in front of us calling, "Halt." I was relieved, as I knew the German police were authorized by the United States to escort refugees from Communist-ruled Czechoslovakia into the U.S. zone of Germany.

The policeman removed his skis, stuck them into the snow, and approached us on foot. He patted us down, asking if we had any guns or money. He didn't want my Czech crowns. Exhausted as I was, I even offered to carry his skis, but he refused. His name was Tchejka, which is a Germanized Czech name.

After the policeman made his inquiries, he pointed to a hill on the other side of a rather deep valley and said in German, "On those hills over there, two weeks ago, the Communists shot to death two refugees, quickly pulled them back into Czechoslovakia, and there was nothing we could do." When I heard that I shivered. Furthermore, I was very surprised that after crossing the brook three times, we were still just a stone's throw from the Czech-German border. We had no idea that we had been walking almost parallel to the brook on the German side. Even in the company of this German policeman, I couldn't wait to get as far away as possible.

Mr. Barta was completely exhausted, he could barely walk, and he still had that worrisome cough. I held his arm and tried to help him as much as I could. The three of us walked quite a while before finally arriving at a police station. There we were asked many questions, mainly about our backgrounds. I was afraid that they would want to look into my briefcase where I had those two dozen pearl necklaces that Karel had given me. To avoid any further questions, I reached into my pocket and handed them some small-denomination Czech bank notes and coins (altogether about Kcs 180, or $6 in US money). I kept Kcs 1.000 in a tiny pocket underneath my belt for a rainy day.

After leaving the police station, the policeman took us to a larger town, Freyung, where an American official issued a pass to each of us bearing the words, "U.S. zone of Germany." This pass authorized us to use rail services, free of charge, from Heidmuehle to Munich.

The big problem was that we still had to get to Heidmuehle, which was two or three miles from Freyung. I was able to walk that distance, but Mr. Barta just couldn't. We were in luck. The local grocer was going to Heidmuehle by horse-and-carriage, and the police arranged for Mr. Barta to ride with him. I was accompanied by a German civilian with a rifle on his back. We walked to Heidmuehle.

It was beautiful to see Mr. Barta sitting next to the grocer on the carriage as the horse trotted down the road. At Heidmuehle I thanked the grocer, helped Mr. Barta descend from the carriage and both of us were escorted by the armed civilian into the Heidmuehle railroad station.

The station was a very small, unheated building and not one other soul was waiting for the train. After we boarded at about 2:30 P.M., the conductor checked our passes-and we were on the way to Munich.

We went through Passau, Landshut, and finally arrived in Munich at about 8:30 A.M. Our pass showed the name of a refugee camp, known as Luitpold Kasserne, which was formerly a military camp. It was not too far from the Hauptbahnhof, the main railroad station, which still had many broken glass panes in the dome caused by wartime bombing.

We finally reached Luitpold Kasserne, where we reported to the camp office. We showed them the passes, which they took. They then gave us some sort of identification cards. We were ushered into a large hall filled with refugees: a mixture of all ages and several nationalities. It was some sight! I immediately inquired about a nurse or a hospital for Mr. Barta. Luckily, there was a Red Cross hospital in the camp, and I immediately took Mr. Barta there. Up until now, he'd been my responsibility, just as I'd promised the Underground back in Prague. But my mission was accomplished.

It was an emotional moment for both of us. I gave him a hug, shook hands, and wished him a quick recovery. He thanked me with tearful eyes and said, "George, I hope that God will reward you for the good deed you did. I hope that you will not have to stay long in this camp, and that soon your dream of going to America will come true. Good luck." I thanked him for his kind words, and said I would visit him the next day. I waved to Mr. Barta as I left, and he raised his tired arm in return.

I went back to the crowded room, where I was given two blankets and a pillow, and a tin dish with a handle. Now it was time for my first supper in the camp. We all stood in a long line, to receive bean soup, a baked potato, browned onions, black coffee, and a hard roll. After I ate and washed the dish, I began to think about getting some sleep. I still was wearing two suits, so I went to a lavatory to take one off. I folded it and put it inside of my heavy overcoat. I also spoke to a couple of other refugees, who had been in the camp for a while. I asked them what would be the next step for me.

Not long after this discussion, I realized I had to do something to keep my things secure during the night. I took off a shoelace from one ski boot, tied my briefcase and shoes to my overcoat through the buttonhole, placed the ski boots and briefcase underneath the coat, and put the coat with my suit inside on top of the pillow, and I placed my black hat over my eyes. At 10:00 P.M. the lights were turned off.

The next day, March 30, was my twenty-sixth birthday. After a simple breakfast and cleanup, I went to see Mr. Barta. He was still sleeping, so I asked a doctor about his condition. The doctor said that Mr. Barta had a tumor, which now had been removed. If Mr. Barta hadn't received medical attention, it could have proven fatal. I knew he was very ill, but I didn't realize it was that serious. Obviously, both Robert and I had saved his life.

The next night they separated all the men from the women and children. I spoke to a Czech man who had been there for some time. When I said that I was part of an underground movement, which opposed communism, he told me not to mention it to the Americans because they didn't like such people. I didn't understand, but I thanked him for his advice.

That afternoon, I had to attend a screening conducted by a U.S. screening officer. The Americans didn't have enough interpreters who spoke Slavic and other European languages, so they had to employ foreign nationals. I was screened by a Ukrainian who knew a little Czech, a little Slovak, some German, and very little English. Because I knew the same languages, we didn't have any problem communicating. He asked me whether I had been in jail or was about to be arrested when I escaped. As we talked, he filled in some sort of form. I told him the truth-that I didn't like the communists for a number of reasons: their forceful methods; the compulsory attendance at their never-ending brainwashing meetings; the paying of party dues; and the inability to get job promotions if you were not a party member.

But I didn't tell him, that I was in the underground movement against communism, or that I escorted Mr. Barta at the underground movement's request or that I had saved his life. He primarily wanted to hear that I had either been in jail or was about to be jailed. But when I didn't say that, he informed me, "I don't think I can recommend you for the IRO (International Refugee Organization) protection. However, you can go to the next building, ask for a form, and appeal to Geneva."

This was a terrible blow for me. I did go to the next building, secured the form, completed it, and gave it back to Madame Dutrepount, a Frenchwoman who was employed there. She told me after several days that I would be transferred to another camp, Hammelburg, where all applicants were sent while waiting for a reply from Geneva. Everyone there would receive an allowance of DM 10 a month. (At that time 4 DM were equivalent to $1.) After three days of waiting, I went to see Mr. Barta. He was progressing very well, and told me that he would soon be released. The next time I saw him, Mr. Barta had completed his screening and had been accepted for IRO protection. Of course, he hadn't been in jail either, so obviously he didn't get the same official that interviewed me.

Neither Mr. Barta nor I had any money. But that shrewd old businessman walked into the city of Munich-and when he returned, Mr. Barta told me that I could get DM 9 for a dozen of the pearl necklaces that I carried in my briefcase. This was great news, since at that point I didn't even have the money for a postage stamp to notify my relatives where I was. After Mr. Barta sold the necklaces for me, I gave him DM 4 and kept DM 5 for myself.

I was informed that on April 12, I would have to leave for Camp Hammelburg, about 250 miles north of Munich. I remembered that there was a map on the wall of the waiting room at the railroad station. I went there, studied the map, and saw that to get to Hammelburg I would have to transfer at the small town of Muenden. One direction would be to Hammelburg, and the other would be to Frankfurt am Main. I also saw that I could go in the opposite direction-to Frankfurt from where I could hitchhike to the British zone. I went back to the camp and didn't mention this to anyone.

On the day before my departure, I was called into the camp office and given a railroad ticket and a paper to hand in when I arrived in Hammelburg. I went to visit Mr. Barta and told him I was being transferred, but I didn't tell him I was considering an alternate plan. I said good-bye and wished him an early emigration to Sweden, where he was to meet his wife. That was the last time I saw Mr. Barta.

On April 12, I boarded the train heading north. It was late in the afternoon when we arrived in Muenden. It was not a large station, and I was surprised to see a Red Cross office there. I inquired about the departure time of the train for Frankfurt, and was told it would leave at 6:00 A.M. I made up my mind, and decided not to go to Hammelburg. I arranged with the Red Cross to stay overnight, gave one of the nuns DM 1, and asked her to awaken me at 5:00 A.M. I still had money from the sale of the pearl necklaces in Munich, so I bought a ticket to Frankfurt and destroyed the other ticket and the paper for Hammelburg. It was a beautiful day, and I decided to go for a walk to kill some time.

Not too far from the railroad station was a large outdoor market lined with trucks. Suddenly I wondered if I could find one that would be going toward Hamburg, 250 miles away in the British zone. I saw a truck with a sign that said, "Bielefeld." That was in the right direction, so I asked the driver and his helper if they would take me along. The driver agreed but said they had to deliver boxes of margarine to several places in Frankfurt. I offered to help.

We rode along in almost total silence, made the deliveries, and left Frankfurt—crossing the main river on the only one of seven bridges left standing after Allied bombing raids. No one ate nor drank a thing. We drove until 1:30 A.M. the next morning, when the driver finally pulled into truck stop station. We entered the restaurant, which was a large room with a bar. The driver and his helper took a table by themselves, while I sat down at the near end of the room. I had used almost all my money on the train ticket to Frankfurt, so I ordered nothing but lemonade. The room was full of smoke and very hot. There were two men standing by the bar, smoking, drinking, and talking. I wasn't really paying attention to them until one suddenly said, "I know where you came from. You are from Czechoslovakia, aren't you? I know the insignia on your jacket. You are one of those who forced me and my family out of your country. I had to leave in 1947 and lost everything—my restaurant, my grocery business, and my tobacco shop." I knew this was true, since the Czechoslovak government had deported all Germans who sympathized with Hitler.

The insignia on my lapel was my bronze Sokol pin, which had been issued by the Czech gymnastic organization. I wore it proudly, and I wasn't going to let this jerk insult me, my pin—or my country.

So after he shut up, it was my turn. I spoke loudly, in German, so that everyone in the room could hear and understand me. I told him that it wasn't I who had ordered him to move his family, and that the Communists who supported the USSR were to blame. I told him that I had escaped because of the Communists, and that I didn't agree with their philosophy or their methods. Also, I told him that he was better off than I was. At least he had something to eat while I had nothing.

Then I pulled out one of the pearl necklaces and showed it to him. I said I would be willing to sell it to him very cheaply so that I could buy something to eat. I set the price at DM 1.50, although in the shops the price was DM 6.00 or more. I suggested that he buy one for his wife. He looked at me, very much surprised, undecided for a minute, not believing what had happened. But it worked. He got out his wallet and bought the necklace. I thanked him, and immediately pulled out another one, showed it to the lady behind the bar, and asked her if she would also like to purchase one. She agreed, and I even sold a third necklace to someone else. Now I had made three sales for a total of DM 4.50. I immediately ordered a salami, bread, and lemonade.

I hadn't realized that before this man had spoken to me, he went to the truck driver and talked to him. Later on I learned that he had asked him not to take me back on the truck.

After I finished my small meal, the man who had provoked the argument came over and offered me a drink. I couldn't believe my eyes, which filled with tears. He probably wasn't sure that I would accept it, but when I did, he asked me to wait. He went back and bought himself a drink, touched my glass and said, "Schuess," which means "Mud in your eye." After we finished the drink, he described more of what had happened in 1947. He also told me that he had spoken to my truck driver and ordered him not to take me any further. I was shocked to hear this, and I asked the driver if I could continue riding with him and his helper. They agreed, so I said, "Auf Wiedersehen," to everyone in the restaurant.

We continued on our trip towards Bielefeld. It was mid-morning when the driver suddenly stopped in front of an overpass. He said it would be better for me not to go into the city, but to climb up on the ramp and try to hitchhike with someone else. I was so grateful for the help of these two men that I gave them both a necklace for their wives. They were delighted, because they certainly had never expected any sort of payment. I thanked them and climbed up the ramp.

On the upper road I started hitchhiking, but no one stopped. I decided to walk until I was on top of the hill and on level road. Finally a pickup truck pulled over. We had traveled quite a distance before the man gestured that I should get off. He advised me that we had reached the station of a streetcar that would take me to Hamburg.

In a short while, the streetcar arrived. I had just about enough money to buy a ticket for Hamburg, and then at last I was in the British zone of Germany.

I asked someone where there was a refugee camp. The man told me it was called the D.P. Camp Zoo. I looked at him and thought he was joking. I repeated my question, and he gave me the same name. To sound more convincing, he explained that it was near Damtor Hochbahn Station, not too far from where I had gotten off the street car. I followed his directions, and sure enough—soon I was standing in front of the sign that said, "D.P. Camp Zoo."

Chapter 12

THE D.P. CAMP ZOO

It was Good Friday, 1949, when I appeared in Hamburg in front of a fenced camp. The entrance had a big gate, and above it there was that mysterious sign, "D.P. Camp Zoo." I didn't know what to think. I didn't realize at the time that the initials D.P. meant "Displaced Persons"-and what about that word "Zoo"? Yes, it was true, it used to be a zoo, full of animals belonging to the famous Hagenbeck Circus. Not long ago, the animals had been evacuated. Now dozens of wooden huts were filled with political refugees.

Near the entrance, I saw a man in a dark uniform standing in a small structure similar to a telephone booth. He didn't pay any attention to me, so I walked in through the open gate and slowly looked around. I knocked on a few doors with signs that read "Office" and "Camp Leader," to no avail. It was after five o'clock, and all the administrative personnel were off for the Easter holidays—which extends through Monday in European countries. Finally, someone pointed out a hut where other Czech refugees were staying. I poked my head in, and saw six beds but only three men. I asked whether someone was in charge of the camp's Czech refugees. One of the men told me his name was Josef Rosa, then demanded to know, "Where did you come from? Which zone did you come from?" I didn't tell him that I had been in the Munich camp, but said that I crossed the Czech-German border in Bavaria and had hitchhiked from there. I don't think he believed me, but he said there was one Czech, Karel Drapalik, who was working somewhere as a roofer, and that maybe he could help.

Outside of the hut, I noticed a vehicle bearing a Red Cross sign and walked over to it. Fortunately, I still remembered quite a bit of English from my college years. I explained to the female driver that I sought accommodations. She turned out to be a British officer by the name of Miss Ryder. As she walked with me to a hut where she had seen an empty bed, she complimented me on my English. We came to Hut F12, where there was an empty steel bed near the door, but no blanket or pillow. Still after all the traveling, I was just happy to find a place to sleep. When I inquired about food, Miss Ryder responded, "Oh, you don't have tickets for meals?" She opened her notebook, removed a couple of blank pages, and made nine paper tickets out of them: three each for breakfast, lunch and supper. She instructed me to stand in line and present a ticket to the kitchen person giving out meals. This was helpful, of course, but she couldn't help me with blankets. She had other business to attend to and responded "not at all" when I thanked her. (In the U.S. zone they had always said, "You're welcome.")

Luckily, I found Mr. Drapalik for help with the blankets. He asked me why I hadn't received any from the camp office. When I told him I'd just arrived, he started questioning me. "How do I know, when I loan you some blankets, that you will then leave, and I might never see you again? What do you have to give me for a guarantee that you will return the blankets? Do you have money?" I replied, "No." He said, "Sorry, I cannot trust anybody without some collateral." I thought of something: my fountain pen with a 14K gold tip. I showed it to him, and explained, "This is my very beloved pen, very valuable to me. I will leave it with you as collateral, and when I do get blankets from the camp office on Tuesday, we will make an exchange. Would that be all right?" He looked at it and tried it out on a piece of paper. Then I said, "I expect to get it back in a few days, OK?" He agreed, and he handed me two blankets. I thanked him and took the blankets to the hut where I was assigned. I was hungry, but the kitchen was closed. I needed a shave, a shower and—most of all—sleep. I was very tired.

Near my hut was a large shower room, where I bathed and shaved. Then I returned to my hut, in which five Polish men had already gone to bed. I introduced myself, made a pillow out of my things, and settled down for my much-needed sleep.

The next morning, I went for my first breakfast, and the line was quite long. The people working in the kitchen were all Lithuanians, so I spoke German to them when my turn came. The breakfast consisted of a dark loaf of bread which was supposed to last for three days, a piece of margarine the size of my little finger, and black coffee with no sugar. I managed to find an empty can of sweetened milk, which I kept in my briefcase for possible use as a cup. I made good use of it now, because I couldn't get any dishes until after the Easter holidays. The meals were not too good-bean soup, potato soup, herring, and some kind of unpalatable hash-but they were sufficient.

On Tuesday I went to the office. Although most of the employees were Lithuanians, the camp leader, Mr. Murphy, was Irish. I registered by filling out the form, and they told me that I had to go for a screening just as I did in Munich. This time the officer was a Dutchman named Dr. Andersen. When I entered the waiting room by his office, there were two other men sitting there. One was Hungarian, while the other one, to my surprise, was Czech. I spoke with them before they were called in. The Hungarian could speak only his native language and Slovak fairly well, so we conversed in Slovak. His turn came first. Soon after, Dr. Andersen gestured for me to come in. He asked if I could help translate his questions for the Hungarian. He also asked if I knew English or German. Dr. Andersen decided to converse with me in German. After several questions, the Hungarian was accepted and was sent to the admitting office.

Next was the Czech who could only speak Czech and Slovak, so again, Dr. Andersen beckoned me to help. I translated Czech into German this time. After being questioned, my countryman passed.

Now my turn came. Dr. Andersen smiled and asked me the now-familiar questions: "Why did you escape?" "Were you in the Communist party?" This time I admitted that I was in the Underground against communism, and that, of course, I wasn't a member of the Communist party. I passed in about five minutes. What a difference in screening compared to the one in the U.S. zone in Munich! I went to the admitting office where I secured meal tickets for a week and two blankets. When Mr. Drapalik came from work that evening, we made an exchange: I returned his two blankets, and he gave me my fountain pen.

I didn't like the men in my room. They drank, were loud and boisterous, and associated with German women who gave them money for drinks. One Polish fellow made curtains out of blankets, which he had hung on wires around his bunk to provide privacy when he was entertaining his girlfriend. But once he didn't close the blankets properly, so we could see them making love. Another time the Polish man, who was an invalid with a bad leg, took out a tin can and urinated in it. One of the other men began to berate him, and the argument turned ugly. The invalid reached behind his bed, took out an ax, swung the blunt end at the other man, and hit him so hard that his pelvic bone was chipped.

I didn't like to spend much time in that room, so I walked around looking for some Czech people. I did find several that lived in different huts. I had my harmonica with me, and a group of us would gather at one place in the camp where there was a picnic bench. I would play Czech and Slovak songs, and the others would sing along. The weather was nice at that time of the year, so we met there almost daily.

One day I noticed three men strolling slowly toward our group. They had on long brown leather overcoats, the kind that German Gestapo officers had worn in Czechoslovakia during World War II. Not knowing who they were, I was uneasy; I hadn't seen anyone wearing that type of coat since the war. To my surprise, they walked over to me, and one of them complimented my playing. I was relieved that he spoke Czech. He asked me which hut I was in, so I told him that I lived in one room with eight Polish men and that I wasn't happy there. I described how the invalid had hit another man with an ax, and told them about the other incident with the tin can. Then one of them asked me if I would consider joining them in their hut. He told me that they had seven beds in their room, but since there were only six of them—all

Czechs—they needed one more man to occupy the spare bed. Of course, I quickly agreed to their offer. They went off to get permission for my transfer from the camp leader's office, and soon I was a resident of Hut H 9.

This room was smaller and lighter than the other hut, but it needed additional cleaning. We rolled up our sleeves and went to work. We scrubbed the floor, washed the walls, and disinfected the whole room, because animals had previously been housed there—after all, that's why the name of this camp was D.P. Camp Zoo. Once the odor went away, we had one of the best and cleanest rooms in the camp.

The others in the room were escapees from Czechoslovakia who had arrived in Hamburg by boat. This Czech boat was operated by a crew of two: the captain, Mr. Novak, and a second man, Vlastik Kopyta. Vlastik had stayed in Hamburg and was one of the men in our room. Captain Novak took five people on his boat with the agreement that he would smuggle them out of Czechoslovakia and through the Russian zone of Germany to the Port of Hamburg. As they were approaching the Russian zone on the Labe River, the five men had to be sealed in the hull, which was full of sugar. At the checkpoint, the Russian control came on and checked the boat.

Down below in the hull, the five of them could hear the controllers walking overhead on the deck. The Russians checked the lead seals on the hatches to the hull, and finally the boat began to move again. There was another check at the point where the boat was leaving the Russian zone for the British zone. This time the captain only had to show his papers, and the trip continued. When the boat was deeper into the British zone, the captain broke the seals and let some light and fresh air into the hull. A little later, the passengers left the boat and asked for political asylum.

Who were these people? Three of them, Josef, Robert, and Jaroslav, were pilots who had flown bombing missions from England during World War II. After the war was over, they returned to Czechoslovakia. But when the Communists assumed power in 1948, they had sought some means of escape. By luck, they found Captain Novak to help them.

The fourth man was Vaclav Kulnaty, who owned a beautiful hotel in Marianske Lazne, the well-known spa in the northern part of Bohemia. The Communists confiscated it and wanted to question him about his other properties, so Vaclav went into hiding until he was able to get on the boat. The fifth man was Vaclav Rezek, a garage owner, who had employed fourteen people in Prague. The Communists seized his garage and were looking for him as well. Eventually Vaclav was able to join the group on the boat, but he had to leave his wife, his teenage boy, and his newborn baby behind. All that Vaclav brought with him were his accordion, and fifty sheets of music, and some money.

The sixth man, Vlastik Kopyta, was the captain's partner. When the boat arrived in the port of Hamburg, Vlastik also asked for political asylum.

The group had managed to accumulate a good supply of canned foods, condensed milk, and one hundred pounds of sugar. Josef, Robert, and Jaroslav had expensive clothes and camel-hair blankets which they had brought from England. Vaclav Rezek had his accordion and sheet music. Vlastik had a true luxury, a little radio. Because our hut contained so many scarce items, it was our policy that one man had to be in the room at all times to protect against theft.

Since I didn't have a cup, I used my empty tin can for weeks. One day Vaclav said, "For goodness sake, George, I can't stand to see you drink coffee from that tin." He went to his bag, pulled out a porcelain cup and said, "Here, take this cup and throw that can away!"

Vaclav was an interesting fellow. He had been a Partisan during World War II, and was awarded a special Gold Liberty Distinction insignia, which he wore on the lapel of his jacket. He also had won some swimming competitions in Prague. Vaclav would be absent from the room very often, even overnight. We eventually learned that he had found himself a girlfriend. When he was in the hut, he played his accordion and we sang along. When Vaclav was at his girlfriend's, I played on my harmonica while the others sang.

We managed to enjoy ourselves, even though none of us except Vaclav had any money—not even for a haircut or postage stamps. There was just one razor blade for all seven of us, which had to be cleaned after each use and put back in its designated place. The rule was well observed, and it was always there when needed.

One day I found out that there was a chance to do some work in an area around Hamburg, which the Allied bombers had leveled. Vaclav lent four of us money for the streetcar fare, and we arose early to go clean bricks from the ruins. The city of Hamburg paid DM20 ($5) for a thousand clean bricks, which then had to be stacked. The supervisor at the site gave everyone a certificate after he counted how many bricks were stacked. We asked for just a single certificate for our group. I took it to the City Hall and received of DM 12.50, which I divided equally between the four of us. Now I had some money for a haircut and postage—and the ability to negotiate with my sponsors in the United States to help me find a job and accommodations.

My sponsors were Mr. and Mrs. Joseph Zack, who lived in New Jersey. I had met them in 1948, while I was still living in Prague and they were there visiting a niece. That came about because they had relatives in the same town where my sister, Frantiska, lived, and she was introduced to them. Frantiska told me when the Zacks would be at their niece's restaurant in Prague so that I could also meet them. We liked each other immediately and they suggested that if I ever wanted to leave Czechoslovakia, they would sponsor me. I was pleased with their offer, but I didn't think anything would come of it.

Still, they came through on their promise. I received my first mail at the camp: the Zacks' affidavit of support and certificate of employment. I immediately decided to walk to downtown Hamburg, where the American Consulate had an office. I registered there for immigration through the quota system. I thought that if the IRO didn't succeed, I could enter the United States through the quota method. Either way, the affidavit and job certificate were necessary, and later on, it proved to be extremely important.

One day when I was walking in the D.P. camp yard, I met a new arrival from Czechoslovakia, Jan Pilar. We talked for a while, and he told me that he had come to the British zone through the Russian zone—carrying ten thousand cigarette lighter flints that he wanted to sell. I told him I might be able to help, if he would give me some on consignment. Mr. Pilar agreed and counted out three hundred flints. We made a deal that I would pay him DM 1.50 after I sold them.

Now I had to figure out how to package them and where to find some buyers. I walked downtown to research where flints were sold and what they were priced at. I discovered that flints cost five for ten Pfenning (DM had one hundred Pfenning). I decided I would sell ten for ten Pfenning. This meant I needed to make up thirty packages.

Some refugees, who had relatives or sponsors in the United States, were getting packages with all kinds of food, clothing, and cigarettes. I found a few people who smoked US cigarettes, and I asked if they would give me their empty packages. Then I walked over to the camp kitchen, where I requested a small cup of flour.

I went to my room and started to make packages. I removed the cellophane from the cigarette packs, cut these up into small squares, made glue out of water and flour, and put ten flints in each of the improvised packages. Now I was ready to go sell them for half the price the shops were asking.

Vlastik had told us about his experiences while on the boat, and I remembered him talking about a big hall in the port area, where dockworkers waited to unload ships. So the next day I arose at five o'clock and walked down to the port. I located the big hall, where sixty or seventy men were coming and going-and smoking. I stood by the door and offered my flints. "Feuersteine, feuersteine-ten for ten Pfenning." Feuerstein is the German word for flint. Before long, I had sold all thirty packages.

Back to the camp, I located Mr. Pilar and paid him DM 1.50. I made DM 1.50, which for me was a great deal of money. I asked him for five hundred additional flints, and Mr. Pilar gladly counted them out. I went to the hut and did exactly the same packaging again. I repeated the procedure for three weeks, and during the third week I added cigarette papers—also at half the price for which they sold in the downtown shops. In those days, many smokers rolled their own cigarettes—which was much cheaper than buying them by the pack—so the papers were a great success.

One morning when I appeared in the hall with my flints and cigarette papers, a man told me that he bought papers from someone who was there before me. When he described the newcomer, I knew immediately that it was Vaclav Rezek. He must have followed me and decided to compete with my thriving business. When I returned to the camp, I asked Vaclav about his presence at the hall. He admitted that he had been there. His argument was that I didn't need as much money as he did, since he had a wife and children in Czechoslovakia. I was a little sore, but because he'd been nice to me in the past, I let it go. After that , I only sold flints, to which he didn't have access. And finally Mr. Pilar's flints were all gone. The time had come to try something else.

There was a very popular soccer team in Hamburg, and its most famous player, George Hanke, was a Czechoslovakian refugee. Somehow he heard about the D.P. Camp Zoo, and one day he appeared there. He inquired if some Czech in the camp knew German and could teach him. I told him that I knew how to read, write, and speak German very well, so I could help him. George gladly accepted my offer, and we set a date for his first lesson. He asked if I could come to his room in lodgings provided by the Hamburg Soccer Club, and we agreed to meet every weekday morning at six o'clock. His club paid for it, but there was a problem: George didn't study very much and he made slow progress. After one month the club stopped paying and that was the end of my teaching career.

I studied the English-Czech/Czech-English Dictionary that I had brought across the border. I decided to learn forty English words a day by writing them down and memorizing them. After a while I was good enough to teach other refugees the fundamentals of the language.

Some of the refugees, who could prove that they had mechanical or other skills, were eligible for an "unemployment compensation" that the British ordered the German government to pay on a weekly basis. A few of these refugees asked me to tutor them in English, for which I charged very little: just DM 1 a week. I stressed the importance of learning as much of the language as possible if they intended to emigrate to Canada, the United States, or Australia. Most of them took my advice and made good progress. This went on for some time, but while I was pleased with my students, I wasn't satisfied with the small income that teaching provided. I desperately needed shoes, razor blades, and postage stamps, yet I couldn't save enough money to purchase these necessities.

One day I went to the camp office and asked for some sort of work. But since all the employees, including the kitchen help and camp police, were Lithuanians, there was little chance for me. However I was told that there was an English Employment Office on the other side of Hamburg, about one-and-one-half miles away. I walked there twice a day for a week, but there were never any openings. Then I discovered that with my identification card and green card I could access the Hamburg streetcars, so the trip across town became much easier.

A German girl in the office, Miss Meyer, agreed to keep an eye out for me, but despite my frequent visits, no jobs were available. She finally agreed to allow me to telephone her, saving a trip. And finally my persistence paid off: Miss Meyer told me there was an opening for a messenger at the British High Court. I jumped on a streetcar immediately and made it to the employment office in record time. Miss Meyer introduced me to a British officer, with whom I had quite a long discussion. I showed him my identification card and told him I was in D.P. Camp Zoo. He took out a form and started to fill it in. I couldn't believe what was happening, and my eyes filled with tears at the idea that I might actually get a job. But it was true! The officer signed the form, put it in an official-looking envelope, and told me to deliver it to the British section of the High Court registrar's office at Strafjustitzgebaeude (German Justice Building). I thanked him and thanked Miss Meyer, who seemed almost as pleased as I was.

In something of a daze, I found the High Court Registrar's Office, where a middle-aged woman introduced herself as Miss Wilkins. She opened the envelope, and after reading it, informed me that I could start work on July 13. I was indescribably happy, and I will never forget that moment. However, July 13 was two weeks away, and I still needed new shoes.

At the camp, a few days later, I noticed a familiar-looking man. Then I realized he was one of my classmates from college, Ladislav Pazdera. What a surprise! He told me he had just arrived from the French zone. We reminisced for hours about our school days. Then I described my new job, and told him my predicament. It was mid-summer, and all I had to wear was my dilapidated pair of ski boots. He asked what size shoes I needed. When I told him, Ladislav said he wore the same size. He would lend me one of his two pairs, which I could return when I purchased my own. They fit great! What luck!

With my shoe problem solved I could concentrate on improving my English for my new job. Because I would be involved with mysterious new words used in court, I studied my dictionary almost every minute of the day. While my roommates played cards, I was busily looking up legal terms like sentence, summons, appeal, and suspended.

CHAPTER 13

MY EMPLOYMENT BY THE BRITISH HIGH COURT

ON JULY 13, 1949, I STARTED MY JOB AT THE HIGH COURT REGISTRAR'S OFFICE. Miss Wilkins had told her supervisor, Mr. Maidment, about me so he already knew who I was. But I introduced myself anyway, and we shook hands.

The first thing he asked me was how I pronounced my name, "Knava." I indicated that the "K" was supposed to be pronounced. Then we discussed my challenging trip to Hamburg.

I had some difficulty understanding both Mr. Maidment and Miss Wilkins. He not only had a Londoner's dialect, but he talked rather softly. I had to concentrate to make out exactly what he was saying. Miss Wilkins was from Avon, and she had a totally different dialect. I was afraid I wouldn't qualify for the job because of my insufficient knowledge of English, but I remained hopeful.

After our discussion was over, Mr. Maidment took me into the storage room. He explained that they had just moved from another location, and the room was a mess, with papers scattered everywhere. He asked me to do some tidying, and indicated a desk where I could sort things out.

I was happy beyond description. I took off my jacket, rolled up my sleeves, and started on one end of the storage room. It took me some time to finish. Since I'd actually been hired as a messenger, I had to deliver and pick up mail between this office and the main headquarters, where Miss Meyer worked. In addition to Mr. Maidment and Miss Wilkins, there were two other people at this location—Mr. Holtzbaum, the senior chief officer over the entire High Court Registrar's Office, and a German lawyer, Dr. Andresen—so there was a lot of mail.

To go back and forth between the two buildings, I would be driven in a Volkswagen "Bug." Mr. Maidment introduced me to the driver and explained that I had to pick up and deliver mail for the main headquarters and the High Court. These trips would be made once or twice a day. Before I received the mail, I was given a control commission passport, which needed to be presented to the watchman before entering the headquarters building.

To my pleasant surprise, the first time I opened the designated door at headquarters Miss Meyer was there to receive the mail. She also had mail ready for me to take back to our office. When I thanked her again for her help, she asked me to telephone her.

I called Miss Meyer the next day, and she requested that I meet her in front of Vaterland, a big business building.

At first I thought she might have romantic intentions. But as it turned out, she wanted me to come to her apartment to dictate from a German book, so she could practice her shorthand. I willingly agreed, and visited her quite often for a while. But eventually Miss Meyer perfected her shorthand, and from then on, we merely exchanged a few friendly words when we saw each other at the office.

I had finally finished straightening up the storage room, so I decided to use my spare time to start memorizing new English words. One day when I was concentrating on my studies, I didn't realize that Mr. Maidment had quietly walked in. He noticed my dictionary, and my notebook in which I was writing words in English and what they meant in Czech. I expected to be reprimanded for studying during work hours. I apologized. To my surprise, he complimented me, and encouraged me to study whenever I had free time.

The next day I was pleasantly surprised again. Mr. Maidment had my desk brought into the office he shared with Miss Wilkins so I could listen to their telephone conversations. He also asked me to keep a record of the incoming and outgoing mail in English. He said this would give me even more opportunity to increase my vocabulary.

I appreciated this wonderful help by Mr. Maidment, and as time passed, we even became friends. Mr. Maidment had a beautiful wife whose name was Betty. They were both twenty-eight, just two years older than I was. They had a nice apartment, and I was invited to a small party there one Sunday.

Betty Maidment was an excellent cook and she loved to bake. All the guests were enjoying her delicious food when Mr. Maidment brought in a Scotsman's kilt. I didn't really know what it was, and I'd certainly never seen one as there was no television. Mr. Maidment asked me if I would like to play a game, and whether I could disregard the outcome. I agreed. He tied this kilt around my waist, which then hung in front of my groin area.

He said, "All you have to do, George, is that after we say something, you reply 'Under a Scotsman's kilt.'" The Maidments and their friends began taking turns, saying this and that, using a little more difficult English each time—and I would answer very seriously, "Under a Scotsman's kilt." At one point somebody said, "she was whispering to him..." and I replied, "Under a Scotsman's kilt." They were rolling around, laughing, and having a great time. I was bewildered.

When this part of the party was over, Mr. Maidment came to me, thanked me for being a "good sport" and said, "I hope you didn't mind, George, it was all just for fun." Of course, I still didn't know what had been so funny, but I was glad everyone had a good time, and I was flattered to have been invited.

One day Mr. Maidment told me that he had received a frozen hare with the skin still on. Knowing that we had relied on rabbits for food in Czechoslovakia, he asked if I could skin and prepare the hare for eating. I agreed, and on the following Saturday at the Maidments, I asked Betty to provide me a piece of string, with a sharp knife, and a large pot of cold water. She did—and then quickly left the kitchen. I tied one end of the string to the paw of the hare, and tied the other end to a window handle, letting the hare hang down.

In no time I skinned it and placed it in the cold water. Mr. Maidment disposed of the skin so that Betty wouldn't see it. After I washed my hands, the three of us had a cup of tea and cookies. Betty looked a little green, and I wondered if she'd ever be able to cook that hare.

On July 31, I received my first pay and I felt like a millionaire. Now my financial problems were solved. I bought new shoes, returned the borrowed ones to Ladislav, and gave him DM 10 as a token for the favor. Not long after that Ladislav vanished from the camp, and I never saw him again. (Later, when I was in the United States, my sister, Anna asked if I knew where Ladislav Pazdera was, because his family in Czechoslovakia would like to hear from him. But I couldn't help, and to this day I do not know what happened to Ladislav.)

I needed many things: shirts, underwear, socks, razor blades, better food, and all the daily essentials. I went shopping, but I bought only the bare minimum of the items on my list. I couldn't help but think my job was too good to be true, and that someday the High Court might let me go for some reason.

Not long after my limited shopping spree, I was surprised that Captain Novak—who helped my roommates to escape—defected and brought his wife. They asked for political asylum, and were given a small room for two in a separate hut reserved for married couples.

I looked them up and became acquainted with them. Mrs. Novak's brother had taken the boat back to Czechoslovakia. He probably had to answer a lot of questions about whether he knew that his sister and brother-in-law were going to defect. But perhaps he had become a member of the Communist party, and if so, he could most likely evade the questions without any problem.

One day, when I went to do my wash in the hut where the showers were, I encountered Mrs. Novak. She told me that her husband had developed a very bad rash and had been hospitalized for several days. Mrs. Novak also mentioned that their finances were depleted, and offered to do my laundry and ironing. I agreed, and said I would give her DM 5 for each wash. I could see in her eyes how happy she was about my suggested payment.

Mrs. Novak had a neighbor, a young Polish woman who had a daughter and no husband. Like most people in the camp, she also didn't have much money so from time to time I gave the little girl candy.

One day this young woman suggested that I come for a visit to play cards. I went over that night, brought candy for her daughter, and wine and pretzels for us. After a while, the little girl went to bed. We continued playing cards for a bit while we drank the wine. We had a nice evening and a little romance.

By the next payday, I was feeling a little more secure in my job, so I bought most of the personal things that I still needed. A month later, I purchased a camera. I didn't have to pay any expenses in the camp, and suddenly I found myself in an unusual position: I had money.

I decided I should send some to my relatives in Czechoslovakia, and I also wanted to repay Millie for financing my escape. But I had no idea how to get money into Czechoslovakia. For the time being, I let the idea pass.

As the weeks went by, more people were leaving the camp because their emigration papers had come through. Our friend, Vlastik Kopyta, decided to immigrate to Norway, and he was the first one that left. He loved the sea, and he wanted to be associated with boats or even large ships. His wish was granted. I remember he immigrated to a city called Tonsberg, which is near the water. We wished him good luck.

There were several nationalities in the camp, including many Slovaks. Some of them didn't like Czechs, and they were called "Separatists." But there were a few Slovaks that I liked.

One day I talked to a young Slovakian, Petr, who was about twenty-three years old. I was twenty-six then, so we had much in common. I told him I had been to Liptovksy Svaty Mikulas, a town near the Tatra Mountains, where I stayed with my cousin's family. Petr was from Zdiar, not too far from the Tatras. He was quite fond of me, most likely because I had visited Slovakia while I was in the Czech army and knew a little about his area. When I mentioned that I'd been a sergeant, he admitted that he was just a soldier with no rank. Whenever we met, Petr greeted me as "Mr. Sergeant."

Some fellows went into Hamburg on Saturdays to drink. They could afford it because they received money from the unemployment office, or received funds from sponsors and / or relatives in America and Canada.

One of our roommates, Vaclav Kulnaty, liked to go to town almost every weekend. Since he had been a hotel owner in Czechoslovakia before his escape, Vaclav enjoyed a busy city atmosphere.

I was the only one in our hut one Saturday night when Vaclav came back rather intoxicated. He slumped on his bed and told me his group had become involved in an argument with some Separatists, so he left early.

A while after his arrival, I heard yelling not far from our hut. That was not unusual on Saturdays, but this time the voices were really loud. Suddenly a man entered our room carrying a yard-long iron bar. Behind him stood another fellow and my friend, Petr.

Obviously trouble was brewing, and I thought they intended to destroy things in our room. My first instinct was to grab the radio, but just as I turned toward it, I felt something strike me in the back.

At the same moment I heard Petr yelling, "No, no, not Mr. Sergeant, he is a good man!" I whirled around and squared off against the fellow standing in front of me holding the iron bar. He looked drunk and was very red in the face. I don't know how I found the courage to do it, but I grabbed the bar from his hands.

In the meantime, the other fellow was beating Vaclav, who was still lying on his bed. I should have gone after him and his buddy with the iron bar, but there was a problem. They were big men, both weighing close to 200 pounds. I was much smaller, so I did the sensible thing.

I leaned out the open window and shouted in three languages: "Help!" in English, "Hilfe!" in German, and "Pomoc!" in Czech. It worked. The three separatists ran through the door-and into the camp police.

Poor Vaclav was almost beyond recognition. His bald head looked split, and his face was covered with blood. He was barely moving, almost unconscious. I ran to the Red Cross building, where someone was on duty twenty-four hours a day. A Red Cross ambulance quickly came to our hut and took Vaclav to the hospital. He was there for several weeks, and had three operations. When Vaclav was finally dismissed he had scars on his face and his left arm was in a sling.

On Monday the three Slovaks were brought into Court. The judge's decision was that they could never emigrate to any part of the world. But since they escaped from the Communists, the British did not deport them back to Slovakia.

Vaclav survived the ordeal and later immigrated to the United States. He was still in the camp when I left for Australia.

One day, Josef, the former pilot, seemed very sad. He kept staring at himself in the mirror. When I asked him what was wrong, he turned toward me and said, "Look at my eye."

I saw that his pupil was extremely enlarged, and he admitted it was painful. I sent him to the Red Cross to have it checked. They gave him drops, and told him that he might have to undergo surgery if the pain didn't subside. It didn't, so in a few weeks Josef had an operation. Unfortunately, his optic nerve was gone, and the surgeon had to remove Josef's eye.

He had a glass eye inserted, but Josef was devastated. He had often talked about his sponsors in England, and how nice they were to him. They, as well as he, were looking forward to their first reunion since the end of the war in 1945. Now he kept saying, "How can I face them? Look at me." We felt sorry for him, but there was nothing we could do to help. Then his friend, Robert, one of the other pilots in our room, was notified that his emigration to England was expected in the near future.

This made things even worse for Josef. At times he would talk about his misfortune and how he shouldn't even join those nice sponsors in England. But he couldn't go back to Czechoslovakia, and he certainly couldn't stay in Germany, the country he had bombed during World War II. He had to accept the condition-and finally Josef did emigrate to England.

Our hut was getting emptier and emptier. Vaclav Rezek was spending more and more time with his girlfriend, and only occasionally showed up in our room. One day he packed all his things, including his beloved accordion. Then he handed me a thick envelope. "Here George, take this sheet music, since it's all in Czech." When I asked what was going on, Vaclav said that he and Jaroslav—the third pilot in our hut-were going back to Czechoslovakia soon to bring out their families.

Sure enough, by a couple of days later, Jaroslav and Vaclav were ready for their risky trip to the east. I tried to talk them out of it, but in vain. Since Vaclav was still in the hospital, I suddenly found myself alone in the large room.

Nobody else knew that Vaclav and Jaroslav had left for Czechoslovakia, so officially our hut was on record as still having four occupants. I didn't like the situation, because I was at work five days a week and my possessions and Vaclav's were in the unlocked room. I was fortunate that my place of work was close to the camp, so I could look in on the hut at lunchtime. To make things appear normal, I was still having lunch at the camp kitchen so no one would realize what was going on.

However, I didn't want to take any chances, so I asked Mrs. Novak if I could put some good clothes and my camera in their room. When she agreed, I left just a couple of boxes, half-filled, with inexpensive things, in the hut to make it appear occupied. The beds of the roommates that emigrated had no blankets on them and looked bare, but this was common; people were always leaving the camp, so many rooms had "vacancies." The rest of the beds still had blankets, so it looked as if four people were living there.

Shortly after Vaclav and Jaroslav left for Czechoslovakia, I was walking through the camp when I encountered a middle-aged man who appeared to be drunk. As I passed him, he said some very bad words to me in Czech.

I couldn't believe what I'd heard. I stopped, looked him over. He was well-dressed, with a long topcoat, a dark hat, a tie, and clean shoes. Not many people in the camp had clean shoes, since they couldn't afford to buy shoe polish and a brush.

I asked him where he lived, so I could assist him back to his room.

He did tell me the number of his hut, but he refused my help. I continued on very slowly, wondering where he was headed. I noticed he repeated the same foul words to others who passed by. I walked away.

Because this man was Czech, my curiosity forced me to find out something about him. The next day I saw him smoking by the window of his hut. I knocked at his door, and greeted him in Czech. Naturally, I asked him if he remembered me. He said, "Yes, I think I saw you somewhere." I expected he would apologize for his bad behavior, but he didn't. I told him what happened, but he still didn't recall the incident. At this point he decided to invite me in. I introduced myself, and he said that his name was Josef Nevrly. His room was only for two people, and I noticed one bed was unoccupied, without blankets. I asked him why the other bed was empty and he explained that the man had just emigrated. I thought that perhaps I should move in with him, but after his conduct the previous day, I wasn't sure I wanted to.

But I kept considering the idea, and the next day I visited Mr. Nevrly again. During our conversation he said that he had lost his wife and that he wanted to immigrate to America. Mr. Nevrly told me that in Czechoslovakia during the war he had saved the life of a Jewish woman, Mrs. Schlosser. He had hidden her in his house behind a brick wall, which could be turned on a pivot. In back of this wall was a windowless room where Mrs. Schlosser was safely concealed from the Nazis. She couldn't leave that room for the duration of World War II—but she survived the Holocaust.

Mrs. Schlosser had immigrated to the United States in 1948. In gratitude to Mr. Nevrly for his valiant act, she had been sending him $5 a week, which he exchanged for DM 20 in Hamburg. Under the dire circumstances of life in the camp, this was a good income for a refugee.

Our talk had reassured me, and within a few days, I asked Mr. Nevrly if I could move in with him. When he agreed, I immediately retrieved my possessions from Mrs. Novak. Fortunately Mr. Nevrly stayed in the room most of the time, so he unwittingly served as our watchman.

Since I was paid in DM, I realized I could trade Mr. Nevrly my

Deutsche marks for his U.S. dollars. That was fine with him, since from that time on he didn't have to worry about any exchange.

Later on, I developed another system. By coincidence, Mrs. Schlosser lived near my sponsors, Mr. and Mrs. Zack—who I had taken to calling my "aunt" and "uncle," although we were not related. I sent my aunt preprinted slips showing an amount of $5. Mrs. Schlosser now paid Mr. Nevrly's weekly $5 to my aunt. She in turn would save the money for me until I arrived in the United States. When my aunt sent me the signed slip, I paid Mr. Nevrly DM 20.

By so doing, I accumulated some American dollars, and we eliminated the danger that letters with money could be stolen. It worked quite well for seven weeks. Then Mr. Nevrly became sick with leukemia, and Mrs. Schlosser somehow arranged his emigration early. He left to undergo treatment in the United States.

One weekend I had an unexpected visitor: Vaclav Rezek's brother-in-law, who lived in East Germany on the border of the Russian zone. This fellow worked for the railroad, so he had no problem getting to Czechoslovakia or to the British zone. He brought bad news about Vaclav Rezek and Jaroslav, who had been caught by Communist guards while crossing the German-Czech border. Now my two friends had been sentenced to fifteen years in prison.

But the story eventually had a happy ending, at least for Vaclav. His cell was located on the second floor, overlooking the prison garage. Vaclav could see everything that was going on there, and since he had once owned a garage in Prague, it was an interesting way to pass the time.

Vaclav noticed that one mechanic had been working on a car, but couldn't get it running properly. When the guard next delivered a meal to him, Vaclav said, "What is that fellow doing in the garage? He hasn't been able to fix that car for the last two days." The guard asked, "How do you know, can you work on cars?" when Vaclav told him about his ability, the guard replied, "I will tell them in the office that you know how to repair cars, and perhaps you could help him."

It didn't take long before the warden asked Vaclav to work in the prison garage. The next day Vaclav discovered that the car the mechanic couldn't fix had a cracked block. He also discovered that the prison entrance was next to the garage. Suddenly a policeman pulled up on a motorcycle and left it standing in front of the entrance, not too far from where Vaclav was working. At the same time the policeman arrived, the phone rang. The guard turned around to answer the phone, and Vaclav saw his chance.

He casually walked through the entrance, started the motorcycle, and rode out onto the street. After a few hundred meters, Vaclav saw a park, hid the motorcycle behind a bush, and ran away as fast as he could. He could hear sirens, so obviously an alarm had been raised. But by now he was quite far from the prison.

That evening, Vaclav managed to get to the River Ohre. He took off his clothes and shoes, bundled them up, then jumped into the river and started to swim one-handed, using his other hand to hold the bundle of clothes in the air. A few hours later he crossed the Czech border into Germany.

I was shocked and delighted when Vaclav reappeared in the D.P. Camp Zoo. But after he'd told me the whole story, Vaclav was off to see his girlfriend in Hamburg. A few days later, he came back to the camp to say he'd fixed me up with a young woman named Karla, a friend of his girlfriend. This was the beginning of a brief but pleasant interlude in my life.

Karla lived in a small apartment with another girl who worked nights. This was very convenient for us, and we enjoyed many evenings together. Occasionally, we would make a foursome with Vaclav and his girlfriend. But I didn't want to get too romantically involved, so I began to see Karla less often.

But now I had developed a taste for Hamburg's nightlife, and I could afford to take advantage of its entertainments. I went a few times to a very popular nightclub that featured a brass band. One evening I met a good-looking German girl there, and she invited me to join her friends at their table. Our foursome had a good time, drinking beer, cracking pretzels, and listening to the band.

Because I knew German, I had no problem communicating with my new friend. She asked me what my nationality was, and I told her I was English. I had an accent, so she accepted it as such. It was a necessary lie, because Germans and Czechs didn't mix well together. Germany had occupied Czechoslovakia for six years during World War II, and this fact was too deeply engraved for either side to quickly forget.

Suddenly it was quite late at night, and time to go home. I offered to escort her. She had her own apartment, and she told me her boyfriend had been killed during the war. We had a short romance, but once again, I didn't want to become too involved.

I also met a girl by the name of Elizabeth Jung. She was from East Germany—the Russian zone—and was also an escapee. She was very attractive, but she lived far outside Hamburg, accessible only by the Hochbahn, which was a tramway. All of our meetings seemed to end up at the tramway station, where I kissed her goodnight. This relationship didn't last long.

I had my eye on a British girl, Miss Hay, who was very pretty. She worked in the High Court, and I exchanged greetings with her when I delivered the mail. She always gave me a nice smile, but she was taller than I was. I knew I was no candidate for her.

Little by little my romantic world slowed down. I didn't want to have any entanglements in Germany, since I intended to immigrate to the United States. But I couldn't as yet, because there was no quota for Czechoslovakians. I corresponded with my sponsors frequently, but they couldn't help; I just had to wait. I was very impatient with the uncertainty of when my chance would come.

One day I went to see Mr. and Mrs. Novak again. Mrs. Novak told me that her brother had visited her very recently, after making another trip on the boat between Czechoslovakia and Hamburg. I mentioned that I wanted to send some money to my family and to Millie. I had heard that there was a possibility to buy Czech money at Valka Camp in the U.S. zone. Mrs. Novak said I could use the service of her brother, and that I should prepare whatever I wanted him to take. I knew she felt obligated to do something for me, because the money she received for doing my wash was her only income.

The following weekend I decided to go to Valka Camp, which was located near the city of Nurenberg. I took the earliest train in the morning so I could manage the round-trip in one day.

When I appeared in the yard of the camp, a man approached me and asked what I was looking for. When I inquired about the possibility of buying some Czech money, he asked whether I wanted real or counterfeit. I replied that I was only interested in real money. That seemed to break the ice, and we introduced ourselves. His name was Josef Dvorak. Josef looked me over and said, "You look too well-dressed, you look out of place in this camp, and it could be dangerous for you." He suggested we walk over to a better area of the camp, where all types of business were conducted. Once there, Josef took me into a building, where I met the "dealer." We exchanged the money and I rushed out of there, just as Josef Dvorak had suggested. My goal accomplished, I took the next train to Hamburg. Nobody, including Mrs. Novak, knew anything about my trip.

I'd become very good at keeping secrets. The camp office had no knowledge that I was working, and I was not about to tell them. I still went to the kitchen for my meals, dressed in shabby clothes. I hid my money and my belongings in the room, and kept the door locked. Luckily my neighbors, Zdenek and Irena Konicek, had a large German Shepherd, which was a good watchdog. Occasionally, I bought bones in a butcher shop when I was shopping for food, and in turn, the dog protected my room.

Some twenty-five years later, when I visited a friend in New York City, I learned that Zdenek Konicek was the headwaiter in the Banquet Room of the Plaza Hotel. Due to emigration, we had become separated in Hamburg, and didn't know each other's whereabouts until all these years later. It was a nice reunion, but rather sad—because Zdenek told me that just after I left Hamburg, his wife Irena had died of leukemia. I think it was due to poor food in the camp, likely the reason for Mr. Nevrly's same illness. We were told in the D.P. Camp Zoo that the International Refugee Organization allocated $3.50 a day for every refugee in every camp. But where did it really go? We saw the kitchen help riding in Jeeps, as did the office employees. The camp leader, Mr. Murphy, had both an English Morris convertible and a Jeep. But the poor refugees in the huts had nothing but inferior food, and—once in a while—some boxes came from the United States.

Just before I started to work, I was given a small package by a camp employee, who said it was donation from America. Inside were a towel, soap, toothbrush, toothpaste and washcloth, along with a return address: Miss Margaret Lee Hutchins, St. Mary's Hospital Wausau, Wisconsin. USA. Naturally, I wrote a letter of thanks to Miss Hutchins, and told her the destination of her parcel. She answered very quickly to say how pleased she was that I had received it, and expressed surprise that I knew English. We then exchanged letters several times, and once she sent me a photo. Miss Hutchins was quite pretty, and I already knew she had a good heart. So in my next letter, I did something extraordinary: I proposed marriage and asked her if she would come to Germany. I was so frustrated waiting for my emigration to the USA that I was willing to do almost anything to get out. She replied, "Thank you, George, for your kind letter and proposal. I am sure you are a wonderful fellow, but I cannot accept because I didn't fall in love with you by simply corresponding." Well, I tried.

One fellow received a parcel from Nebraska, and the return address said Mary Ann Zeleny, a Czech name. He asked if I would write his thanks, which I did. Soon after I received a letter from Mary Ann, with an enclosed photo. We exchanged a few letters, and—not having learned any lesson—I also proposed to her. She replied that she had a boyfriend. I didn't receive any more letters from either of those women.

Several days later I was given a small package from Norway. In it were articles similar to those in American parcels, and a name, Nana Stephensen, with her address in Oslo. There was also a large tube of some sort of salve, manufactured from fish—and it smelled like fish. When I sent a thank-you note, I asked Nana about this salve. She was very pleased to receive my letter, and responded that the salve could be used as a body ointment. We exchanged a few letters, but I didn't ask Nana to marry me because I didn't want to go to Norway.

One day I also received a parcel from England. Unlike the others, this one contained only canned food, a box of tea, and a can of coffee. It came from a young man by the name of Howard Routledge, who had visited Prague in 1947 to attend the World Festival of Youth. I wrote Howard to thank him, and to ask if he had any contact with the others who had been with him in Prague. But disappointingly, I didn't receive a reply.

I was also disappointed in my sponsors, the Zacks. They sent me only one package that contained a used winter coat, two pairs of socks. a used towel-and no food.

I did, however, receive a letter from Mrs. Zack—my aunt—which included a request that she had received from the citizens of Trhova Kamenice. Since this was the town in which my sister, Frantiska, had lived since 1931, I assumed she was one of the citizens involved.

The request was for information about a church bell that was removed by the Nazis during World War II. Hitler had ordered the collection of all church bells throughout Czechoslovakia, so that they could be melted down and used for the production of ammunition.

The bell from Trhova Kamenice had been manufactured in 1875, and was of course treasured by the townspeople. Now they wanted to find out if it had indeed been melted down, or if it could perhaps be located somewhere in Czechoslovakia.

In the letter was also enclosed a photo of the bell, showing its inscription:

RANNY USVIT PULI DENNI,
PRICHOD NOCI HLASAM VAM,
ZEHNAM VASI PRACI PILNE,
NEBES MATI POZDRAV VAM.

IN THE MIDDLE OF THE DAY,
I AM ANNOUNCING THE ARRIVAL OF NIGHT,
MAY YOUR DILIGENT DAY'S WORK BE BLESSED,
BY GREETINGS FROM HEAVEN.

I found out where an inquiry could be made, and sent a letter there. But after almost a month's time, I received a negative response: the bell had vanished. I wrote the result to my aunt and uncle in America, who in turn informed my sister, Frantiska. I also sent the mayor of Trhova Kamenice a copy of the disappointing response.

Whenever I saw Mrs. Novak, I discussed the possibility that her brother might take money to Czechoslovakia for my relatives and Millie. She assured me he would do so on his next visit.

Encouraged, I wrote a letter to my brother in Prague, asking him to distribute the money to our family and to Millie. I also asked Vincenc to retrieve my stamp collection from our farmhouse and give it to Mrs. Novak's brother, so that he could bring it to me.

Soon Mrs. Novak's brother appeared in the camp, and we arranged a meeting to discuss the details. I gave him the letter and package of money for Vincenc. After having a cup of coffee and some pastry, we said good-bye.

I knew it would take quite a long time before I could expect to receive my stamp collection, and I could only hope that it would actually happen. There was always a chance that Mrs. Novak's brother might have to surrender the collection if the Communists decided to search his boat. The package wouldn't be easy to hide, since the stamps were in seven albums. In spite of Mrs. Novak's brother's willingness to help me, I considered it a gamble.

Weeks later, I came back to the camp from work, and because it was my day to pick up the wash, I went directly to Mrs. Novak's hut. She had it ready as usual, but after I paid her and we chatted for a bit, I noticed she was looking at me with a strange expression on her face. Suddenly Mrs. Novak smiled and said, "I have very good news for you. My brother was here, and he brought you this package."

I couldn't believe my eyes when I opened it. There were my postage stamp albums—but only six of the seven that I had expected—and also my book about growing and pruning trees. I also looked for another treasured gardening book, but it wasn't there. There was no way of knowing why one stamp album and the second book were missing, but

I was overjoyed with what I had received.

It was decades before I learned how my stamp collection got out from behind the Iron Curtain. I was told the story by my nephew, Jan Knava-son of my late brother, Frantisek—when I visited Czechoslovakia in 1995.

Jan was 15 years old when Vincenc unexpectedly showed up at Frantisek's home. After a brief visit, Vincenc said he was going to walk over to our family farm, about one mile away. Jan decided to accompany him, and during their walk, Vincenc shared his secret.

One day during the lunch hour, Vincenc had been alone in his office when a man came in, wearing overalls and carrying some tools and a bag. He walked around pretending he was checking the air conditioner. Suddenly he placed the bag on Vincenc's desk and said, "Your brother, George, from Hamburg has asked me to pick up his stamp collection." It was, of course, Mrs. Novak's brother. He set up a place and time for them to meet in Prague, and told Vincenc to bring him Kcs 2,500 (approximately $100) for his travel expenses. There was no other conversation, and he left.

My brother was shocked, speechless, and frightened beyond imagination. He told Jan that just a few days earlier, the police arrested two of his office colleagues for some anticommunist activity. Vincenc thought someone might be setting him up, since it was a well-known fact that I had escaped, probably with help from the Underground.

But in spite of his fear, Vincenc took the risk. He went home to pick up my collection-keeping back one stamp album and one gardening book-and returned to Prague to rendezvous with Mrs. Novak's brother. When they met, the brother requested another Kcs 2,500 for his expenses, stating that the first amount was insufficient. After the payment was made, Mrs. Novak's brother left. He wouldn't accept a letter, but would verbally convey Vincenc's message to me, since any correspondence would be disastrous if the Communists caught him.

Now Mrs. Novak's brother had to smuggle my stamp collection through the Russian zone to the port of Hamburg. To be honest, I didn't appreciate then how dangerous the whole affair would be for both her brother and mine.

When I visited Czechoslovakia in 1990 and saw Vincenc we talked very little about what had happened so many years before. During one of our conversations, he did mention that he had given the missing stamp album to a plumber as payment for work. My brother's reasoning was that he didn't think we would ever see each other again, or that communism would ever be defeated in Czechoslovakia. I thanked Vincenc for his courage and for following through on my request. I also apologized to him for the anxiety I had caused, simply because I didn't know how bad conditions were. My brother was an inspector in a large insurance company, and I thought he was greatly respected and well-paid. I never realized how inadequate his salary was, or that my sister-in-law had to go to work splitting bamboo into strips for fishing poles. The Communists had also forced them to leave their apartment and move into a smaller one after their son married. All this, of course, was sad news to my ears, and I felt guilty for having asked Vincenc to run such risks for me back in 1949.

One day I received a surprising letter from Jan Kriz and Henry Moulis, my former coworkers at the Poldi Steel Co., notifying me that they had escaped to the U.S. zone. They were now in a refugee camp at Ludwigsburg, West Germany, where thousands of refugees were living in terrible conditions. They had no money, but somehow Jan had managed to send a letter to my sponsors. He wrote the Zacks to give him an affidavit of support and a certificate of employment, the same documents they had sent me. In the package, the Zacks had also included my address of the D.P. Camp Zoo.

I was overjoyed to learn that they had escaped. After reading about the bad conditions in their camp, I immediately sent Jan DM 5 and Henry DM 2 in separate letters, as a trial to find out if the letters would be received unopened. But I didn't get a reply as suddenly I was in the process of emigrating to Australia. When the letters weren't returned, I assumed Jan and Henry had received them.

CHAPTER 14

APPLICATION FOR EMIGRATION TO AUSTRALIA

THE AUSTRALIAN SCHEME HAD COME ABOUT THAT SUMMER. (THE WORD "scheme" actually meant recruiting for workers.) Refugees of any nationality, men, women and children (although there were very few children in the camp), could go to a building near the camp and apply for emigration. I did so as soon as I heard about it.

The procedure was quite thorough. Each applicant had to go through a complete physical examination. Those who were healthy-regardless of sex-were later notified to appear in front of the Australian Commission. I was one of those called, and met with an official who explained the procedure.

Applicants were offered emigration under the condition that they would work in Australia on any job offered by the government for a period of two years. If the applicant agreed, he or she would sign a contract to that effect, and the Australian government would then provide free passage from Germany. Most of the applicants qualified, except for those who were unhealthy or had a police record.

I qualified, so now it was only a matter of time until I would be notified to leave for a camp in Fallingbostel, from which the emigrants would be transported to a ship. Nobody knew how long this would take, and it turned out to be several months.

CHAPTER 15

EMIGRATION ANTICIPATION

AROUND FEBRUARY 15, 1950, MR. MAIDMENT, ASKED ME IF I HEARD anything about my chance to immigrate to the United States. I hadn't, and when I told him, he brought up a subject that worried me. He said something about his government's intentions to "cut down on forces" in the British zone. Mr. Maidment assured me that it wasn't imminent, but he wanted to inform me about the possibility that my job would be eliminated. He mentioned Canada, and asked whether I would go there before my quota number for the United States was called. I told him I would agree to go to Canada, and wait there for entry to the U.S. Then he mentioned that Australia was another prospect.

After returning to the camp, that conversation with my boss preyed on my mind. I immediately wrote my aunt in New Jersey to ask if she could find out something about my chances to immigrate to the United States. I suggested that it might be a good idea to write to Washington, D.C. I explained about my conversation with Mr. Maidment just to make her understand the urgency of the situation.

Things were normal at work in the days that followed, and there were no other alarming conversations with my boss. Still, I was worried, and started asking other refugees about their emigration plans.

After some time, I heard that Canada had a scheme. I mentioned it to my boss, and asked him for permission to investigate. He agreed, so I went to the building where the Canadians were interviewing refugees.

But the whole thing turned out to be a total waste of time. Canada was only interested in large men—weighing two hundred pounds or more—to work as loggers. Since I had a slight build, I was immediately disqualified. Quite frankly, I took it as an insult.

I couldn't understand why such a large country wasn't interested in educated people, regardless of their weight. But there was no use arguing about it, so Canada was out of the question for me.

Now Mr. Maidment decided to apply to Australia on my behalf, although I already had applied. On March 15, he personally typed a letter to the Australian Consulate General in Marienburg, asking for visa application forms and a landing permit. I was very grateful, and valued his kindness and concern.

Life and workdays and weeks continued. I didn't hear any more about a work reduction, and I was even promoted to court clerk and interpreter, which I did in addition to my messenger duties.

One day two Czech youngsters carrying firearms were caught by the police at the Czech-German border, and were brought to the High Court for a hearing. Since the boys didn't know English, and no one in the court knew Czech, I was called to act as interpreter. I advised the pair to plead guilty, and say they would only have used the firearms in self-defense if they were attacked by Communists at the border. They were sentenced to six months in jail, but based on their plea of self-defense, the sentence was suspended and the youngsters were placed in the refugee camp.

When I returned to the office, Mr. Maidment asked me how my countrymen had fared. I told him the result, and explained that the boys had been sent to the camp. He congratulated me for my service to the court, and said he was happy to learn that the two young men were not behind bars.

Later in March, Mrs. Zack sent me a copy of a letter her husband had received from the Displaced Persons Commission in Washington, D.C. It stated that I did not qualify for admission to the United States because I hadn't entered Germany between January and June, 1948. The writer's suggestion was for me to apply for emigration at the nearest

U.S. Consulate. Of course, I had already done this the first few days I was in Hamburg. But I made further inquiries, and learned that my number, in chronological order, would be valid no matter what part of the world I was in; when my number came up, I would be notified.

CHAPTER 16

GOOD-BYE HAMBURG

ONE AFTERNOON WHEN I CAME HOME FROM WORK, I HAD A LETTER FROM THE Australian Recruiting Office: my emigration procedure was underway, and I was soon to leave for the camp in Fallingbostel. The date of the transfer from my D.P. Camp Zoo would follow.

At the office the next day, I showed the letter to Mr. Maidment, who congratulated me that some action had finally been taken regarding my emigration. Everyone in the office quickly knew about it, and I kept hearing jokes about sending them a koala bear or a kangaroo. I had mixed feelings, knowing that I would have to say good-bye to the Maidments—the most wonderful people one could ever meet.

About a week later, I received word to appear at the Australian Recruiting Office for relocation to Fallingbostel. When I told Mr. Maidment, he said that before I left, he and his wife would like me to have breakfast with them.

On my last day of work, I went around to the offices to say my farewells to Mr. Holtzbaum, the chief registrar; to Mr. Bishop, the prosecutor; to Dr. Andresen, a German lawyer; and to several German women employees. They all wished me bon voyage, and asked me to write them from Australia. Although I was happy that my emigration finally had become reality, it was quite an emotional experience to leave these people who had been so very nice and kind.

The morning before I left the camp, I visited Mrs. Novak to thank her for everything she had done for me. I also asked her to thank her brother for his valiant job, and hoped that her husband would soon be in good health. It was a very sentimental moment, and we both had tears in our eyes as I gave her a kiss on the cheek.

The time had come for me to depart from the D.P. Camp Zoo. It turned out to be a simple process; all I had to do was sign some papers and return my blankets. Mr. Maidment picked me up early that morning, and I showed him the "paradise" in which I had lived for the past two years.

When we arrived at his house for breakfast, Mrs. Maidment asked me what I would like for breakfast. I replied that anything would be welcome. She made bacon and eggs, biscuits, and a cup of tea. We had a nice visit and I was surprised to learn that they were expecting their first child. They also insisted that I had to address them as Ray and Betty, because they considered me a friend. Finally, I faced another emotional moment: saying good-bye first to Betty. I gave her a big hug and, trying not to weep, walked out to the car.

Ray and I left to go to the Australian Recruiting Center, which was nearby. Since he wasn't allowed to drive inside, we said our farewells in front of the camp. This was perhaps my saddest moment of all, because this man had done so much for me. We shook hands, and I thanked him for his kindness and help. Then I walked into the yard through the gate, dropped my luggage, looked back, and waved good-bye.

The yard was filled with emigrants. There were several uniformed guards directing all of us into nearby buildings-men separately from women, even married couples. Inside, the camp commander looked at our papers. When he read that I spoke five languages, he gave me a "non-paying job," as a camp policeman, with a band on my arm that indicated I was a translator. I was also told to keep an eye on order and cleanliness, because there were hundreds of emigrants in the camp.

There was a large dining area, and I noticed that at every meal, the same couple was sitting at the next table. I also noticed that the very attractive woman looked at me constantly. She was about thirty-five years old, and the man, whom I assumed was her husband, was about forty-five. After a few days, the man approached my table and said to me in German, "We Hungarians have a great deal of liberty. My wife would like your company." Then he left. I was shocked, even though the woman had been making eyes at me throughout every meal. I knew what room she was in because as a camp policeman, I had to make rounds. But there were many other women lodged in the same room, so any attempt to socialize was virtually impossible. Well, it was interesting to learn about Hungarian customs, although I didn't think it was like that for all Hungarians!

After several days in Fallingbostel, we were notified that we would be taken to the seaport of Nordenham. Each emigrant was assigned a number, which had to be visible on his clothing. My number was 366, written with ink on a tag with a string attached. In order not to lose it, I tied it through the buttonhole of my coat.

We were transported by buses to Nordenham, where we would board the Fairsea, a large but not luxurious ship. During World War II, it had served as an aircraft carrier, and had now been rebuilt to transport refugees. The crew was Italian, but there were also many International Refugee Organization officers, doctors, and other personnel.

Before we entered the ship, every passenger had to place their number on their luggage. I didn't feel too comfortable about this, because it reminded me of a film that I had seen about the Nazis transports to concentration camps. However, I soon learned that our numbers indicated the location on the ship where we would be accommodated.

As we boarded the Fairsea, its crew directed us to our quarters. I was located in the hull at the front of the ship, in a room with thirty-five other men.

CHAPTER 17

VOYAGE TO AUSTRALIA

WE SAILED FROM GERMANY ON DECEMBER 20, 1950. THERE WERE 1,909 displaced persons on board: 766 men, 620 women and 523 children from all over eastern Europe.

We were headed for the English Channel, which was approximately twenty-three miles wide. When we arrived there, the weather was clear, and we could see the White Cliffs of Dover. Despite some high waves and the constant rocking of the ship, I felt fine.

But on the second day, as the Fairsea headed into the Atlantic Ocean towards the Bay of Biscay, I was seasick. We were told to eat very lightly, if we ate at all. Most of us munched crackers, walked on deck to get some fresh air—and "fed the fish" over the rail. My seasickness lasted thirty-four hours. Fortunately, as we approached Spain, almost everyone recovered.

The dining room was downstairs near the center of the ship. I finally felt as though I could eat and had a light meal. Then I went up to the deck, from which I could see the coast of Portugal on the left side. On the right side, the ocean appeared to be two different colors, dark green and light green. It looked as if someone had stretched a long line in the water and divided it into two parts. Everyone on deck admired this unique sight.

I stood there a long time, reflecting on my life in Germany. Even though I had met many wonderful people there, it wasn't difficult for me to leave since I'd never wanted to remain in that country permanently. I was looking forward to Australia, which represented a stepping-stone for me on the way to America—my ultimate future home. I knew that I would have to face another beginning, but no obstacle could discourage me.

Our next port was Gibraltar, the entry into the Mediterranean Sea. We could see in the distance the city of Malaga, Spain. Then we were in the open Mediterranean, and there was nothing but water, waves, and sky.

The next day, while I was having lunch in the dining room, a lady approached me and asked me if my name was George Knava. With a certain degree of surprise, I said it was. She introduced herself as Mrs. Codrington, an Australian education officer. She said that she'd heard I knew English, and asked if I would teach a group of refugees some fundamentals of the language.

I agreed, and she took me to an area where a class of nineteen people would be assembled for their first lesson. Mrs. Codrington said there would be a blackboard, chalk, and a small table for my use. We agreed the class would begin at 9:00 A.M.

Because I had the experience of teaching English in the D.P. Camp Zoo, I decided to use a similar method with these students. The next morning, I went to the dining room and borrowed a bread basket. I filled it with a fork, a tablespoon, a teaspoon, a knife, a napkin, a cup—twenty items in all. I took the basket upstairs to the classroom, where the students were waiting for me.

I introduced myself and went to work. There was a stack of notepads with pencils on a small table, which I quickly distributed. For me there was a small booklet to be followed as a teaching schedule. It started with the alphabet, so I taught the class how to pronounce the letters A through Z, and made them repeat it over and over again to become familiar with the pronunciation.

Mrs. Codrington eventually appeared to check on our progress. By then I had already switched from the alphabet to the names of the articles that I had in the basket. I wrote each word on the blackboard, and told the students to write them in their notepads, and next to them the meaning in their native language. After we finished with the twenty items, I had the class repeatedly pronounce each one out loud.

Then I asked them to cover the side with the English words and to try to translate the words into their language from English. I emphasized that they must have patience, since it was difficult to learn a new language. I stressed the importance of knowing some English when they arrived in Australia, and how helpful it would be for them if they knew even a few words.

Mrs. Codrington stood for some time in the back of the classroom and listened to my explanations in German. I knew most of the refugees spoke that language because they had lived in Germany for months or even years. I was surprised that among the students were two Czechs, Mr. and Mrs. Obdrzalek, whom I knew from the D.P. Camp Zoo in Hamburg. They had been my students in the camp, and therefore were ahead of the rest of the class.

Before the end of that first session, I told the students to memorize each word and to continue practicing their pronunciation. I added that at class the following morning, I intended to teach twenty more new words.

When I was at lunch in the dining room, Mrs. Codrington approached to thank me. She said she was very pleased with my method, and asked if I would take another class of twenty students every afternoon. I accepted.

At the appointed time, I met the new class and proceeded with the method I had used with the morning class. Mrs. Codrington appeared again, but this time she stayed only a few minutes. I gave the students the same pep talk that I had given to the morning group, stressing the importance of learning as much English as possible.

After class, I raced up on deck to view the African coastline. All I could see was just one tree that looked like a large bush with a flat top. At first, I was surprised that there were no more trees along the coast, but I soon remembered that northern Africa was mostly desert. Then we were in the middle of the Mediterranean, and our only view was of the calm sea.

Since there wasn't much to do on the ship, I was happy to pass the time teaching. According to Mrs. Codrington, our journey would last four more weeks, which would give the students a golden opportunity to learn English at no expense. And it would give me a feeling of satisfaction that I could be of help.

A few days later the Fairsea was scheduled to stop at Port Said, Egypt. Now the water was getting rough, and several miles out of Port Said, we suddenly experienced a hurricane-like storm.

The captain announced on the intercom that everyone should go to their rooms. The top of the ship was closed, completely sealed by closed hatchways. The Fairsea halted and dropped anchor. Huge waves flew over the ship like clouds. Like all the other passengers, I was frightened. The storm lasted four endless hours, and there was a collective sigh of relief. A loud noise indicated the raising of the anchor, and the ship proceeded to Port Said. In the morning, the Fairsea stopped about three hundred feet from the platform of the harbor.

We had breakfast, then went on deck to look at the harbor and the city. Within a short time, several small rowboats, filled with all kinds of gift items-mainly Egyptian rugs with pictures of camels, tigers, pyramids, and sphinxes-started to surround the ship. The merchants were shouting one word, "Tashe, tashe," lifting the articles and indicating the price with their fingers.

Incredibly, payments and purchases were made by throwing on strings back and forth. These strings had a kind of pouch mounted in the center, where the money was placed and lowered to the merchant. As soon as he received his payment, he carefully fastened the purchase to the string, which was then pulled up onto the ship. This business continued almost half a day. We didn't even have classes because there was too much commotion.

Finally, the ship left harbor, and we headed toward the Red Sea through the Suez Canal. On our left side, in Saudi Arabia, similar sales were taking place. Arab men were walking barefooted, holding containers in which they had American cigarettes-Camels, Chesterfields, and Lucky Strikes—at a very reasonable price. The business with Arabs occupied our time for several hours.

The weather was getting warmer and warmer. In the morning I took a picture of the Red Sea, although it was not too clear because of the fog. I couldn't believe the Red Sea was so wide; looking at a map, it appears much narrower.

On January 1, 1951, we arrived in Aden, where the ship stopped to get fresh water. It was a hot and windy day. On the upper deck, we were served a New Year's dinner in wide, heavy dishes, because the ship was rocking back and forth.

After the Fairsea had taken on supplies, we headed for the Indian Ocean. One evening, I watched some dolphins following the ship. There were about four or five of them, and what a fascinating sight they made!

After the excitement of Egypt and Saudi Arabia, everything was back to normal. My number of students increased to over fifty for both sessions. And since they were all doing well, I was very pleased with the results, as was Mrs. Codrington.

On January 7, a celebration was planned to commemorate our crossing the Equator. This celebration included a show that had to do with shaving one man before his christening by Neptune. The "shave" was simulated by the use of heavy cream. The next event was a shower before the christening. The same unwitting victim sat on a chair while another man poured a bucket of water over him. Then came the christening by Neptune, who was dressed in a decorative costume. In one hand he held a three-point fork, while with the other hand he tapped the man lightly on the head with an ornamental cane.

After this part of the celebration, Neptune distributed a certificate of baptism to every passenger. I was baptized and given the name "Stella Maris" on a form printed in Latin, dated January 7, 1951, and signed by Neptune. During the festive evening, everyone was served cake and drinks.

This event took place on Wednesday. But the next day was Friday! We had not only crossed the equator, but the international date line. Until that point, the ship's captain had navigated according to the North Star; from now on, our course was determined by the Southern Cross.

Occasionally, we had a chance to see the captain of the Fairsea, whose picture I took leaning against the railing on the upper deck. We could also sometime see creatures that looked like birds flying in and out of water. These flying fish, which flew many yards before they hit the water again, were very interesting to watch.

The ocean was very calm, and we had no more storms. Teaching made the days go by quickly; otherwise—despite the glimpses of flying fish—the long trip would have been monotonous. Now my number of students had increased to over sixty for both sessions. Although this increase made the classes crowded, the students' progress in English was rewarding both to them and to me.

Two weeks later, we could dimly see the northwest coastline of Australia on the horizon. Everyone was excited, because most of the passengers were looking at their new homeland; some people even clapped their hands. But we still had some three thousand miles to go before landing at Melbourne in southeastern Australia.

During the last week of classes, I taught my students the well-known Australian song, "My Bonnie Lies Over the Ocean." It sounded wonderful, much to the surprise of Mrs. Codrington. She had never known such classes before!

On Saturday, January 20, three days before landing in Melbourne, the classes ended. I felt very proud when I counted a total of eighty-six students in both sessions. My mission was accomplished. I wished the students lots of luck and a happy future in their new homeland. I would never see most of them again, but I felt great satisfaction knowing that I had helped them get a successful start on their lives in Australia.

The passengers received instructions to pack their luggage and bring it on deck before supper. We would be given permits to leave the ship on Sunday evening, January 21. Since each passenger had a number, we would be called in numerical order to report to the International Refugee Organization office with our documents. Vaccination certificates had to be taken with us when we went for a medical examination.

And then we would be ready for transportation by train to Bonegilla Camp, hundreds of miles inland.

PART II

AUSTRALIA

CHAPTER 18

MELBOURNE

ON MONDAY, JANUARY 22, 1951, AFTER THIRTY-THREE DAYS ON THE SHIP, WE ended our long voyage in Melbourne harbor. It had been a fantastic experience.

While the Fairsea was being pulled to dock by pilot boats, many things came to my mind. I knew that I would have to live here for at least two years under my contractual obligation to the government of Australia. I also had no idea of what to expect in this huge continent, which is almost as large as the United States. Why did I have to be so far away from my dreamland America? I certainly had mixed emotions, but at least I was out of the D.P. Camp Zoo. For the first time since leaving Prague, I could see the horizon of real freedom. In Germany, I was supposed to feel free—which I did to some extent—but I had also felt shackled in that refugee camp, never knowing what the next day would bring.

When the ship came to a full stop at the pier, we were instructed to stay in our area until further notice. We knew that the customs inspection would take a long time for so many people. However, after about an hour, an announcement was made that we could go on deck. Everyone was curious, but all there was to see were just some buildings that looked like cargo warehouses.

Then I suddenly spotted my friend, Jan Kriz, standing on the pier. He saw me at the same time and began to wave. In his hand he held something like a ball with a long string attached to it, which he threw up onto the deck. When I unwrapped it, I found inside a welcoming note and his new address. I wondered how Jan knew that my ship would land that day, and assumed he read about it in the newspaper.

We were instructed to tie tags with our personal numbers to our luggage, get it ready near the exit for customs, and stay on the ship. Because there were so many bags to be inspected, we had to stay on the ship overnight. I was worried about my stamp collection, which I had placed in the bottom of my suitcase.

The next day we were allowed to go into a large area where our luggage was arranged in numerical order. When I found my number, 366, I noticed that the end of a red necktie was sticking out of my bag. That was puzzling, since it wasn't mine. Someone had lost a tie, and I had received a gift.

CHAPTER 19

BONEGILLA CAMP

AFTER WE PICKED UP OUR LUGGAGE, WE WERE TOLD TO BOARD A TRAIN. WE were on our way to the Bonegilla Camp, some 380 miles away in what the Australians call bush country.

It was very hot in Australia at that time of the year—over one hundred degrees, in fact, just the opposite of the January climate at home. Everything was new and different compared to Europe. When we were out of Melbourne, all we could see was dry grass and hundreds of sheep and rabbits. I was told that to thin the rabbit population, the government had offered 5 pounds sterling for 144 rabbit noses. However, the government didn't succeed with this bounty program because hunters felt that it wasn't worth their time or the cost of the bullets.

It was a long nonstop ride, but late in the afternoon we finally arrived at the camp, far inland near the Murray River, the longest in Australia. The camp was comprised of many huts, built from corrugated tin. We were assigned quarters in those round huts, which were quite cramped. The only square and spacious building was for office and living quarters of the camp leader.

I was given a bed and blankets and assigned to a hut with about two dozen other immigrants. Ironically, the man next to me was a Czech, Ivan. He was about forty years old, and came from a small town in Moravia.

Nearby was the kitchen hut, where the next morning we went for a breakfast of eggs, biscuits, and grapes. For lunch we had mutton chops, mashed potatoes, carrots, and a roll. For supper we were served pork sausages, biscuits, and vegetables. Generally the food was good, and there was certainly a lot of it.

When I was standing in line for lunch the next day, I suddenly heard my name on the loudspeaker: "George Knava, please come to the office." When I reported there, a man dressed in a tropical-style outfit announced, "On behalf of the Australian government, it gives me great pleasure to award you four pounds—one pound for each week of teaching English to immigrants on the ship. Welcome to Australia." He gave me the money and shook my hand. I was very surprised that I had already earned my first income in Australian money!

After this pleasant incident, I went back in line for my mutton lunch, which was about the same as the day before. The weather was hot but dry, which made it tolerable. Some immigrants decided to go for a walk to the nearby Murray River; but I decided to get a little sun and stretched out on a blanket.

Later I walked to the railway station to get the train schedule to Melbourne. I had heard that if you could find a job and accommodations in that city, you could remain there and get out of the bush country. It was worth a try.

In the morning I took an early train to Melbourne. When I arrived, I immediately bought a newspaper, the Melbourne Chronicle, and read the want ads. Since I was born and raised on a farm, I thought I should look for a job connected with farming. I saw an advertisement for help at the Melbourne Tomato Company. I went to try my luck.

As I entered the yard, I was astonished by what I saw. The huge hopper-type trucks were bringing in tons of tomatoes, which they unloaded in a sloppy manner. They opened the sides of the hopper and dumped the tomatoes on a large waterproof canvas. From there the tomatoes were loaded on a pocketed conveyor and pounded into a grinding machine, obviously to make juice. I didn't like the idea of working here, because the odor was overpowering due to the heat and the hygienic conditions left a lot to be desired. However, I was just curious to see if I could get a job. I entered the office and a young woman, with that unusual Australian accent, inquired if she could help. When I replied that I was looking for a job, she gave me a form to fill out and asked me if I could start work at once, because they were very busy. I said that I would return as soon as I finalized some personal matters, thanked her, and left.

My next task was to find accommodations. I looked in the newspaper and saw an ad for a room for rent. I phoned from a nearby "milk bar," similar to a variety store in the United States. A gentleman answered, and I learned that the room wasn't too far away. When I found the rooming house, a Mr. Neumann introduced himself and showed me around. He asked me when I would like to move in, and I replied that it would be a little later, when I had a job. I added that what I needed now was a certificate stating that I had a room available. I said that I would like to pay him for the certificate, even if he wouldn't have the room in the future. I repeated that for the time being all I wanted was the certificate. He hesitated a bit, but he did write a note stating that I had a room available whenever I needed it. The price was ten shillings, and I paid him, thanked him, and left. (In Australia at that time the rate was twenty shillings to a pound, and one shilling was worth twelve pennies. The conversion rate in American money was $2.20 for one pound.)

As soon as I received the certificate, I rushed to the railroad station in time to return to Bonegilla. I arrived too late for dinner. Fortunately, I had some grapes to hold me over until the next morning.

I noticed that the camp leader kept the nationalities together, regardless of the size of the group. There were many Polish, East German, and Hungarian immigrants, but only two Czechs, Ivan and myself. Little by little, I could see that certain groups were leaving the camp on assignments. It was noticeable because the line for meals was getting shorter.

CHAPTER 20

JOB NO. 1: MERBEIN

ONE DAY IVAN AND I WERE CALLED TO THE OFFICE AND NOTIFIED THAT THE next morning we would be sent by train to Mildura, where a grape grower would pick us up. Strangely enough, only Ivan and I were assigned to this job, and we had no idea what it would entail. I was given a letter addressed to Mr. Maurice Power, Merbein.

When we reached Mildura, I saw a man standing near an old beige car, looking as if he were expecting someone. When we stepped off the train he approached and asked, "Are you from the Bonegilla Camp?" I replied that we were and handed him the letter. He said he was indeed Mr. Power, and told us to follow him to the car. I couldn't believe that we, the assigned fruit pickers, would be picked up by the farmer himself. Ivan knew only a few words of English, so I had to do all the talking. Mr. Power said that his farm was in Merbein, only about two miles away.

Soon we arrived. I had expected to see something similar to an agricultural farm such as the ones I knew in Europe. But this was vastly different: rows and rows full of grapevines extending as far as we could see. Mr. Power invited us into the house to meet his wife, who was quite friendly. She asked me where we came from, and gave us a cup of tea with some wafers.

When we finished our refreshments, Mr. Power offered to show us his grape vineyards. There were no animals—just the house, a couple of sheds, some kind of chicken—wire racks, and miles and miles of vineyards. Between some of the rows there were irrigation canals branching off from a main canal, which in turn branched off from a river.

After Mr. Power gave us the grand tour, he showed us our sleeping quarters. It was a square shed with two beds, a toilet, and shower. It had electricity, but no cooking facilities, because the government had ordered Mr. and Mrs. Power to provide our meals. The shed also had no windows, only some large openings with wire mesh to keep out the mosquitoes.

Mr. Power said that because it grew extremely hot around lunchtime, we would work from 7 A.M. to 11 A.M., and then from 2 P.M. until 6 P.M. He said we'd be paid by the bucket instead of by the hour, and recommended that we retire early to be ready for the next day. We were told to be at his house at 6:15 A.M. for breakfast.

I set my traveler's alarm clock for 5:30 A.M. It was a very hot night, and we could hear the "music" of mosquitoes trying to get a bite of us. Much later, when it finally cooled off, we fell asleep.

The alarm clock sounded all too soon, and we blearily shaved and washed before breakfast. Mrs. Power served porridge, tea, and a biscuit. It wasn't a very hefty meal, but we couldn't complain since the food was being provided for us. During breakfast both Mr. and Mrs. Power asked me questions about my past, which I answered gladly. Afterwards, we thanked Mrs. Power and went outside. I was surprised to see six additional—obviously local—people, waiting there: four women and two men. Mr. Power briefly introduced us by first names only, and we were ready for work.

There were two kinds of grapes to be picked: currants—which were used to make raisins—and seedless yellow grapes. The currants were dark and small; the yellow grapes were large. There were dozens of metal buckets, stacked on top of each other. We separated them to use for the currants, which we would pick first, because the yellow grapes were not yet ripe.

We were instructed in the art of picking: to gently nip off the grapes with our fingertips, so that they didn't lose any juice by being squeezed. The buckets were supposed to be filled to the top, to show a slight hill. There were two pickers for every row of vineyard, one on each side.

When the buckets were full, they were put on the side next to a strip of road, from which the farmer and two other men collected them. One man picked up the buckets and placed them on a large platform, where the other man stacked them on a wooden pallet. The buckets were arranged in a five-by-five grid, with twenty-five on the bottom, twenty-five on the next level, and twenty-five on top. When those seventy-five buckets were ready, the pallet was placed on a flatbed pulled by a tractor, and transported to the dipping basin.

There it was lifted by a crane, then lowered into the basin—which was full of a disinfectant that would kill insects. The insects floated to the surface, and one of the men picked them up with a mesh scoop, similar to those used to remove bugs and leaves from swimming pools.

When the surface was clean, the crane pulled the pallet out, placed it on the flatbed and the farmer took the grapes to a drying rack in the yard. This rack was approximately fifty feet long, five feet wide, and had several stories of chicken wire. The farmer drove slowly along the side of the rack, as one man on top passed the buckets to a man on the ground, who emptied them on the top story of the chicken wire. When all the buckets were empty, they were spread on the flatbed to dry. The buckets had to be completely free of moisture before they were used again, because otherwise they would pick up the sandy soil when they were placed on the ground for the pickers.

While this procedure was underway, the pickers had a number of full buckets ready for the next round, and this went on and on, all day long. The grapes, spread on the top story of the rack, were exposed to the strong sun. Soon the grapes would shrink and gradually fall lower and lower through the chicken wire until they ended up on a wide canvas placed on the ground underneath the rack.

The nearly-dry raisins were then removed from that canvas and transferred to a larger canvas, where they were again exposed to the sun. The farmer used a very long rake and moved the raisins back and forth to allow complete drying. This process repeated itself day after day until the harvest was completed.

There were a couple of reasons why the picking was done in the morning and again in the afternoon, with a three-hour pause between. First, it allowed the farmer, with the help of two men, to bag or box the raisins and stack them in a shed during the driest time of the day. Thus, the raisins would not pick up dampness in the late afternoon or evening. The other reason was that the pickers got a break and did not have to work in the extreme heat, which sometimes reached 117 degrees Fahrenheit.

After three hours of experience in fruit picking, we stopped to eat. We didn't have to go to the house since Mrs. Power made sandwiches and brought them to us. The breakfast hadn't been very hearty, and I was wondering what we would have for lunch. Soon we found out. It was a sandwich which had one slice of bologna, one slice of tomato, and a touch of mustard. To top it off, she gave us homemade lemonade and commercial pastry. That certainly was not a sufficient diet for hard workers like us!

That first day of picking was something new for me, and therefore somewhat interesting; but the heat during the last hour in the morning and the first two hours in the afternoon was extremely intense, almost unbearable. I had to wear a shirt with long sleeves to avoid a severe sunburn. The women and the farmer also wore large straw hats to protect their heads and necks from the sun. I only had a small, hot winter cap which I had brought with me from Germany. Yet I wore it, and to avoid burning my neck, dangled a handkerchief from under the back of the cap.

It was only natural that we were thirsty. Of course, we could eat as many grapes as we wanted to quench our thirst, but soon even the grapes were not enough. The farmer knew that, and he had a special remedy for our problem. He brought two steel rods, about the thickness and length of a broom handle, with a hook on top of each one. He drove the rods into the ground, and placed a few pieces of dried eucalyptus wood between them. Above the wood, Mr. Power hung a tin billy (the Australians use the word "billy" for an ordinary tin bucket), filled with water, from a wire that was strung between the rods. Then he put a match to the wood, and in a few minutes, the water was boiling. He opened a can of tea, and dropped some loose tea leaves into the water. After a minute or two, he unhooked one end of the wire, took the billy off the flame, and asked each of us to take one of the mugs that he had on the flatbed. He poured this boiling tea into our mugs and told us to drink it as hot as we could, without any sugar or milk. I thought the man was crazy. But when I saw him and the Australians drinking it, I looked at Ivan, and we also started to sip it. Almost immediately I was sweating bullets all over my body. By the time I'd finished drinking the hot, bitter tea, I had lost my thirst and felt almost as if I was shivering. The hot tea had brought my body temperature up to match the heat of the atmosphere.

After the tea break, we finished our workday. I was looking forward to supper, hoping it would be more substantial than lunch. But it wasn't much better, because Mrs. Power served us just two small pieces of pork sausage, one egg, a biscuit, a cup of tea, and some leftover pastry. After this skimpy meal, Ivan and I decided to walk into Merbein to see what an Australian village was like—and to buy some food.

The village was small, and we quickly saw a sign for a milk bar. We went in and bought salami, bread and milk. Ivan and I were relieved that we had discovered this milk bar, for now we could add extra food to Mrs. Power's meager servings.

The currant picking lasted two weeks; then we started on the yellow grapes. Picking currants had not been too hard, but because I had rather small and delicate fingers, the tips were quite sore. I worried about the yellow grape clusters, some of which weighed three pounds or more. We decided that Ivan, with his stronger hands, would do the actual picking, and that I would use my knife to clean the stems. Our pay that week was much higher, because the yellow grapes were larger than the currants, and it didn't take as long to fill the buckets. As Ivan and I refined our system, we became faster and more efficient. I remember that one week we picked a record of 213 buckets.

One Saturday afternoon, Ivan didn't feel well and decided to stay in the hut. So as not to bother him, I decided to go for a walk and see more of the village. It was an extremely hot day, and when I spied a pub, I went in. The interior was full of smoke, and many men were standing by the bar, talking with that Australian dialect to which I couldn't become accustomed. I certainly understood their strong swearing, however; every other word was "bloody." I approached the bar and ordered a glass by pointing to one the man next to me had. When the bartender asked, "One pot?" I nodded. He placed the "pot" (a glass of about 10 oz.) of beer in front of me and said, "One bob." Since I didn't know what a "bob" was, I took some change out of my pocket and placed it on the counter. He looked at me rather strangely and took one shilling. Now I knew what the word "bob" meant. I wasn't much of a drinker, but the beer was refreshing.

When I finished, I walked out and saw a large car in front of the pub. On the passenger side sat a heavy-set woman with a dark complexion and thick, bushy, untidy hair. I immediately thought that she was an aborigine. She was perspiring and breathing heavily, and looked thirsty. In the back of the car were two teenaged boys about thirteen and fifteen years old. Because aborigines were not allowed in bars, I went inside the bar and bought two pots. I took them out to her, assuming that she would drink one and give the other one to her sons. Instead, she quickly drank both of them, not giving the boys even a drop. She handed me the glasses, and I don't remember if she even thanked me. Then a white man—probably her husband—walked up, stepped in the car, and drove away. When I returned home I told Mr. Power the story. He said that if a policeman had been nearby, I would have been arrested for buying her the drinks!

Sunday was our day off—a day of rest. Ivan felt better, but he opted to stay in the hut. I walked around the Powers' property, to learn how the irrigation system worked. As usual, it was very warm, so after making the rounds I decided to take a nap underneath an almond tree, the only spot of lawn in the shade. I stretched out and fell asleep. When I awakened and looked up into the crown of the tree, I was shocked. About three feet above my face was a large, ugly (or perhaps beautiful for nature lovers) lizard some sixteen inches long, pumping his cheeks and staring at me with huge eyes. I wasn't sure who was more afraid of whom. I didn't move, and neither did he. Finally, I started to edge away, a few inches at a time, until I'd put enough distance between us so that he couldn't jump at me. I had no idea what he might have done, but he looked fierce—like a prehistoric animal.

One Saturday, there was to be a gathering, or perhaps a dance, in the local hall. Ivan and I decided to go. When we arrived, we saw about fifteen people in their late teens. They had a radiogram (called a phonograph in the United States), which was playing totally unfamiliar music. But there was no dancing; everyone just stood in small groups talking. There were bottles of soft drinks on a table, but no bartender. We sat down on a bench and no one paid the slightest bit of attention to us. Not one of them approached us to ask who we were or where we came from. We were well dressed and clean-shaven, so there was no reason for them to ignore us. But they did, so after about an hour, Ivan and I left.

The harvest season ended after nine weeks. We were released from that assignment and had to return to Bonegilla to wait for another one. Before we left I thought about telling Mrs. Power that in the future she should be more generous with food, but I decided to keep it to myself and not spoil the relationship.

Mr. Power drove us to the railroad station, and complimented us on being very good workers. In a few minutes the train came, and I thanked him on behalf of Ivan and myself. We shook hands and said good-bye. Another experience was behind us. What was next?

When we arrived at the Bonegilla Camp, we reported to the office. An official said he would show us our new living quarters, which were even closer to the kitchen hut. Obviously, the immigrants were getting assignments in other areas and were leaving this camp, because the population was much lower than when we'd left the camp in late January.

CHAPTER 21

JOB NO. 2: BUSH COUNTRY

A few days after we returned to Bonegilla, I was called to the office and told that the next day I would join a group going to an area about forty miles from Melbourne to help install telephone lines. The officer gave me a list of names saying that there would be fourteen Polish immigrants and one Russian. He chose me for this assignment because my records indicated that I spoke Polish, and he needed someone to act as interpreter. He said that we were not going to any particular town, just the bush country.

In the morning, I said good-bye to Ivan and joined my new work group. We had to go to Melbourne to report to the stationmaster, then be taken by truck to our destination in the bush country.

When we arrived in Melbourne, I checked in at the stationmaster's office. He told me that a truck would come for us, and soon it arrived. The driver introduced himself as Mr. Mason.

About an hour later, we pulled into a clearing surrounded by eucalyptus trees. There were several tents set up, rows of telephone poles lying on the ground and crates of supplies for putting up the phone lines.

Mr. Mason gave us each a sheet of paper to fill out. Unfortunately, the men could only fill in their names, since they didn't know English. Mr. Mason asked me to help, so I completed the forms and returned them to him. He checked them against a list, and discovered that he has them all except mine. When Mr. Mason looked at me questioningly, I told him that I didn't want to stay in those woods, with all those men, because I felt isolated and very much alone. I preferred to go to Melbourne, and said that since I had helped him, he should help me. Mr. Mason responded that he couldn't do anything unless I had employment in Melbourne and a certificate of accommodation there. I reached into my wallet and showed him the certificate that Mr. Newmann had given me. He read it skeptically and asked, "What about a job?" I replied that I had a job with the Melbourne Tomato Company. He obviously didn't believe me. He put on his climbing hooks, hung the buzzer in his belt, climbed the telephone pole, hooked up the alligator clips, asked for directory assistance and waited. When he was given the number of the Melbourne Tomato Company, he dialed it and inquired if I had a job there. They verified the fact. He came down the pole, looked at me, and said, "Put your luggage on the truck and let's go. I will talk to George in South Yarra." (South Yarra is a suburb of Melbourne.)

CHAPTER 22

JOB NO. 3: SOUTH YARRA PMG

MR. MASON DROVE ME TO THE SOUTH YARRA PMG—POST MASTER General—which handled telephone operations in the Melbourne area. He introduced me to George Smith, the manager, who said they needed one person for a work crew. However, it was now late afternoon, so George said I should start the next morning.

When he asked where I was going to stay, I showed him the certificate of accommodation from Mr. Neumann. He said that was too far from South Yarra. But he knew of a vacant room for rent at Mrs. Pierce's home on 12 Fawkner Street, just three streets away, and suggested I inquire about it. George informed me that work would begin at 7:00 A.M., and said he'd see me then. Mr. Mason offered to take me to Fawkner Street in his truck, and we were on our way.

When I rang Mrs. Pierce's bell, an elderly lady appeared. I told her that George Smith at the PMG Depot said she had a room for rent. She looked at me closely, perhaps thinking about my foreign accent. But in a few seconds, she agreed to show me the room. It was perfect: light and airy, with a window facing the street.

She explained that the rent was one pound, 10 shillings a week, or six pounds a month. I said I would take it immediately. I excused myself and went outside, where Mr. Mason had waited in his truck. He was happy to learn that I had rented the room, and helped me unload luggage and briefcase. Mr. Mason wished me a good life in Australia and drove away.

I returned to the house and told Mrs. Pierce I would rent by the month, since it was more economical. Then Mrs. Pierce introduced me to her husband, and we had a lengthy talk. I learned that she was retired, but that Mr. Pierce worked at the hospital as a chef. They had one daughter who was married to an American and lived in Florida. Mrs. Pierce also informed me that there was another tenant in the room next to mine: a Greek fellow, named George.

After our long conversation, Mrs. Pierce offered me a cup of tea and some homemade pastry. She said that I could use the stove for simple cooking and showed me the utensils. When we finished the refreshments, I thanked Mrs. Pierce for her hospitality, and went to my room. It was wonderful to sleep in a real bed.

The next morning I reported to the PMG Depot, where George Smith was talking to three men. He introduced me to them: Bill, Jack, and Norman. George said that I would report to Bill, the foreman of the linemen crew. My title would be a lineman. He said that our group took care of telephone repairs, the installation of new lines, and laying underground cables. He said that Bill would explain how to do these various tasks, and that our group had a truck filled with all the necessary supplies.

Before getting started, George asked me to fill out some forms. He said that I would be paid the basic wage of 9 pounds, 10 shillings per the government's rules. Since the exchange rate then was $2.20 American dollars for one pound, I would make almost $20 a week. (Australia's currency is now in dollars and cents.)

It took me only a few minutes to finish the forms. Then our group was sent out on an assignment, which was to install a new line in a customer's house only a few streets away. My seat on the truck was a wooden case behind the cabin, while the other three sat inside. I was surprised to know that neither Jack nor Norman had a driver's license, while I—an immigrant—had my license from Czechoslovakia. Of course, I didn't know anything about the technical aspects of this job. I helped by holding wire, getting the gaffs (climbing hooks) off the truck, and doing other simple tasks—primarily for Jack, who was the main installer and tester.

Day by day, I learned various skills—including some messy ones, like stripping cable covered with tarpaper. The tarpaper was stuck to steel wires that protected the cable, and both the paper and the tar-coated wires could only be removed by working bare-handed. Our hands then had to be washed with kerosene, which wasn't very pleasant. Since Norman and I were at the bottom of the crew's pecking order, we were always stuck with this job. Norman was a very nervous and tough worker, and he liked his drinks. As a matter of fact, all three men liked to drink. We were supposed to work until four o'clock, but a few minutes after three, we would pack up and head for the nearest pub—and stay there until it was time to go back to the Depot. This was the routine every afternoon.

Now that I had a permanent address, I dropped a line to Jan Kriz to let him know where I was. He visited me as soon as he received my letter. We had lots to talk about, so after that we saw each other almost daily after work. Jan was very pleased that I was living in the metropolitan area of Melbourne. He told me that he had landed in Sydney and was in a camp there until he got a job at NASCO, (National Automotive Service Company), a large auto-parts warehouse in Melbourne that was owned by General Motors.

I was surprised to hear that our friend, Henry Moulis, was working there with him. Jan said they played tennis together almost every other day, and suggested I buy a racquet and play with them.

One day George Smith called our crew into his office and showed us an enlarged map of the area near the Hawthorn railroad station, where aerial telephone lines were to be pulled down and installed underground. He told me that I would operate a jackhammer to open the holes and tracks for the telephone cable to be buried. I was very happy to hear this assignment would take some time, because it reassured me that my job was secure.

When we started work on the project, Bill showed me how to operate the compressor. The sidewalk was already marked by blue lines, so all we had to do was to follow those lines and dig out the tracks with the jackhammer. He gave me gloves and goggles and I started. It was noisy, and the vibration was hard on my arms, but luckily the soil underneath the paved surface was soft, and the digging progressed very well.

Norman was assigned the job of cleanup, while Jack and Bill were preparing the telephone cables that had to be buried underground. Soon I was far ahead of them, so Bill asked me to help strip the cables. I hated that tarpaper wrapping, but I didn't say anything because I was still a newcomer to the crew.

Soon we came to the point of covering the spliced cables in the pits. The individual splices were inside tiny paper tubes, which formed a sizable bulk that had to be covered by lead sheeting to protect it from dampness. This task was both time-consuming and delicate. The sheet had to be formed into a tube, and its edges tapped by a mallet to make it as thin as possible.

By using a blowtorch, the blend of lead and some kind of fat had to be carefully and smoothly applied to the seam while it was still hot. After it cooled, the ends had to be tapped into a conical shape to meet the cable, again making the edges as thin as possible. Jack was doing this part of the operation, but he wasn't happy about it. He had some close calls with the flame from the torch, and sometimes he almost burned his fingers.

I did some more work with the jackhammer and helped to bury the cables. When it came to covering the spliced individual lines in the pit, I offered to do the job that Jack had been doing. I did everything he did, only I did it better: the edges were smoother. Bill was happy, and from that point on I was assigned to do them all.

One thing that helped me work so well was the cool weather. What a change in temperature from the time I was picking grapes! Winter was now just around the corner, but the temperature had seldom gone below 53 degrees Fahrenheit.

As the assignment progressed, I noticed that the three men in our crew were growing friendlier. Norman in particular seemed more eager to help me. Now when it came to cable stripping, he wouldn't let me do it because it was tricky and dirty work, and one could easily get hurt. He could do that part, Norman said, but not the covering of joints. That was welcome news to me!

One day after work, I went to the post office to buy some stamps. Since I now had a permanent address, I had to write several letters to my relatives in Czechoslovakia. While standing in line, I noticed a well-dressed man ahead of me. When his turn came, he asked the clerk how much his overweight letter would cost to send. I recognized his accent and asked if he was from England. I introduced myself, told him that I had recently arrived in Australia, and that I had worked for the British High Court in Germany. He said, "Oh, really, that sounds interesting. My name is Norman Fig. I haven't been here too long myself and have a position as Superintendent of the Melbourne Hospital. Pleasure to meet you."

We talked for quite a while, and he asked me where I lived. I told him a few streets away, and he offered me a ride. Mr. Fig drove an old convertible, a 1939 Vauxhall, and it seemed to run well for its age. Before I stepped out, I asked him if we could have some other chance for a chat. He gave me his card and asked me "to ring him up." I thanked him and left.

Mrs. Pierce must have heard me enter my room, because she immediately knocked at the door. She said she'd placed some wood in the bathroom, which I could use to heat up water in the old-fashioned water heater. She undoubtedly had realized that my taking cold showers was not very pleasant at this time of the year!

I wanted to become better acquainted with Mr. Norman Fig so I phoned him one Saturday. He invited me for supper at the hospital and offered to pick me up. I accepted and thanked him.

Mr. Fig arrived late that afternoon and took me to his office. It was very clean, with sunlight coming through the large windows. He asked me to sit down, and we continued our talk where we left off at the Post Office. About 5 P.M., a very nice-looking woman came in and brought us some servings of canned fruit. When we finished eating it, she carried in a tray with the main course-broiled fish with several side dishes. Later, she served us tea and pastry.

When we finished the meal, Mr. Fig suggested that we go for a drive near the ocean. During the ride, I asked him how long he'd owned his car, and he replied, "Not too long." Mr. Fig said that he hadn't wanted to buy an expensive car when he first came to Melbourne, since he wanted to make certain that his job would be secure. But now he was very pleased with his position, and was thinking of selling his car and buying a later model.

We had quite a nice ride. When we arrived back at my place, I thanked him and told him I didn't know when or how I could reciprocate his kindness. He replied, "Not at all," and drove away.

I was surprised at Mr. Fig's friendliness, and compared him to my former employer and friend at the British High Court, Mr. Maidment. Then it dawned on me that perhaps he was looking for a buyer for his car. Well, I thought, it wouldn't do any harm to ask him how much it would cost.

I decided to phone Mr. Fig Monday. I had saved some money, and it was difficult to live in the city without a car. I asked Mrs. Pierce if she would allow me to park a car in front of their house. When she agreed, I became excited and I decided to call Mr. Fig the next day. I had about three hundred pounds in savings, although I didn't want to spend the entire amount. Mrs. Pierce let me look at her newspaper, where I found that used cars varied in price from two hundred pounds and up.

The next morning I decided to make myself scrambled eggs. When I entered the kitchen, Mr. Pierce was reading the paper. When I reached into the refrigerator for the eggs, Mr. Pierce—being a chef—asked me how I broke the eggs. After I showed him, he offered to demonstrate how he broke dozens of eggs on his job. He took an egg, cracked it open with one hand, dumped it next to mine in the pan. I smiled at him, and said that I would try it the next time. I did; it worked. I still do it that way.

After breakfast, I called Mr. Fig and asked him the price of his car. He thought for a minute or so, then said 225 pounds. Now it was my turn to think. Finally I told Mr. Fig that I wanted to spend a maximum of 200 pounds for my first car, because I had to become accustomed to driving on the left side of the road. I was glad we were speaking by phone; I wouldn't have had the courage to tell him that face-to-face after he had been so nice to me.

To my delight, Mr. Fig agreed, but added that he would first have to buy another car because he needed transportation. He asked me to call him in a few days. I was overjoyed. Since my weekly wages were 9 to 10 pounds. I had saved over two weeks' pay with my bargaining over the price.

I thanked Mr. and Mrs. Pierce for allowing me to conduct business in their kitchen. I told them that I had made a deal with Mr. Fig, and they joked a bit about my negotiating skills.

On Monday, I was back at work on the Hawthorn assignment. Everything was progressing smoothly there, but my mind kept wandering. On Wednesday, as agreed, I called Mr. Fig to find out if he had bought another car. He said he had, and that he would have it the next day. He would pick me up after work in his new car and we would ride to the hospital, where I could pick up the Vauxhall.

Everything went just as arranged. Mr. Fig asked me if I had a driver's license, and when I told him it had been issued by the Czech military, he said I should find out if it was valid in Australia. When we arrived at the hospital yard, I paid him the two hundred pounds. He gave me a receipt, the papers needed for the transfer, and the car keys. I told him that since I now had transportation, I could play tennis with my friends as soon as I bought a racquet. Mr. Fig said he also liked tennis, and suggested we get together for a game. I agreed, we shook hands, wished each other good luck with our new cars, and said good-bye.

I really had no idea whether I'd made a good deal or not, but I was very happy to have a car. It was a small red convertible with a radio. I parked it in front of the house so that I could see it from my window.

Now I had to start saving again. My next purchases had to be a tennis racquet, tennis shoes, socks, shorts, and a T-shirt, and all that would be another sizable expense. I planned to go shopping on Saturday. Even though it was not the season for tennis, people were already playing.

The next day was another routine day at work. I didn't tell anyone that I had bought a car. I wanted to wait until someone noticed it. I was afraid that Jack and Norman, the two Australian-born workers, might be envious that an immigrant, who had arrived only a few months ago, now owned a car. I thought it was better not to seem forward.

Our project was progressing very well, George came to visit and found everything satisfactory. He appeared when I was using the jackhammer. When he passed out the pay envelopes he said I looked like a pilot in my goggles. He was a very mild and pleasant man.

On Saturday I went shopping downtown at a sporting goods shop. When I walked in, I saw a large display of tennis racquets and balls. I knew the name, "Slezinger," tennis racquets and found some. In particular I liked a very shiny one with nice decals and a good handle. But when I looked at the price, I was shocked. It cost nine pounds—my weekly wages! I looked at some others which were cheaper, but I didn't like their appearance, I decided to buy the expensive "Slezinger" and a can of tennis balls. (I still have that racquet, and I've only had it restrung once.)

On Sunday, I surprised Jan Kriz at his place. He asked me how I arrived there, and he couldn't believe his eyes when I showed him my car. I told him I had bought a racquet and balls, and that now all I needed were shoes, shorts and a T-shirt. Then I could play tennis with him and Henry.

I asked Jan to show me the area. He lived across from Luna Park, an amusement place near the ocean in the St. Kilda suburb. He said he liked it there very much, because he could go for a walk after work and enjoy the sound of the ocean and the sea air. He had the same kind of arrangement that I had—a room with kitchen privileges. But since he didn't like to cook, he often ate in the Bohemia, a Czech restaurant, and made sandwiches at home for lunch. He added that the Bohemia had very good food, and that there were usually several Czech immigrants there. A violin player entertained during mealtimes on Sundays. As it was now nearing the lunch hour, I suggested that we have a meal there.

When we arrived the violinist was playing, and there were quite a few guests. It was music to my ears to hear the Czech language. When the waiter came to our table, I promptly ordered one of the most popular Czech meals, viennerschnitzel and potato salad, which I hadn't eaten for a long time. Jan ordered another very popular Czech meal: pork, dumplings, and sauerkraut. The meal was delicious. Better yet, it wasn't very expensive. All this was a great delight for me. Jan told me about two other Czech restaurants, the Praha and the Moravia. I never expected this, and it indicated there must be a number of Czech immigrants in Melbourne.

After we left, I invited Jan to go for a ride. He suggested that we drive to Fisherman's Bend, about three miles outside Melbourne. That was where he and Henry worked, and also played tennis.

When we arrived, I saw a huge warehouse with the sign, NASCO: A Division of General Motors Holden. I asked Jan about the sign, and he said that Australia had its own car called "Holden."

Behind the building there were three tennis courts and shower rooms for the employees. This pleasant facility was closed since it was still wintertime. Jan said it would open in the spring—in September. That still sounded strange to me!

After viewing the area, we drove back to St. Kilda where I dropped Jan off. The afternoon had turned cool and cloudy, so we decided to call it a day. I returned to my room and wrote letters to Ray and Betty Maidment, and to Mr. Holtzbaum, the Chief of the High Court in Hamburg.

After work on Monday, I went to a nearby police station to find out what to do after the purchase of a car. I was told I had to have it transferred to my name by the magistrate's office where I could also get a driver's license. I took care of this the next day, so now I was licensed and registered.

Because of the car, I was able to visit Jan often. One day he told me that he had met a young girl, Maxine, at work. She belonged to the Youth Hostel Association, a group of young people who met every Friday. She gave him the meeting address and invited him and me to attend one of their meetings. Since Jan and I were both alone and lonely, we decided to go sometime in the near future.

I also asked Jan to accompany me to buy the last items I needed in order to play tennis: shoes, shorts, and a T-shirt. After I made these purchases, we strolled through the downtown area. Through one window we noticed a large machine making doughnuts, one every three seconds, all perfectly uniform. We stopped to watch for a moment, then couldn't resist going in. We ordered tea and doughnuts, which were really tasty.

Afterwards, I invited Jan to see my room and to meet Mr. and Mrs. Pierce. As I was driving Jan home, I suggested that we go to a dance to become acquainted with some Australian girls. I had heard of a place called Trocadero, so we decided to go there on Saturday. I told Jan that I would pick him up at 7:00 P.M.

So Saturday night, Jan and I went to our first dance in Australia. When we walked into the Trocadero, it was very noisy. Although there were several tables in the large hall, most people were standing—men on one side and girls on the other. We stood in the men's group for a little while, curious about this Australian custom.

After a couple of tunes were played, I heard the sound of a tango. I approached a table where two girls were sitting, and asked one of them if I might have a dance. She was very nice-looking, and I was delighted when she consented. During our dance, I asked her if she was from Melbourne, and she said she was from the Toorak area (a wealthy section). She said she didn't come to the Trocadero very often. When she inquired where I was from, I told her I was Czechoslovakian, and that I had just recently arrived in Australia. After the music stopped, I led her back to her table.

When I rejoined Jan, he was standing in the same place. I asked why he hadn't danced, and he said he'd asked the other girl at the table, but she had turned him down.

When the music began again, I approached the same girl, but this time she politely refused: "No, thank you." A couple of minutes later, a husky fellow sat down next to her. Although he was poorly dressed in a work shirt and had a bandage on his cheek, she seemed quite friendly with him. I realized it was fortunate that she hadn't danced a second time with me, since I probably wouldn't have left the hall in one piece. Both Jan and I asked several other girls to dance, but when we were consistently rejected we gave up and left. Even though I had been in Australia for only a short time, it was apparent to me that Australian girls didn't like foreigners.

We decided to go to the "pictures" (Australian usage for movies), so at least the evening wouldn't be wasted. The show was Three Coins in the Fountain, and the theater was very beautiful, with hundreds of stars painted on the ceiling. Since the admission was not expensive, I began going to the pictures at least twice a week.

One day Jan and I decided to try the Praha, a downtown Czech restaurant. The manager was a Mr. Cerny who welcomed us personally in Czech. He gave us a menu with a nice selection of meals. I ordered pork, dumplings, and sauerkraut, while Jan chose sauerbraten-beef and dumplings in a thick gravy.

For dessert we had coffee and homemade cake. Everything was delicious, and it was no wonder that the restaurant was very crowded. Because people were waiting for tables, we didn't want to prolong our stay. But I did stop to ask Mr. Cerny who had baked the delectable torte. He said it was Mirek Kostal, a Czech immigrant, who had opened his own confectionery shop in South Yarra. This was good news, since I worked near his business.

When I was in college in Czechoslovakia studying English, the professor had said, "Sunday is the dullest day in England." Now that I had been in Australia for several months, I observed that Sundays there were also very quiet. Most stores were closed, streets were half-empty, and traffic was light. When I bought the car from Mr. Fig, he told me to make certain to buy petrol (gasoline) on weekdays, since even the pumps were closed on Sundays after 6 P.M.

After our disaster experience at the Trocadero, Jan and I decided to go to the Friday meeting of the Youth Hostel Association. When we entered the hall, a tall, good-looking girl came to greet us. She said her name was Margot. We introduced ourselves, and I told her that Maxine, a coworker of Jan's, had invited Jan and me to join the group. In a few minutes she returned with Maxine, who was quite pleased to see Jan. There were probably twenty or more lively young people in the room, and Maxine asked for silence to announce that these two newcomers were from Czechoslovakia. She introduced us to all of the members. It was interesting to hear the names—such as Rae, Gwen, Maxine, Margot, Evelyn and June—which were quite different from those at home.

I talked to Margot for quite a while, telling her about myself. She said that her ancestors were Russian, added some details about her background, and explained that she was chairman of the Youth Hostel group. Then she excused herself, walked to the far end of the hall, and again asked for silence. This time she brought up some unfinished business from the previous meeting, regarding a hike which was planned for the near future. When the discussion ended, Margot returned and apologized that no entertainment had been planned; she explained that the purpose of the meetings was primarily to arrange hikes and other trips. All in all, it was a nice evening. But I felt it would have been more congenial if they had music and perhaps some dancing. I decided I'd suggest it for the future.

Gradually my life in Australia became more diversified. I visited all three Czech restaurants and met more Czech immigrants. Sometimes I phoned Norman Fig, and I often saw Jan. But one evening when I arrived at Jan's rooming home to take him to a Youth Hostel meeting, he told me that a girl he had met there the previous Friday was going to pick him up. He said her name was Evelyn Menzies and that she was about twenty-seven years old. I was happy he had made a friend, and said that I would see him at the club.

That night Margot had arranged some races as entertainment. These entailed cutting a wide ribbon with scissors. Two people stood in one place and two others about twenty-five feet away. Between these pairs was the tape, and whoever split it first was the winner. A stopwatch was used to measure the precise moment that the tape was cut. I happened to be one of the first pair competing, and beat my opponent by a good margin. There were several races over the course of the evening. Afterwards, I was pleasantly surprised that I was declared a winner. I was awarded a prize, a small metal kangaroo, and was congratulated by my many new friends.

The weather was improving. It was October, and more and more people were playing tennis. One evening after work I picked up Jan, and we went to the General Motors courts, which were now open for employees and guests. When I was a boy, I had used wooden racquets to hit balls. But it was rather different using my new tennis racquet with its much longer handle. However, I kept improving, and before the evening was over, I could hit the ball well enough to keep it within the lines. I promised myself I'd be better next time! After the game, I took Jan home and asked him if he would be at the club on Friday. He said that he and Evelyn had decided to go to the pictures.

The days were getting longer, and because I liked to play tennis, I decided to play as often as I could. But because Jan now had a girl friend, he didn't have time. Instead he arranged for me to play with our friend, Henry Moulis, at the GM courts. The problem was that Henry lived on the outskirts of Melbourne and commuted by train, so we always had to make arrangements ahead of time. However, despite that small inconvenience, we had fun. The company not only allowed us to use their courts free of charge, but on certain days even provided tennis balls. There were showers, and occasional competitions with prizes. Tennis was the number one sport in Australia, and many families had their own private courts.

On the following Friday, I assumed that Jan would be picked up by Evelyn. When I arrived at the club, I saw her—but no Jan. I asked Evelyn where he was, and she said that they had stopped seeing each other because Jan was becoming "too serious." I didn't ask any more questions. That night's meeting was about a trip that was being planned to Phillip Island, located in the southern waters of the continent. While everyone was discussing this trip, I noticed that Evelyn stood next to me and kept giving me a look as if she were interested in me. At the end of the evening, I asked if she would like to go on a date, and she agreed. Evelyn was very pretty, but I still felt rather uneasy, thinking about Jan's reaction. I asked her why she would go out with me and not with Jan. She repeated that he was too serious, and added that her parents had a very luxurious car—a Citroen—which they wouldn't allow her to drive at night. Evelyn said that my having a car would make it more convenient for her. I evaluated her reasons, which I found very practical, although not very flattering!. We set the date for Saturday.

On Saturday afternoon, I drove to pick up Evelyn at her parents' residence, No. 12 Cuba Street, in a very nice suburban area. When I arrived, Evelyn greeted me and asked me to come in to meet her parents. She introduced me to Mr. and Mrs. Menzies, who invited me to sit down for a little while. Evelyn had informed them that I came from Czechoslovakia, and they were curious. They asked me a number of questions: how I had left home, where I had been before I arrived in Australia, and so forth. Naturally our conversation took quite some time, and Mrs.

Menzies offered me a cup of tea and pastry. While we sipped our tea, I glanced out the window and saw a beautifully landscaped garden. I complimented them and mentioned that I liked gardening, but especially vegetables, which we had grown at home by the thousands of pounds. Then I thanked Mrs. Menzies for her hospitality, and Evelyn and I went for a ride. I complimented her on her nice parents and their lovely house.

The prime minister of Australia was named Menzies, and I was astonished when Evelyn informed me that she was his niece. No wonder her parents had wanted to quiz me!

We drove to the other side of Melbourne on the coastal road, which was rather narrow and winding. I noticed a photographer on top of a high rock with his camera mounted on a tripod, directed at the curved road with its double line. I asked Evelyn why the man was there. She said that he was a policeman taking pictures of drivers who went over the line. The police would develop the film, locate the name and address of the offender by his plate number, and mail him a fine. It was good to know this at the early stages of my driving in Australia.

After about an hour, we saw a flat plateau area. I drove close to the edge, where it offered a spectacular view of the ocean. Because I had a convertible we could hear the sounds of the breaking waves. The beach was absolutely beautiful and clean, a beige color that stretched out on both sides of us as far as we could see. We talked about many subjects: her work as a saleslady in a large clothing store downtown, my experiences, our likes and dislikes.

As we sat in the car, I watched both the ocean and Evelyn. It was a warm, sunny day with not a cloud in the sky. She was dressed in light casual clothing—a pretty blouse, shorts, and, to protect her hair from the wind, a colorful kerchief. She had a beautiful figure and a peaches-and-cream complexion, which tempted me to touch her. However, I considered the remark Evelyn had made about Jan being "too serious," so I decided to control my impulse and limit my romantic ideas to holding her hand. She was the first girl I'd been out with in Australia, and I didn't want to spoil my image on our first date. After a while, we drove back to town, and decided to go to the pictures that evening.

It was nice to have a date with a girl from an affluent family, but I had a problem. I didn't have any suitable clothes to wear in the evening. The clothes that I had were out of style, because fashions were different in Europe. I wore the best suit I had, with a shirt and tie.

At 7:00 P.M. I picked up Evelyn, who looked very attractive. She didn't make any comment about my appearance, so I could only hope that I was dressed appropriately.

The theater was packed. There were many American films in Australia in the fifties—one better than the other—and the theaters were almost always sold out. During the picture, I held Evelyn's hand, which she didn't resist. It seemed like a step in the right direction. The film was very entertaining, and I was happy.

After the show, I took Evelyn home. We sat in the car for a while in front of her home, discussing the picture. Then I asked her if I could kiss her good night. When she did not reply, I leaned over and kissed her anyway. Then I asked if I could see her on Sunday, but Evelyn said that almost every Sunday, she took her parents for a ride. I told her that I would call her during the week for our next date.

Because I couldn't see Evelyn on Sunday, I visited Jan, and we went to play tennis on the GM courts. We spent a nice afternoon, and Jan introduced me to some of the other players. After a few sets, we left and I took Jan home. On the way, I suggested that we go to the Czech restaurant Moravia for dinner. Jan thought it was a good idea. I went home to change, and later picked him up.

When we entered the restaurant, it was full of Czech immigrants. There must have been a soccer game that afternoon, because the restaurant was filled with young men talking in Czech about the game. The atmosphere was very congenial, and the meal was delicious. And somehow, Jan and I went through the day without mentioning Evelyn's name.

On Monday, I went back to the usual routine. We were making good progress with the Hawthorn assignment, and the area where we buried the aerial lines looked changed. By now we were involved with more than cables and jackhammer work. We also had to repair the sidewalks. Some places even required concrete and brick reinstallation, because the individual cable lines had to be brought underground into buildings, disturbing the landscape. When George came to see how we were doing, he expressed great satisfaction. I was making a joint in the pit when he approached me and said, "George, you are doing fine work. I know this was not your profession in Czechoslovakia. But just imagine: these pits will remember you for years to come." We both laughed—but I was flattered.

On Tuesday, I called Evelyn's home to arrange another date. Her mother answered and said Evelyn wasn't there because she had to work overtime. I thanked her and asked her to give my regards to Mr. Menzies. Since I had nothing else to do, I washed my car, and wrote letters to my sisters and brothers in Czechoslovakia and to my sponsors in the United States.

On Thursday I called Evelyn again. And again Mrs. Menzies said Evelyn was working overtime. But I thought I'd see her the next day at the Youth Hostel meeting, and could arrange for a date.

When I arrived at the club on Friday, Evelyn wasn't there. I asked her friend Margot where Evelyn was, and she said that Evelyn was dating someone occasionally, so perhaps this was their night out. Well, it made good sense, but I couldn't understand why Mrs. Menzies would lie and cover up for her daughter. At the meeting there was a discussion about a future hike, but I was too distracted to pay attention. During my drive home, I decided that I had to find out if anything was going on between Evelyn and someone else.

On Saturday morning, I called Evelyn at home. I invited her to a matinee that afternoon, and to my great surprise she agreed. I told her that I would pick her up at 1:30.

Evelyn was dressed very nicely as usual, and I had on a hound's tooth jacket with a white shirt and tie. She said the jacket made me look too young. I told her I didn't have much suitable clothing and added that I was gradually buying Australian clothes. I wasn't certain my answer satisfied her, but I noticed by the expression on her face that she wasn't in the best mood. I didn't say anything more and just kept driving.

After the pictures, I suggested that we go to the Bohemia restaurant for Czech food, and was again surprised when she accepted.

At the restaurant, Evelyn looked at the menu and was undecided. I offered to select something she would like. I ordered viennerschnitzel and potato salad for her, and pork, dumplings, and sauerkraut for myself. I purposely ordered different meals so she could see two examples of Czech cooking. Everything was delicious, and the atmosphere was quite lively as the violin player played melodious songs. We stayed for a long time enjoying the music.

Little by little, the guests were leaving, so about nine o'clock we left, too. The night was still young, but the way things were, I didn't expect any romantic conclusion to this date. I drove to Evelyn's home, and when we arrived, I didn't offer to kiss her. Evelyn must have sensed that I was out of sorts. She thanked me for the picture and dinner, and we quickly said good night.

On the way home, I reviewed the events of the day and still couldn't understand Evelyn's mood. My final analysis was that Evelyn, the daughter of affluent parents, thought she was too good for me. I was a poor immigrant, a telephone lineman with no handsome clothes and an old "Bessy" car—just not up to her standards. I wasn't angry, but I was disappointed. She was very pretty, and I had looked forward to enjoying her company. But now I decided Evelyn was a closed chapter and that I wouldn't call her again.

On Sunday morning, I had to do my weekly wash. I had learned from Ludmila how to starch the collars of my shirts and how to iron most of my clothing, including handkerchiefs. Because I was so busy, I overlooked the time, and suddenly it was almost noon. I shaved quickly and decided to go for my weekly Sunday meal at the Bohemia. I put on light clothes and took my tennis equipment with me. I went to invite Jan to have lunch with me, but when I arrived, he had just finished eating. I suggested that after I ate, we could play tennis. He agreed, and added that Henry would be there also. I drove to the restaurant, and had lunch, and went back to pick up Jan.

When we arrived at the GM facility, only one court was occupied. We began to play, and soon Henry arrived. To keep all three of us involved in the game, we played what I called "progressive" tennis—two players on one side using the full width of the court, and on the opposite side of the net, one player using only the inner width. This worked very well, and we changed partners after each set. It was quite enjoyable, and we had a good game. We took showers, then I drove Jan and Henry to show them my rooming house. I made them drinks and we sat reminiscing about our past in Prague. We couldn't believe we were together after two years' separation. It seemed as if fate had brought us together again so very far from Czechoslovakia.

The following week Jan and I found time for more tennis. It was now November, so the weather was getting warmer and the evenings were getting longer. We took advantage of this and played quite often. I asked Jan if he was planning to go to the next Youth Hostel meeting, but he said he couldn't because he had volunteered to help one of his coworkers with a moving job.

So on Friday I went to the meeting alone. The people attending were all regulars, except for one girl who was talking with Margot. When Margot saw me, she introduced me to this new girl, Jean. She was quite good—looking, and we had a short chat. Then Margot called the meeting to order. A couple of trips were discussed: one to Phillip Island, southeast of Melbourne, and one to Lorne, an oceanside camping area to the southeast. The Lorne outing would require a tent, a sleeping bag, and camping equipment. That trip was scheduled for early December, while the Phillip Island trip was planned for early January.

It was warm in the hall, and I had a soft drink with Jean. While we were sipping our drinks, a girl approached us. Jean introduced her as Robin, and said she had ridden to the meeting with her.

Jean asked me where I came from, which triggered many other questions. She was extremely interested to hear about my experiences, which took up the rest of the evening. When it was time to leave, we were still deep in conversation. Jean said she would like to hear more, perhaps at the next meeting. I suggested that if Robin wouldn't mind, I could take Jean home and continue with my story. She looked at me, a little surprised, but said she would check with Robin. When she returned, Jean said it would be all right.

We walked out to my car, and I told Jean that I hoped she wouldn't mind riding in old "Bessy" as I now called the Vauxhall. Jean smiled and said that she didn't mind at all. I asked her where she lived, and she replied that she lived with her parents in a suburban neighborhood, Glen Iris, about five miles from the downtown area where we were. As far as I was concerned, it wasn't too far at all!.

During the trip, I continued with my story and soon we were at her parents' home. I asked Jean for her telephone number, and suggested that perhaps we could see each other before the next meeting. She reached into her handbag, took a page from a notebook, and wrote down her phone number. I went around, and opened the door for her, whispering that I knew how to close it silently so that her parents wouldn't be awakened. I told Jean how much I enjoyed talking with her, and I would call her soon. She said good night.

Well, perhaps this was another chance to have a girlfriend! During my trip home, I decided I would call her first thing in the morning. I hoped she didn't have a boyfriend. I was young, alone, and looking for company—and Jean seemed to be very pleasant and friendly.

On Saturday morning, I called to ask Jean if she had any plans for the weekend. She said she had invited some friends to play tennis on her parents' private court that afternoon. Jean asked if I played tennis, and when I said that I did, she immediately invited me to join them. This was a pleasant surprise.

It was another pleasant surprise to discover that Jean must have been watching for me, because she came out to greet me as I drove up to her house. She asked me to follow her into a large living room, where the other guests were seated. Jean introduced me to two men and two girls, and to her parents. Jean had told me that her father was sixty-seven years old and still played tennis often.

That afternoon, Jean didn't play, so her father took me on. Since he was almost forty years older than me, I wondered if I should let him win. We started to play, and to my shock he gave me a tough time. He couldn't run as well as I could, but he placed his returns in the corners of the court so that very often it was impossible for me to return the ball. In the end, we didn't finish the complete set. We called it fifty-fifty, and I congratulated him on a great game.

It was a very enjoyable afternoon. We finished about 4:30, just in time for tea. Now I knew why Jean didn't play—she'd been busy setting a large table. The cups were upside down in the saucers, obviously to keep them free of any dust. There were several plates full of homemade biscuits and pastry, a real treat. This was another affluent home; Jean had told me during our chat the night before that her father had a large machine shop, with seventeen employees, including her as bookkeeper.

One man at the table, Doug Leonard, was very comical, always joking. He "had the floor," most of the time, and he kept all of us entertained. Jean had introduced Doug as a long-time family friend, and explained that he owned a delivery business for express shipments. I sat quietly, enjoying the friendly atmosphere as well as the pastry. A little later, however, Doug noticed my silence and asked me where I came from. When I told him that I was from Czechoslovakia, he asked how had I managed to leave a country that was under communist rule and hemmed in by well-guarded borders. I told him that it would take a long time to describe my dangerous escape, but he insisted that he would like to hear it. When the others chimed in to agree, I began to tell my story. I talked and talked, while everyone stayed very quiet and looked at me intently.

No one realized how much time had passed, until at 7 P.M., Jean reminded Doug that he would be overdue for a date with his girlfriend. He looked at the clock and said, "I can always have a date with her, but I will never have another chance to hear anything as interesting as what George is telling us. I'll explain everything to her later." He told me to continue, and asked me a few questions now and then. About thirty-minutes later, I finally finished. Everyone thanked me and said they'd been totally absorbed in my story. In turn, I thanked Jean and her parents for inviting me. I told them how much I had enjoyed the visit, shook hands with her parents, and then Jean accompanied me to my car.

While standing outside, I asked Jean if she had any plans for Sunday, and said I would like to take her for a ride. She agreed and we set a time. I thanked Jean again for the invitation, and left happy that I was going to see her the next day.

On Sunday I went to the Bohemia for my usual meal, and then went to pick up Jean. When I arrived, she came to the gate of their garden. I stepped out of my car and opened the passenger-side door. I asked if she liked the ocean, and suggested that we go for a ride along the coast. She agreed, and we were on our way. I chose the same scenic road that I had taken with Evelyn, and stopped at the same plateau. We sat in the car for a long time, and Jean wanted to hear more of my experiences. She told me she had read a lot about Czechoslovakia and other central European countries, so she was familiar with them geographically.

On our return, as we were approaching Melbourne, I invited Jean for dinner at the Bohemia. I had become acquainted with several Czech immigrants who ate there frequently. I also liked the violin player and the atmosphere. By now, the Bohemia was almost my second home in Australia. When the waiter brought us the menu, Jean admitted she didn't know anything about Czech food, so I ordered for both of us. When we finished the meal, Jean said she'd loved it. We sat there for quite a while longer, until the restaurant was half empty.

Finally, we decided to leave, and I drove her home. When we arrived at her parents' house, I helped Jean out of the car and accompanied her to the door. I sensed that a kiss would be in order. She didn't show any resistance, and I thought my kiss had been acceptable. I said good night and left.

For me to have a native-born Australian girlfriend was a big problem, because I didn't want to stay there. My dream was America, and the only girl I would marry had to be a Czech willing to accompany me. But that was almost impossible, because there were no single Czech girls in Australia! I needed to have a girl as a friend until I could emigrate to the United States. That was very difficult, and perhaps even unfair to ask of anyone.

It was hard for me to divide my hours after work: I wanted to play tennis with Jan and Henry, date Jean, and go to the Youth Hostel meetings. I was very busy, but that was good, since the weeks went by quickly. I knew that someday I would be granted a visa, and I just needed to fill the time while waiting.

The work around the Hawthorn Station was nearing completion. The area looked better and better every day. Now we were behind schedule in installing new lines into private homes, so there was plenty of work ahead.

I thought I'd been neglecting Jan and Henry, so I made arrangements to play tennis with them every other day, weather permitting. The evenings were longer, and we stayed on the courts until dark. During one of these evenings, Jan told me that his employer, NASCO, planned to have a company picnic on October 28, which friends of the employees could attend. I accepted Jan's invitation. Coincidentally, the date of the picnic was also a very important anniversary for all Czechs and Slovaks, because on October 28, 1918, the new Republic of Czechoslovakia was established, finally liberating it from the Austrian-Hungarian monarchy. The date is celebrated every year, just like July 4 in the United States.

I was also seeing Jean during the week and playing tennis on her court. Perhaps I played too much, because the wrist of my right hand was aching a bit. However, I didn't pay much attention to it, since I enjoyed the game tremendously.

The work was finally completed at the Hawthorn station, and we had a small party at the PMG Depot. George was happy; he thanked us and was our host for the day. I asked him what our next project would be. He said the first job was a small one. A manhole was causing a problem, and we would have to work on it the following week. After that, there were all those new phone lines that needed to be installed. I liked to hear that, since I wanted to stay in the Melbourne area—and as long as we were busy, I was not in danger of being transferred. I had heard about these transfers from a Czech at the Bohemia, who told me that the government transferred immigrants from one place to another on the spur of the moment.

On October 27, Jan, Henry, and I played tennis all afternoon, which was not exactly the best thing for my aching wrist. The next day I picked up Jan and we went to the picnic, which was held in a large area near an athletic field that had a racing oval for runners. When we arrived, they were selecting groups of runners for individual heats. The man in charge was asking for young men to line up for the heat runs. Jan and Henry refused, but I agreed. I was in the third heat, with four men to each heat.

Because I had been playing tennis often, I was in good shape. I won the heat and became eligible for the final race.

We lined up for the race according to ages. Because I was twenty-eight, some of the younger chaps were positioned several yards behind me. At the starting gun, we ran around the whole oval. I was first almost to the end, but in the last couple of yards a young man pulled ahead of me. I received second prize: a handmade and beautifully painted boomerang.

When I joined Jan and Henry, I was introduced to several of their coworkers and we all sat down to eat. After our meal, Jan introduced me to the head of the warehouse, Mr. O'Keefe. He was already feeling no pain, and asked me if I could sing. Without replying, I burst into the popular Australian song, "Waltzing Matilda," and everyone joined in. When the song ended, I started another one, "She'll be running round the mount'n when she comes..." and again everyone joined in. After that, I began singing, "My Bonnie lies over the ocean...." At this point, Mr. O'Keefe hugged me around my neck, weaving us both from side to side in time with the song. Then when the day was winding down, Mr. O'Keefe said, "George, I am very pleased to meet you. If you ever need any help, just come and see me." I thanked him, and shook hands with him and some other people. Jan and I waved to all and we left.

Jan was bewildered by my contribution to the singing. As long as I had known him, even in Prague, we never had a chance to sing anywhere. He asked me where I had learned those Australian songs. I explained that when I was accepted for emigration, I decided to learn some Australian songs just in case I ever got a chance to sing—and obviously that had paid off at the picnic. Jan listened, then shook his head, perhaps with some degree of admiration. Henry smiled but didn't say anything. We had a very good time, and I will never forget the NASCO picnic in Australia.

On Monday we met at the PMG Depot as usual, and George told Bill to take care of that manhole problem. We loaded a restraining railing onto the truck, and drove out to examine the manhole. I could see that the cover, which was supposed to be flush with the street level, was a few inches low, thus creating a drop like a large pothole. It was necessary to put the railing around the spot. I tried to unload the collapsible railing off the truck with Norman, who somehow misjudged the timing. The railing hit my right wrist just at the spot where it ached. Now it really hurt, and I thought a bone was cracked or chipped. Bill and Jack were looking on while we were unloading, and when this happened, they quickly came over and checked my hand. Bill was concerned, and asked me to get into his truck. He took me to a hospital clinic to have my hand examined, but since there were several people waiting ahead of me, I told him to go back to the job.

When my turn came, the elderly doctor asked to see my arm. I showed him the aching spot on my wrist where the railing had hit me. He looked at it and gently tried to work it. He didn't say anything, but went to the door to the next room and called in a younger doctor. That doctor saw the little blue spot on my wrist, shook his head, and said, "It looks like a tennis elbow." Having made his diagnosis, the young one went away, while the elderly doctor took out some plaster of paris, gauze, and a bowl. In a little while, my wrist was in a cast and sling, and the doctor told me that I should not do heavy work for two weeks to give my wrist a chance to heal. I asked him if he would be kind enough to give me a note stating that I should not do any hard work, and he agreed. I was surprised he didn't give me a bill or ask for a fee. I thanked him and left.

I went back to the Depot to see George. He already knew what had happened, obviously from Bill, but he was surprised to see my arm in a sling. I showed him the slip from the doctor. He read it, and said, "George, we have a slight problem. I just received a note from PMG Headquarters that you've been released from this branch. You are assigned to work for PMG at Kew, a suburb outside Melbourne. We are supposed to take you there tomorrow." He scratched his head and said, "We will have to do what this release says. When you get there, show them the slip. They will most certainly send you home, and you will report back there when your wrist is healed." I thanked him for being so kind to me all these months and said good-bye. There were still several hours left to the day, and I had a simple lunch. After lunch, I sat on the porch in front of my room and had a welcome rest, enjoying the bright sunshine.

When Mr. Pierce came home from his job at the hospital, I asked him why I didn't receive a bill from the doctor at the clinic. He said the hospital took care of minor cases at no charge.

The next morning I went to the PMG Depot as usual. When I greeted the crew, they all said they were sorry about my injury, and sorry that I was leaving. We had a short chat, then it was time for me to say good-bye to Jack, Norman, and George. Bill told me to get into the truck, and we were off. I waved good-bye, and that was the end of my stint with PMG South Yarra.

It was quite a ride to Kew. When we finally pulled up to the PMG gate, the office was almost invisible because the yard was piled full of heavy equipment, telephone poles, and cables. Bill swerved around all those stacks and stopped in front of the field office. We both entered. Inside was a heavyset man, who stared at my sling in surprise. I gave him the note from the doctor. He said he would register that I had reported, but if I couldn't work on heavy equipment or lift cables, he obviously would not be able to use me. He told me to come again after my hand healed, wished me a quick recovery, and politely said good-bye. Bill took me home.

When we arrived at my rooming house, Bill saw my car parked outside. He asked me whose car it was, and when I said it was mine, he looked rather startled. He stepped out of the truck to inspect it closer, then he smiled and wished me luck. We shook hands—me using my left hand—and I thanked him for being nice to me all these months. Bill stepped into his truck, waved, and drove off.

My arm wasn't very sore, just uncomfortable if I tried to do any lifting. But I could use it for writing letters, and this was a good chance to catch up on my correspondence. In a couple of days, I could probably even drive. Still, I didn't want to be too active, since I didn't know if someone would check on me, even though I had the doctor's note.

One day, I stopped at Kostal's Confectionery near my rooming house. When I entered the shop, there was a Czech lady talking to Mirek Kostal—the owner, whom I had looked up after learning he made those delicious pastries for the Praha restaurant. I stood a couple of steps away, listening to their conversation. When she was about to leave, I asked her what part of Czechoslovakia she came from. She replied that she was from Moravia, near the Slovak border. While we were talking, I ordered some pastry. After I paid, we introduced ourselves. She told me that her name was Anna Fischer, and that she had run a laundry and cleaning business in Czechoslovakia. But after the communists confiscated it in 1949, she and her husband had escaped. When I inquired if she was in the laundry business here, Mrs. Fischer shook her head and said that they didn't have enough money to start a business. Since I couldn't do any wash with my arm in a sling, I asked if I could pay her to do some laundry for me. Mrs. Fischer said she would be glad to help, and gave me her address, which was just around the corner. I told her I would bring my wash very soon.

When I returned home, I called Jean and asked if she would like to go to the pictures with me. She accepted, and we made a date for Saturday at 7:00 o'clock. I didn't say anything about my arm, thinking it would be easier to explain in person.

Early on Friday evening, I drove to Jan's rooming house. He was shocked to see my arm in a sling. I told him what happened and asked if he wanted to go to the Bohemia. He said that he already planned to have a simple supper at home, and invited me to join him. As we ate, I mentioned that Mr. O'Keefe had told me to go see him if I ever needed help. Jan listened, then said I had a good chance to get a job at NASCO, since they were very busy. He asked me how I would go about making the change from PMG. I told him about the doctor's note that said I shouldn't do any heavy work. I could present that to the magistrate downtown, where I would have to go anyway to ask for a transfer to NASCO. Jan thought that was a good idea. I thanked him for the supper and left.

On Saturday, I picked up Jean. After I told her about my wrist, we went to see the pictures. I wanted to watch every American picture that was shown in Australia. They were not only superior films, but I wanted to hear American English so I could understand it when I arrived in the United States. I was determined to emigrate, and I couldn't wait until the day I could get my visa.

After the picture, I took Jean home. Even though I knew she would probably never leave Australia for America, I wanted to become better acquainted with her. When it was time to say goodnight, I accompanied her to the door of her house and kissed her.

I decided not to go to the Bohemia the next day to have my usual meal, because I didn't want to explain to people why I was wearing a sling. But Sunday dragged by, and my stomach growled at the thought of the sauerbraten I was missing.

It was hard to fill the days that following week. I wrote many letters to my relatives in Czechoslovakia during the mornings. In the afternoons, I sat on the porch enjoying the warm sun and thinking about my next date with Jean.

On Thursday I went to the hospital clinic to have the cast removed. The same elderly doctor was there, and he gently took off the cast. Then he moved my hand several times and asked if it was aching. When I said it wasn't, he released me from his care. I was glad it was over as I could be active again.

On Friday, I went to the NASCO to see Mr. O'Keefe and check with him about a job. When his secretary announced me, he came out of his office smiling, shook my hand, and asked what brought me to see him. I was relieved that he remembered me, since he'd been a bit soused at the picnic. I told him that I had some very good friends who worked for his company, and that I would like to change jobs from PMG to NASCO. Mr. O'Keffe rubbed his chin and looked at me for a few seconds. Then he said he'd like to help me, but that there might be some difficulty because the government needed workers at PMG. However, he promised to try to do something. He dictated a few lines to his secretary, saying that NASCO was in need of manpower and that the company would be willing to give employment to George Knava. When he finished speaking, he glanced at me to see my reaction. I nodded my head, and he told the secretary to type it.

In a few minutes, she handed the typed letter to Mr. O'Keefe. He read it, signed it, gave it to me, and said, "George, I hope this will help. I would like to have you here." I thanked him, we shook hands, and I left.

Since it was still early in the day, I drove to the magistrate's office in downtown Melbourne to ask for my transfer. It went surprisingly well.

The magistrate asked me the purpose of my visit, and I told him I had been working at PMG, doing heavy jobs that had caused an injury to my arm. I explained that I'd been just released by a doctor at the hospital clinic, who recommended that I refrain from further heavy work. I showed the doctor's note to the magistrate. He read it and asked me what kind of employment I would like to have. I replied that I had a job promised to me by the manager of the NASCO warehouse, and handed him the letter from Mr. O'Keefe. The magistrate thought for a few minutes, then gave me a form to complete, stating that my job was terminated with PMG. I filled it out; he took it; I signed it; and he filed it. Then he filled out a shorter form—declaring that I was released from PMG-which I was to take to NASCO.

On the following Monday, I went to the NASCO personnel office to apply for a job. I filled out an application, and was told that they would let me know. Probably somewhat smugly, I immediately said that Mr. O'Keefe had agreed to hire me last Friday. Of course, the personnel officer wasn't at all sure I was telling the truth. She phoned Mr. O'Keefe, who gave his permission for me to start a week later.

CHAPTER 23

JOB NO. 4: NASCO

ON NOVEMBER 14, I REPORTED FOR WORK AT THE PERSONNEL OFFICE. THE foreman of the warehouse came in, introduced himself as Eric, and asked me to follow him. He showed me what my new job would be: pulling car parts from hundreds of bins, placing them on a trolley, and delivering them to a long counter to be checked. The title of this job was "picker." Eric handed me some loose tickets that indicated the location of the bins in which the parts were stored. To protect my clothing from grease, he gave me a long coat and gloves. He took a felt ink pen and marked my name on the pocket of the coat. Then Eric showed me where to pick up the trolley and how to search for the parts. Now I was on my own.

When I filled up the first trolley, I delivered it to the counter to be unloaded. To my great delight, the checker was my good friend, Henry. We were both astonished to see each other. He welcomed me, and joked, "You again?" Henry was grinning from ear to ear. "Wait until Jan sees you. He's somewhere among the bins." It didn't take long before Jan appeared, pushing a trolley filled with parts. He spotted me, ran over, and said, "Welcome to the club!"

The job seemed easy but it required constant attention to pick the correct number shown on each ticket, which had to be wired to each part. The checkers, in turn, monitored the quantity, which had to be verified from a long list of parts. It usually took several months before a picker could move up to this position. Fortunately, Eric soon needed another checker—and I got the job.

There were seven checkers: Henry and I, one American named Bruce, one Englishman, and three Australians. At first, the work seemed easy: The checked parts were handed to packers on a rear counter who then placed them in boxes to fill orders to automotive stores all over Australia. But after a few months, the checkers were asked to do their own packing. It required skill to prevent breakage, because we were packing fragile items such as cork gaskets, bulbs, and cigarette lighters next to heavy steel parts. We were provided with specially-made wooden cases, that were constructed on the premises. I soon realized there was a way to make this process less risky, and asked for boxes a little larger than were required. That way I could place the heavy steel parts on the bottom and separate them by cleats, usually made from two-by-fours. I then closed off that section with strong cardboard. On top I packed the fragile items and covered them with wood chips. Last came the shipping list, before the lid was nailed on. The boxes were finally strapped with steel belts that were applied by a special hand machine. They were extremely heavy and had to be handled by a crane, which placed them on trucks. Due to my method of packing, no breakages ever occurred in any of my packed boxes. Much to the astonishment of Eric, I sometimes even placed fragile parts on top of engines.

I was very happy at NASCO, but one night something terrible happened at home. A thief broke into my car and stole my radio and my beautiful leather briefcase that contained a box of tennis balls, a towel, my socks, my tennis cap, and sunglasses.

When I told Mrs. Pierce about this, she said she thought there had been some noise during the night—but not loud enough to make her get up and check. Since both she and her husband liked to drink, perhaps they'd been sleeping very soundly. I also got little more satisfaction from the police, who rather off-handedly informed me there had been forty thefts reported that month. They said they would keep my case on record, and they would notify me should they recover the radio,.

The theft of the radio and my briefcase made me very upset and made my stay at No. 12 Fawkner Street unhappy . Because I also had to travel to NASCO daily, almost four miles one way, I decided to look for a different room, somewhere closer to my work. I was lucky, and in a couple of days, there was an opening at No. 6 Cowderoy Street in the St. Kilda suburb, not too far from where Jan lived. I told Mrs. Pierce that I would finish the month of November and then I would move. She said she was sorry to lose me, but as it was more convenient for me elsewhere, she understood my decision.

Now that my arm was free from the cast, I could resume my usual activities as before. Jan, Henry, and I stayed after work every other evening and played tennis. In the meantime, I dated Jean, who was happy that I had been successful in changing jobs. I told her I would move to St. Kilda on December 1 in order to be closer to my new job, and to try to forget the neighborhood where I had been robbed.

On the following weekend, I invited Jean to go on a different ride. I wanted her to show me other suburbs around Melbourne for a change of pace. We took a drive to see the wealthy section called Toorak, then North Melbourne, ant other areas that she knew.

Later in the evening, when we were on a large hill outside of Melbourne, we sat in the car enjoying the beautiful view of the city with its millions of lights. We talked about different events: my family, her family, and more of my experiences. I could see that she was becoming very fond of me, which made me a little worried.

During our conversation, we also talked about our ages. I told her I was twenty-eight, and she said she was thirty-four—although she didn't look her age. I told her about my sponsors in the United States, and my plans to go there someday when my visa was issued. She listened patiently, and at one point, I told her that I would like to be her friend, but that I didn't want to stay in Australia. My dream was to go to America. I added that I would be her friend under these conditions, and that's how it would have to be. She said words that I will never forget: "That's all that matters." I tried to be fair about my intentions.

I expected that Jean would be upset and perhaps would ask me to take her home right away, but it was not so. She probably expected that I would be aggressive earlier, but now, when I explained my position, she leaned toward me. I put my arm around her, and she put her head on my chest not saying anything. The fact was we hadn't known each other very long, but because my experience was that Australian girls didn't like foreigners, I decided to be honest with her, even at the risk that she would never want to see me again. Now that she understood, a heavy load was lifted off my chest. The explanation was very difficult for me.

A little later, we ended our conversation with a kiss and were on our way home. When we arrived at Jean's parents' house, I accompanied her to the door, gave her a kiss, and bade her goodnight. On the way back to my room, I had plenty to think about. I had told Jean of my future plans and now it was up to her, whether or not she wanted to see me again.

The end of November arrived, and it was time to leave Mr. and Mrs. Pierce, a very nice couple. I noticed that Mrs. Pierce had wet eyes. I gave her a hug and a kiss on the cheek and shook hands with Mr. Pierce. I wished them both good health, said good-bye, and went out the door. After my briefcase was stolen, it was an easy move for me. I had only one piece of luggage, my clothes were on hangers, and I placed my shoes, towels, and other small articles in a couple of boxes.

I made arrangements with Mrs. Hall, my new landlady, who didn't actually live at No. 6 Cowderoy Street. Her stepdaughter, to whom I paid the rent, occupied the best room in the front. Another single girl, Phyllis, rented a room, and we all shared the kitchen, as well as an adjacent bathroom. Upstairs was a married older couple, Mr. and Mrs. Gunstone, with a complete apartment.

When I moved in, no one was at home, except for the lady upstairs. She must have heard my car and came down to check on who it was. She introduced herself as Mrs. Gunstone. She had a strong accent that wasn't Australian. I told her that I was born in Czechoslovakia. I found it interesting that two foreign people were living in the same Australian house. After our chat, she said it was nice to meet me, and returned upstairs.

I put my things away and made myself at home.

"Here we go again," I said to myself. Another relocation—but still not to the United States. I knew that it couldn't come soon, as I had more than one year to go to fulfill my contractual obligation to the Australian government.

My room, with its one window, faced a narrow street between two houses; it was not a very nice view. But the absence of a landlady in the house allowed us free reign of the kitchen and the opportunity to do some cooking anytime I felt like it. I checked the kitchen—the cupboards, drawers, and refrigerator—and everything was there, fully equipped. There were groceries and other supplies that belonged to the other renters. I decided to go shopping for some basic groceries. I asked Mrs. Gunstone for directions to the nearest milk bar which was just a few streets away.

When I drove towards the milk bar and turned into the street, I was pleasantly surprised. There were about a dozen of hard-top tennis courts only partly in use. This was very welcome as Jan was within walking distance. We could play there, which would save time instead of driving to the General Motors courts. At the milk bar, I did some shopping and returned home to put away the groceries.

Now that I had a new address, I notified the American Consulate General downtown again. I wanted to make certain that they knew my location in case my visa would arrive. I also sent my new address to my relatives in Czechoslovakia and to the Zacks in New Jersey.

Later in the evening, everyone returned from work. We introduced ourselves. The stepdaughter's name was Robin, and the girl in the room next to mine was Phyllis. Both the girls were quite pretty. I also met Mr. Gunstone, a tall man, who told me that he was a car salesman. He immediately joked that I should replace my old 1939 Vauxhall with a new one.

I didn't use the kitchen for any cooking the first day because I wanted to observe the traffic there. Robin left the house soon after she came home, and Phyllis was the only one who used the kitchen. Now that I knew what time they arrived home from work, everything could be arranged to eliminate being in each other's way. Phyllis didn't give me the opportunity to have a few words with her. I wanted to become acquainted with my neighbors, but obviously she wasn't curious about who moved in.

Now I had to swing into the regular routine and to find out what the mornings would be like. I set my alarm clock to get up earlier than at the

Pierces' home, both to make sure I wouldn't oversleep and to survey the kitchen situation. Because I was tired after moving and organizing my new living quarters, I went to bed earlier than usual.

In the morning, there was no kitchen activity at all. I must have been the first one in the whole house who was up. It was very quiet. I had a feeling that living in this house would work out fine. I had my breakfast and drove off to work.

We were very busy at the warehouse, because orders were piling up. Later in the afternoon, Eric asked if I would work three hours overtime. I would receive time-and-a-half pay. I quickly agreed, and thanked him. Then he asked Henry, the Englishman, and Bruce, who also agreed.

I watched to see what the Australian chaps would do; they declined. No wonder that General Motors employed almost all foreigners in this large warehouse. The people from overseas appreciated the extra money more than Australians did.

To prove my point, every time I walked by a pub, I never saw a foreigner standing by a bar drinking beer. There was a law that pubs must not sell drinks after 6:00 P.M. One day when I was standing in front of a pub, a bell rang from 5:55 P.M. to 6:00 P.M. It rang and rang, and through the door, I could see how men were asking for pots and pots of beer that they lined up in front of them. As long as the bell was ringing, they still could order drinks, but when it stopped, no more drinks could be served. The drinks that were in front of the guests were allowed to be finished. The only way that one could get drinks after 6:00 P.M., was with a meal in a restaurant or in a hotel where one was registered.

On Friday, I picked up Jean and we went to the club. It was decided that we would go camping the next weekend at Lorne, approximately seventy miles from Melbourne. Doug Leonard was hired to take us there early Saturday morning at 7:00 o'clock. We would stay overnight in tents on the beach, and return Sunday evening. There were twenty people interested.

I bought a tent, a rubber sheet to cover the sand inside the tent, and a sleeping bag. I was equipped, and looking forward to the trip. Jean was going also. Jan wasn't going since he didn't want to buy a tent and equipment. He would spend the weekend playing tennis with Henry, who wasn't a member of the Youth Hostel Association. Henry told me that since he lived outside of Melbourne, it was rather inconvenient for him to attend the Friday meetings at the club.

On Saturday I invited Jean to the pictures. The theater was completely sold out as usual. I was glad that Jean liked American films, which at that time were flooding Australian theaters. The film was very enjoyable, and it offered not only nice entertainment, but a welcome rest for my legs, which ached after standing hours and hours at the warehouse.

On Sunday I invited Jan and Henry to try the tennis court near my new address. We played our usual progressive game and had a nice afternoon. Since we were not properly dressed to go to the Bohemia, I offered them a bachelor's snack,—coffee and pastry—at my new room. We compared the bad news we had received from our homeland. The communists were pushing their doctrine even harder, confiscating property and replacing business people who didn't want to join the party. We were sorry for our relatives, but glad we had escaped. At the end of the day, I took Henry to the train station and drove Jan home.

The next Saturday morning, I picked up Jean early, and we drove to a large parking lot behind the club, where the group for our Lorne trip was gathered. Doug Leonard arrived with his large van equipped with benches inside. When he saw us, he offered Jean and me seats up front. He asked us to put our equipment in the back to have more room, and told me how much he enjoyed the story of my escape which I had shared with him at Jean's home. He said he would like to hear more about my experiences during our relatively long trip. I told him I would be glad to do so, and thanked him for allowing us to sit in the front. From there, we would be able to enjoy more of the ocean scenery. Margo checked off the names of the participants, and when all were present, we were off.

It was a beautiful day, not a cloud in the sky—a bit hot for me, but I knew that it would be cooler by the ocean. During the trip, I described my life at the D.P. Camp Zoo in Hamburg, and my employment at the British High Court. Doug was shocked that humans were placed in huts previously occupied by animals. He listened quite intently to my story.

In a few hours, we arrived at a large camping ground. Doug parked his van as close to the beach as possible, and everyone looked for a spot to put up their tents. Jean and I put up our tents side by side. Then everyone went swimming. The ocean water was cool and refreshing, and the mild breeze provided some gentle waves that splashed us. It was great fun, and I admired this beautiful beach with its fine, beige-colored sand. The beach extended as far as the eye could see in both directions and except for us, there was no one there.

Jean warned me not to stay too long in the sun, but I told her that I had been exposed a lot while picking grapes. She explained to me that the sun inland was different than the sun by the ocean, where one could get dangerously burned. She put some suntan lotion on me, and urged me to wear my shirt and cap as well.

For lunch, she prepared sandwiches and tea for herself, and I made some sandwiches and coffee. There was an outside grill made of stones, but it was too hot to start a fire.

It was so enjoyable! I just couldn't have enough of the ocean. But I had no experience with the power of the sun near the water. I gladly accepted any advice Jean gave me, since she was born in Melbourne and had been going to the ocean since her childhood.

I was surprised how cool it became in the evening after the sun set. The breeze from the ocean provided cool air, and we had to wear jackets while gathering around the fire. A couple of fellows started the grill and roasted sausages. There was no doubt that everyone was having a great time. We sat in a circle, talking, joking, and singing until late that night. Finally the fire went out, and it was time to get into the tents.

It was fascinating to listen to those waves crashing on the sand, something I had never before experienced. They were like music to my ears and, being unaccustomed to that wonderful sound, I stayed awake much of the night.

It was a pleasant morning, and I sat in front of my tent waiting until Jean and others emerged from their tents. We had a camp-style breakfast: juice, hard boiled eggs, biscuits, and fruit. Jean took care of the food as she had more experience with camping. Some chaps went in for an early morning swim, but I didn't. I asked Jean if she would like to go for a walk along the edge of the ocean, to splash water on our feet and to pick up some seashells or other possible "treasures" washed up on the beach.

When we returned, the sun was becoming stronger. In spite of all Jean's warnings and precautions, I still got sunburned. I had to wear a shirt and cap to avoid any additional burning. What was most difficult was to protect my insteps, which were already sunburned and painful. I had to cover my feet with a towel and stay on the blanket.

At lunchtime, someone started a fire in the grill, and I could smell food cooking. Doug was there, and he fried a large batch of pork sausages. To my pleasant surprise, he invited Jean and me to share them. Doug did a great job, and we enjoyed the lunch.

In the afternoon, most were inclined to go swimming, to talk, and—for those who could—to sunbathe. That was out for me, but Doug and some other friends encircled me on their blankets and wanted to hear more about my experiences.

I was happy that everyone was very friendly, and I had the opportunity to tell these friends something that they probably would never hear anywhere else. I emphasized the precious quality of freedom, particularly for those who had not experienced it. Most people take it for granted. I was a little older than many of them, and I was happy to see their interest in what I had to say. Doug took every opportunity to ask most of the questions. I liked him very much, and I could sense that he knew what freedom meant for me.

By 4:00 o'clock we were on our way home. Most people had red faces, which gave everyone a healthy glow. I was told that I would feel more pain from my sunburn in the evening, and would probably have a difficult time sleeping.

Back in Melbourne, time came to say our "cheerios"—good-byes. I thanked Doug for being exceptionally nice to Jean and me, and told him that I had a most wonderful and unforgettable time. He said that he enjoyed hearing my stories and was looking forward to seeing me again. We shook hands, and I thanked Margot for arranging the trip.

When we arrived at Jean's home, I helped her take her camping equipment into the garage. She asked me if I would like to come in, but I declined, since I needed to take a shower to wash the salt off my back. I gave her a kiss, thanked her for her pleasant company, and left.

On the way home, I reflected on the events of the weekend and felt very happy that I had experienced a nice change from my city routine. I had enjoyed the sound of the ocean waves, the smell of the salt air, and the sea breeze.

Everything was back to normal the following week. Because we were still busy in the warehouse, I agreed to work overtime.

Every day two young women would pass by in front of our long counter on their way to lunch. I knew one of them, Connie McKenzie, a pretty blond, whom I had met at the GM picnic. I hadn't met the other girl, but she always gave me a friendly look and smile.

One day on their way to lunch, Connie's friend came to the counter in front of me and said, "My name is Vicki, I know your name. I have never done this before, but there is a General Motors ball before Christmas for which I have purchased two tickets. I wonder if I could invite you to be my escort, because I don't feel like attending it alone." I was very much surprised, and flattered, and wondered how to answer her. After a few seconds, I said, "Thank you, Vicki, I appreciate your invitation. But I cannot accept it as I have a girlfriend, and it wouldn't be fair to her."

I could see she was disappointed and perhaps a little uneasy that she had approached me. Connie was listening from a short distance away. When Vicki approached her, she put her arm around her, and they walked away. I felt sorry for her disappointment. I felt I had to be true to Jean's friendship and love for me, despite the fact she knew I didn't want to remain in Australia. It was hard for me, but I couldn't be alone, and I didn't want to be some kind of a drifter.

Christmas was around the corner, but it didn't feel like it. The spirit wasn't there as it was in countries with snow and cold weather. People were walking around in shorts and playing tennis, and all kinds of outdoor sports. I said to myself, "What kind of Christmas do they have here?"

However, the calendar said the date, and Christmas had to be celebrated. Jean invited me to spend the holiday with her and her parents. She had three sisters and one brother, Bill. One sister, Ruth, lived at Kerang, a small town in the bush country. She and her husband had a hardware and sports shop there. The other two sisters and Bill lived in the suburbs of Melbourne. Until now, I hadn't met any of her siblings.

For me, Christmas was spent among strangers. But they knew about me and were very friendly. Everyone received presents, too many to mention. I gave Jean some nice perfume, and she gave me a T-shirt, tennis balls, and socks for tennis—very practical and welcome gifts.

We had a most pleasant and enjoyable day. Jean's relatives asked me many questions when they noticed my accent. Ruth wanted to hear my stories, but she helped her mother in the kitchen and didn't have a chance to listen. She said I would have to visit them at Kerang where we would have more time to talk. Her husband, Walter, and their daughter, Gwen, their only child, listened patiently. They couldn't understand why ugly, merciless actions were imposed on innocent people under communist rule. I could see that they—living in the bush country and away from the culture of Melbourne—wouldn't get as much information as people living in the city.

Since Ruth and her family weren't staying in Melbourne for New Year's, she invited Jean and me to visit them at Kerang. I thanked her, but I told her I didn't think I should take a chance driving my old car on such a long trip. Jean's father overheard our conversation and offered to loan us his car, a Holden, a very recent and reliable model.

Early on New Year's Eve, I drove to Jean's home. Her parents allowed me to park my car in their garage. They wished us a safe trip, and we were on our way, with Jean acting as navigator. It was a long drive, and the weather was very warm. But the car was very comfortable and quiet, so it was a pleasant ride.

Twenty-five miles before Kerang, in the land of nowhere, we suddenly approached a pickup truck on the side of the road. When we were closer, we saw two dead sheep lying on the road covered with blood, and a man sitting on a box near the truck, with blood on his face and a cloth on his forehead.

I stopped and asked him what had happened. He said he hit a flock of sheep that had run in front of his pickup. Some were wounded and crawled away, but these two were killed. When I asked him if I could take him to the nearest town, he said that someone else had already stopped a long while before and was arranging help for him. He thanked me and we drove away. I couldn't understand why the man didn't stop in time when he saw so many sheep so close to the road. He must have misjudged their speed, didn't slow down, and then it was too late.

Finally, we arrived at Jean's sister's home. When we went in, the dining room table was set and I could smell the aroma of something cooking in the kitchen. We received a warm welcome and were asked about our trip. Jean started to talk about the accident we'd seen. They listened and said that once in a while they heard about such incidents, but were surprised that it had happened in such an open area. Walter said that the driver must have been either drunk or half-asleep behind the wheel.

Soon Ruth served the meal: lamb stew with potatoes and vegetables, followed by tea or coffee and homemade pastry. Later, Ruth confessed that Jean had told her what I liked to eat, so she had prepared this delicious meal especially for me.

After dinner, while the women were cleaning up in the kitchen, Walter offered to show me their property. They had a very large shop full of hardware, sporting goods, guns, and canoes.. He also had a van for delivering merchandise. When I asked him why he sold canoes in the bush country, he replied there was a large swamp rich with fish nearby, and that people came to either buy or rent a canoe to go fishing there.. He asked me if I would like to see it. I readily accepted.

When we returned from the "shop and property tour," Walter told the ladies that he was going to take me for a canoe ride. We loaded the canoe into the van, and off we went. Sure enough, in a few minutes, we were at the swamp. The water was clean, deep, and full of dead, standing trees. We launched the canoe and were paddling along. We disturbed several herons, who obviously liked fish.

There were a few homes around the area but very far apart. Walter told me everyone bought many acres. Land was extremely cheap, and the government liked to see it occupied. As a matter of fact, immigrants were told that after our two years' obligation to the government was met, we could apply for land at a certain distance from the city and would receive 950 acres to live on. After fifteen years of living on that land, it would belong to us, free of charge. I wasn't interested, but I heard some immigrants say that they couldn't wait to see the day when their obligation was fulfilled and they could live on that land.

After we returned, we put the canoe in its place and went inside the house to join the ladies. They asked how I liked the swamp. I told them that I was surprised how large the area was and how clean the water was. Walter told me they had their own well which would never go dry. It was unbelievable to see that in the middle of nowhere.

Walter and Ruth's daughter, Gwen, a very pretty girl of about 18 years old, worked with her parents in the store. I was told she did the bookkeeping and waited on customers. She asked me if I would like to have some iced tea, and we all sat down with our frosted glasses of tea.

Now Ruth wanted to hear about my experiences. To avoid repeating the same tales that Jean had already heard, I tried to tell different ones—but the basic stories, such as my escape, I had to repeat. I also had to repeat the events of my life in the D.P. Camp Zoo, and the voyage on the ship from Germany to Australia. Well, I certainly had enough to talk about until supper time.

After the meal, we saw in the New Year with a drink and a toast for good health and happiness for 1952. We talked some more and finally retired in the wee hours.

The next day, we took a short ride to see the town and left after lunch. We thanked Ruth and Walter for a pleasant visit and their hospitality. We returned to Melbourne in the evening, and I thanked Jean's parents for the use of their car and expressed my pleasure at having visited their daughter, Ruth, and her family.

Now that the New Year had begun, I made a resolution to bring my life a little more up to date and to take care of several priorities. I needed a telephone installed as soon as possible, since I wasted a lot of time driving around in my car to contact people. I had to buy a radio, my car needed repairs, and I needed additional shoes and clothes. All these would require money, and I had to look for a part-time job. I also had to have money put aside for my fare to America, in the event that the United States issued me a visa. I established a list of priorities and decided to take care of them, one by one.

The following week started on a regular basis, the only difference being that we were asked to work less overtime. Because I had some education in commercial science, I had a feeling that the company wanted to close the year with a good profit to satisfy the shareholders. That was probably the reason we were working a lot of overtime to fill orders.

I contacted PMG and ordered a telephone, and in a few days, it was installed. This made a world of difference to me. I started reading the want-ads and realized how convenient my phone would be when applying for a second job.

I noticed that the Lewton Radio Shop, located in downtown Melbourne, was looking for a part-time salesman on Saturdays. When I phoned them, they asked me to come for an interview. I decided to go dressed like a salesman: a white shirt, a tie, and my hound's-tooth jacket. To make certain that no one would be ahead of me, I even appeared at the store before it opened.

At 8:00 A.M., a man unlocked the door and asked me to come in. It was possible that he thought I was a customer. Then he asked me what he could do for me. I immediately told him I was interested in the part-time job as a salesman, and had come for an interview. He introduced himself as Ron, and asked me to see Mr. Lewton, the owner, who was in the office in the rear of the shop.

Ron announced me, and Mr. Lewton introduced himself. When he asked me if I had any previous experience, I told him that I used to sell for an agricultural corporation in Czechoslovakia. After he looked me over, he asked me when I could start. I said right away. Rather surprised at my quick answer, he stated that I would work only on a commission basis—the more I sold, the more money I would make, whether I sold items in the store or from house-to-house. I was then introduced to Mr. Hamilton, the store manager.

Mr. Hamilton took me around and showed me the variety of merchandise on display: radiograms, refrigerators, clock radios, regular radios, cabinets for radios, and recordings. Since everything had price tags, there shouldn't be any problem, he said.

He acted very business-like, and from that point on, he was primarily in his office, taking telephone calls. At one point, Mr. Hamilton hung up the receiver and called Ron to his office. I was standing nearby, and I overheard Mr. Hamilton telling Ron that some lady from Toorak had called about purchasing a refrigerator. Mr. Hamilton suggested one for £800, but if she didn't like that one, there was another one for £600.

Ron listened and in a minute he was on the way to take care of the sale. A little later, Mr. Hamilton came to me with a page from the newspaper on which he pointed out a second-hand radiogram, and said, "George, we advertised this radiogram, but we do not have it. Mrs. Smith called that she would like to purchase it, even if it needed repairs. As her brother-in-law is a mechanic, he could repair it."

When I looked at the price, it showed £30. He then showed me one for £70 on the floor, and said, "Put this one in your car and try to sell it to her." He gave me a diagram how to find her house, which was several miles outside of the city. I didn't like that kind of business, but I did what he said.

When I found the house, it was on a steep hill, about seven miles outside of Melbourne. When she saw me on the bottom of the hilly driveway, she asked me if I brought the radiogram that the Lewton Radio Company advertised. I had to tell her what Mr. Hamilton asked me to say, that the one in the ad was sold and that I had brought a very nice one that was a little more expensive.

She said, "Don't even take it out of your car, I don't want any other one. I wanted the one advertised. Goodbye."

No sale, and I returned to the store. When Mr. Hamilton saw that I had brought the radiogram back, he said, "What is the matter, George, you couldn't talk the lady into buying this one?" I told him what she said, and he replied, "You're not too good a salesman," and he walked back to his office.

A little while later, the phone rang, and after Mr. Hamilton finished talking, he called Ron again and sent him on another sale. Apparently those two were dealing together, with the good sales going to Ron.

After a little while, a man walked into the store and started to walk around the display of radiograms. I let him look for a minute or two, and then asked if I could help him. He said he wanted a good radiogram with a fine sound. I asked him to follow me, and a few steps away, I showed him a very nice one. Mr. Lewton saw me showing this radiogram. He quickly walked up to us and from a short distance away, he gestured to me by a movement of his head and a wink of his eye to disappear. I did, and he took over. He talked to the man for a couple of minutes, put on a recording of a Strauss waltz, and started the radiogram. He turned the volume up, down, up, down, and the sound was really very fine.

The man listened patiently, looked at the sides for possible scratches, examined the finish, and after a few minutes, said he would buy it. Mr. Lewton took him to his office, they made a deal—and no sale for me. Now I saw that this was another way to steer me away from a potential commission, but I had learned something.

In a short while, a nicely-dressed younger man came in, carrying a briefcase. He walked straight to the office without any sign of buying or looking. I asked if I could help him but he declined. Because Mr. Hamilton was on the phone at that moment, the man couldn't talk to him. He introduced himself as Stanley Cermak, a salesman. I was shocked—a Czech? I introduced myself, George Knava, and he, too, was very surprised. I told him that I had just started the job and didn't get much help from the office, just junk sales. He told me that I would never get good sales, and that's why he decided to go on the road to sell. I was certainly glad to meet Stanley, as he gave me a good warning. By this time Mr. Hamilton had stopped talking and could see Stanley.

When Stanley finished with Mr. Hamilton, he asked me where I came from in Czechoslovakia. I told him Tunechody near Chrudim, where I had graduated from the Commercial Academy. I also told him that I still corresponded with some of my classmates and with Professor Vasina. When I mentioned the name Vasina, he was surprised and said that he had been dating a girl that Professor Vasina took away from him and later married.

What a coincidence: thousands of miles away, and we had so much to talk about. He wished me good luck, gave me his calling card, and recommended that I start selling on the road.

I was very happy that I had met Stanley, and was convinced that I was wasting my time in the store. There was very little foot traffic because it was the wrong time of the year—very hot, and people were out by the ocean, playing tennis, or on picnics. I stayed until the end of the day, and never showed up again. They were unfair, all of them.

On Friday, I went to the club, where the final arrangements were to be made for the trip to Phillip Island. This outing would be longer than our previous trip, and it was decided to leave an hour earlier.

Margot made out a list of all people interested, and Doug again was willing to take us there in his van. It was recommended that we take flashlights, since we would be walking through low brush on the edge of the beach, where penguins slept.

Jean was with me at the meeting and agreed to go. But like the last time, Jan preferred to play tennis with Henry.

There was no meeting planned for the following Friday evening, because we were all getting ready for the trip. I visited Jean, and we checked off items on a list that we had prepared together during the week. We agreed that I would pick her up early Saturday morning to be at the club's parking lot by 6:00 A.M.

When we arrived, Margot was already checking off each member on the list. When everyone was present, we left. Doug invited Jean and I to sit up front with him, which I appreciated, since it gave us a better chance to see the sights.

It was a long ride, very enjoyable, with perfect weather. When we drove onto the island, I noticed how well the roads were paved. On each side were numerous trees, almost all eucalyptus. At one point I noticed a couple of koala bears close to the road, one high in the crown of the tree, one very low. I asked Doug to stop so I could take a photo of them. I stepped out of the van and very slowly walked to the tree with my camera. When I was close to the bottom of the tree, both of the koalas were looking down at me, but not frightened and not moving. I started to climb—or almost walk—on the trunk of the tree, which was leaning, ready to fall. When I was close enough, and the koala wasn't moving, I took a picture and set the camera for another one. At this point, he decided to climb higher, so I also climbed higher. Just as I snapped the picture, he must have become frightened and dropped a chip from his rear end down at me. I had to laugh as obviously he didn't like me. However, I loved him. Both of my photos came out well. I had them enlarged and put them among my mementos.

After this lovely encounter with the koala bear, I returned to the van. I thanked Doug, and told him and Jean about "the chip." We had a good laugh. I will never forget it, and every time I see a koala on TV, I can't help but remember the incident.

When we arrived at the tip of the island, we had to find a place to set up our tents. It was a very warm day, but a pleasant breeze from the ocean made it comfortable. The surface was sandy with a cover of brush.

As there were no married couples in the group, everyone had to find a suitable spot to set up their tents. Girlfriends and boyfriends set up next to each other, side by side. Jean and I looked for a spot, but because of the bushes, it wasn't easy to find. Finally, I noticed an opening between a couple of bushes, and saw behind them a sandy area. When I walked through the opening, there was a fat snake about four feet long basking in the sun. Bringing it to Jean's attention, I immediately told her to find Doug to ask him if the snake was dangerous.

In a few minutes, Jean and Doug appeared. When he looked at it, he wasn't sure whether or not it was dangerous. To resolve the situation, he found a wooden stick, killed the snake, and took it away. Although we were still a bit shaken, we decided to use the area as it was large, pleasant, and suitable for two tents. To eliminate the possibility of any snake entering our tents, we buried the edges fairly deep into the sand. When we finished, we went to the van to inform Margot of our location.

Not too far from our campsite was the beach with its very fine, white sand, bleached by the sun. A powerful breeze came off the ocean and created strong waves. What a spectacular sight!

Everyone was ready for a swim in the pleasant water. As I wasn't familiar with large waves, I watched the others, who were ducking under them rather than fighting them. When the large waves were behind them, the swimmers simply jumped up and waited for the next one. Following the others, I plunged in deeper, and soon was confronted with a large wave. But I didn't know there was quite a strong undertow under each wave. When I wanted to jump up behind the passing wave, the sand was fast running away under my feet. It was very difficult to jump up, but somehow I managed just in time before the next wave came. By using the same method, I soon mastered the art. It was a great deal of fun, but when I left the water, I was told the undertow was very dangerous and people often drowned. Not having been warned about this danger, I was lucky that I watched the others. Jean forgot to tell me as she took it for granted I knew. For the Australians, it was like handling a toy.

Danger or no danger, I enjoyed that afternoon tremendously, and will never forget it. It was a great experience. Jean didn't go into the deep water as she just wanted to cool herself off. Her best advice to me was to protect myself against a severe sunburn by keeping on my cap and covering my body with a towel. In spite of that, I did get sunburned, and later my skin peeled. Another experience!

When everyone had enough swimming, we returned to our tents and had something to eat. Margot told us that later in the evening we would go to another location to watch the penguins emerging from the ocean. We were told to bring our flashlights. The reason was that the penguins slept in very low, thick brush. There were hundreds of them and without a flashlight, we might step on them. Tourists had wounded and even accidentally killed them.

Shortly before dark, our group went closer to the shore, where we watched hundreds of these lovely creatures swimming and diving in the ocean. It was a very beautiful sight. Some of them were trying to stand at the edge of the water, but the approaching waves swept them off their feet and back into the water.

Just before dark, as if they were on command, they started to get closer and closer to the beach. Soon, they walked with a wobbly motion uphill into the brush. We waited until all of them left the ocean, then carefully walked through the brush, back to our quarters. Doug had a bright floodlight mounted on his van, which gave us a chance to gather around and enjoy chatting about our day in this beautiful part of the island. Later, it was time to get into our tents for the night.

The next day, everyone was awakened by the sound of the swishing waves. Obviously, the swimming and walking had made us tired. Doug had equipment to make tea in a large volume. We reached into our dwindling supplies of food to have breakfast. We were told that we would leave around 2:00 o'clock, so there was still time to go on the beach to enjoy watching the waves, sunbathe, and swim.

After lunch we packed our tents, and we left this beautiful place. We were lucky; the weather was perfect, and the trip back was very enjoyable. Later that evening, we arrived back in Melbourne. Everybody was happy after a wonderful excursion.

During the ride back to Jean's home, I talked about the undertow that I had experienced, and I asked her if she previously had taken this trip. She replied that she had not. Now I knew why she hadn't warned me about the danger. When we arrived at her home, I thanked her for providing the food, helped her unload the tent in the garage, and gave her a kiss.

When I arrived home, I couldn't wait to have a shower, because my hair was full of sand and my body felt sticky from the salt water. However, that was a very minor detail. All in all, it was a very successful and unforgettable trip. A weekend like this could spoil anyone. When I went back to the warehouse, it took me a while to get into the tempo of work. My body was sore from the heavy beating of the waves and my face was sunburned. During lunch, I told Jan and Henry all about the trip.

When I returned home, I visited Mrs. Fischer to discuss the matter of her doing laundry for me and others, if it could be arranged. She offered to provide affordable laundry service if I could find enough customers. We arranged that I would deliver the wash on Mondays and pick it up on Fridays. The Fischers, who had a meager income and two children to feed, welcomed the extra money. I left my wash with her and told her I would scout around for other prospects.

When I discussed the idea with Jan the next day, he liked the idea, although Henry already had someone else. At the Praha restaurant, I introduced the idea to several Czech single men, who also agreed to have Mrs. Fischer do their wash.

The restaurant manager offered the use of a designated area, where boxes for the laundry would be filled every Monday, and the money left there on Fridays. This plan worked out well. Soon I had enough customers to keep Mrs. Fischer busy, and I had my wash done without charge.

One day I received a letter from my oldest brother, Frantisek, in which he informed me that his friend, Mr. Hasek, had escaped and emigrated to Melbourne, Australia. I managed to contact him, and was invited to visit him and his family at their home in South Yarra.

Mrs. Hasek very hospitably offered me coffee and some homemade Czech kolace, a nice surprise for me. We had lots to talk about. On my second visit, I helped Mr. Hasek with his income taxes, since he was not well-versed in English. My brother was very pleased when I informed him of my warm reunion with the Haseks.

When I had no Sunday plans, I enjoyed going to the Praha restaurant for a good meal, and occasionally met new Czech immigrants there. It's customary in Czechoslovakia to take any vacant seat at a table in a restaurant, unless someone expresses a desire for privacy. One Sunday, I elected to sit at a table next to an older gentleman. As usual, it didn't take me long to start a conversation, first about the weather, then about any subject.

Mr. Weissman, who was Czech, had come to Australia a number of years earlier and had established an office as a real estate broker on Burke Street, in downtown Melbourne. I asked him if it was difficult to become a real estate salesman. He said that to get a license, it was necessary to be a college graduate. I told him that I was a college graduate, and would like to try to sell real estate. He gave me the necessary information—where to go, what to do—and soon I obtained a license.

When I received it, I went to Mr. Weissman's office to inform him. He was quite surprised, and invited me to work weekends. The next Saturday morning, I went to his office about 9:00 A.M. Mr. Weissman had his desk covered with a newspaper, obviously checking to see if his ads were in it, and probably looking at other ads. In a short while, the telephone rang. When he finished his conversation, he told me that I could show one of his advertised houses, the one that the woman on the phone wanted to see. He gave me the directions where to pick her up and the location of the house. I took his notes and followed his directions.

I arranged to meet the prospect, a middle-aged lady, at the house. I introduced myself, and we went to see the house. It was quite a distance away in a suburban area. But when we arrived, we saw that the house was very unattractive, unkempt, and unappealing. Consequently, the woman was not interested.

The benefit that I gained was that I saw a part of Melbourne that otherwise I would never have seen. And on the return trip, I noticed one old house that also looked empty, unkempt, and most likely condemned. I kept it in mind, and started to think about what could be done with it.

I dropped off the lady and returned to Mr. Weissman's office. He asked me how I made out. I told him the lady wasn't interested. He shook his head, and said, "Better luck next time." Then he added, "I had good luck today. I sold the house we advertised for £50,000.00." He showed me the picture of it in the newspaper.

I congratulated him but wondered why he hadn't given me a chance to sell that one or some decent house in a nice neighborhood. But perhaps the best leads were reserved for the more experienced salesmen.

Curious as to how many houses Mr. Weissman advertised, I asked him if I could see the ads in the newspaper. The advertised houses were marked with a red pen. Not too many telephone calls were coming in, and those that did come proved to be dead ends. He suggested that I go see the houses he advertised to get an idea what we had to offer.

He further suggested that I buy a newspaper when I went to lunch, rather than waste time copying the ads. After lunch, I could drive around to see the houses. I decided to mark the addresses next to the ads and study the city map for their locations. I bought the newspaper and went to a nearby restaurant to have lunch. While waiting, I opened the newspaper to the page that I had already seen in the office, and made small

George picking Sultanas grapes in very hot weather (117°).

Using a crane, George (far left) and two other workers dipped 75 buckets into a special solution.

Above: George working as a compressor operator.

Right: George operating a jackhammer.

Right: Jan Kriz and George (far left) with friends during one of our many tennis meetings.

Below: After the click of George's camera, the Koala, probably scared, climbed higher and dropped a chip down at George and just missed.

Above: Evelyn and George in her parents' garden.

Right: Jean and George in her parents' garden.

Race at NASCO Picnic.

Right: Jan, Henry and George (kneeling) at NASCO picnic race finish line.

A good friend and tennis partner, Jan Kriz (left) and George.

Job completed—12 jets finished and one to go. (George kneeling second from left.)

Above: George mingling with the natives on Fiji Island.

Right: Bananas before harvesting.

Above: George sightseeing at the Sydney Bridge in 1955.

Right: George waiting for a Bus Tour into a mountain in Auckland, New Zealand.

marks next to our ads. I was curious to see what kind of houses were on the market, and what their prices were.

I returned to the office after lunch and marked the prices and locations of the houses. When I finished, I told Mr. Weissman I would go to see the houses. I also told him that I would not return to the office until Sunday, unless I was fortunate enough to find some prospective buyers.

After I looked at the advertised houses, I realized they were not a good value, and to find buyers for them would be very difficult. With my other busy endeavors, I wasn't certain whether selling real estate would be practical or profitable for me, but I decided to leave it open just in case.

As the new week started, all was back to normal on my regular job. During the tea break and the lunch hour, I kept thinking about what had happened. Somehow the whole idea of a future selling real estate didn't seem too promising, since it required a lot of time on weekends and even some evenings. But I remained fixated on that empty, perhaps condemned, house that I had seen the previous week. I decided to look into it. In case my visa was granted, I needed extra income for my fare to the United States.

One evening I took a ride to the house. The driveway was narrow, curved, and made of cobblestones. The deteriorating fences along the boundaries were constructed with wide wooden planks. The gate to the backyard had been removed, with only the posts remaining. The property was split in two halves. On the left was a carport, covered with corrugated sheets, several of which were missing—and its entrance was blocked by a huge palm tree. Behind the carport was a shed. On the other side was a stucco house, surrounded by three large peach trees, two of them dead and the third with just a few live branches. The trees took a lot of space in the yard, making it very difficult for a vehicle to turn. The house was shabby, everything was neglected. I tried the door, which was locked. I looked through the windows, and saw vacant rooms. Obviously the house had been condemned. Now the question was, what could be done about it?

I decided to find out who the owner was. A neighbor lady told me she knew the owner, an older man with no children. After the owner's wife died, he had moved to a new location on the other end of the city. She gave me his name, Mr. Jennings, and his telephone number, and added that she visited him occasionally because he was a very nice man. I thanked her and decided to call him. I couldn't buy the house, of course, but I had an idea that I could clean it and rent it.

On the way home, I stopped by the Fischers for the laundry. Mrs. Fischer offered me a cup of tea and some pastry. I mentioned the house to Mr. Fischer who indicated that he would take a look.

After we saw the place together, Mr. Fischer suggested the carport could be used for car repairs, the shed to store tools, and the yard to park cars waiting for repairs. He knew a mechanic, Antonin Brychta, a Czech immigrant who might be interested in sharing the vacant carport and starting a business. Perhaps I could find some people who would need cars to be serviced or repaired. It seemed like a good possibility, but the place was not suitable in its poor condition. For the present, it was just an idea.

I called Mr. Jennings and I asked him what he planned to do with his property. He couldn't give me any definite answer at the moment, but he asked me how much I would be willing to pay a month. I had a feeling that he knew that the place would have to be eventually demolished. I dared to give him a very low, almost ridiculous offer of £ l-10-d (pound, 10 shillings, and no pennies—one pound was worth 20 shillings and one shilling was 12 pennies). Mr. Jennings hesitated a little, but he agreed. I asked him if I could send him a money order on the first day of each month. Much to my surprise, he accepted my offer.

Now it was up to me to see what I could do with the place. It needed a lot of work. Luckily, it was early spring. The weather was not too hot, the evenings were getting longer, and I had time to make repairs after my regular job. This new enterprise interfered, of course, with my other activities, but I needed to save as much money as possible to prepare for my possible trip to America. I decided to make work my first priority.

I needed tools. Luckily, my landlady had some in a shed, and I borrowed them for the job. I started with the carport, having in mind the possibility of car repairs as Mr. Fischer suggested. It required a lot of work. The roof was constructed with corrugated sheets, many of which had been blown off by the wind. I knew I would have to buy some to complete the roof .

Another problem was that huge palm tree, which would prevent a car driving into a carport. I decided to dig it out. Little did I know what a mammoth job this entailed! I wonder how many people know that a palm tree has hundreds of thin roots the size of pencils, bound together and tough as dry cane. My ax could barely cut it, even though I had sharpened it very well. To speed up the process, I decided to work by moonlight. It took a long time, but finally I dug it out. It wasn't too high, but it had a lot of branches on the top which were very tough to remove. As I had a convertible, I decided to take them to the dump in my car.

When I arrived at the dump, I couldn't believe my eyes. Obviously a shed or some small building had been demolished, and a lot of corrugated sheets were piled up. Some were in fair condition, some were bent and had to be straightened out to be usable. I unloaded the palm branches, I backed my car to the area where the sheets were and started to load them. As I was loading them, a man drove in next to me with some junk and started to unload it. I told him that I needed some sheets to cover a carport, but I didn't like them in such poor condition. He listened to my story, and after a moment, told me I had no problem, because around the corner near the dump was a lumber yard where they had a special machine that straightened corrugated sheets. And not only was there a machine there, but one could do it by himself for a very low fee. I fed the sheets through it, and within a short time, the work was accomplished, costing me only 10 shillings. I considered myself very lucky, as I had expected the roof would give me bigger problems. Two or three days later, I installed the sheets on the roof, cleaned the floor, and now I had one space ready for a car that needed repairs. When this was done, I informed Mr. Fischer and invited him to see the place. He agreed that there was ample space for a car next to a long workbench located by the wall.

Now that I had a key, I could inspect the house inside. The house contained three rooms with many spider webs. To give the rooms a fresh look, I decided to use whitewash. I was pleasantly surprised that I didn't detect any stains or spots on the floors from the leaky roof. The rooms looked much better, and I decided to rent them for storage since the house was not to be used for living quarters.

My next project was the yard. There was all kinds of debris and a couple of mounds of gravel. The biggest job was to dig out the peach trees. Whenever I saw a bright moon, I drove there and dug and cut the trees to a manageable size that could be loaded on a truck. I expected the job to be more difficult, but the sandy soil made it easy. When this was done, I hired a large truck to take out everything from the yard, then raked it to make it suitable for turning vehicles around and for parking.

All these activities with the property kept me away from my social life. I gave the project top priority, hoping that my hard work would pay off in the near future.

When I had finished my work on the property, Mr. Fischer introduced me to Mr. Brychta, who wanted to see the property. I took them there in my car, and showed them what I had done. Mr. Brychta hadn't seen it before, but Mr. Fischer had, and he couldn't believe how the whole place had changed. Mr. Brychta wasn't pleased with the carport, because it was too open and couldn't be locked. However, he knew someone who owned a Czechoslovakian car, a Skoda, that needed repairs. Since he had no place to work on it, Mr. Brychta was in favor of using the carport and of forming a threeway partnership to repair cars. I was supposed to provide the carport and find the customers who needed repairs, while Mr. Brychta and Mr. Fischer would do the work. I wasn't too enthusiastic about this idea, but because my rent was so low, and because Mr. Brychta had no place to repair the car, I decided to give it a try.

I allowed Mr. Brychta to bring in the Skoda. But the idea of forming a business met with complications. Mr. Brychta had a full-time job and could work on cars only in the evenings. Mr. Fischer had just lost his job and was in need of income, but as yet there were no cars to be repaired except the Skoda. Both men expected me to find customers. This was very difficult, since very few immigrants had cars. As time went on, Mr. Brychta blamed me for the inability to find work for them, and consequently the whole idea of the partnership stayed in limbo.

Because I didn't have any luck in soliciting car repairs, I concentrated on improving the rooms inside the house and improving and clearing the yard area. The individual rooms needed door keys. I hadn't arranged for electric service on the property; so activities had to be done during the day, or the tenants would have to use flashlights. Basically, the property was ready for renting, and now I had to find suitable tenants.

I decided to buy the Melbourne Chronicle daily to watch for ads of someone looking for space. I was lucky. My first tenant was a large hardware store that needed storage space for steel and merchandise. I set the monthly rent at £4, which was agreeable to the tenant.

Within a month I had all the rooms rented. My hard work started to pay dividends. I collected £12 monthly, and I paid £1, 10 shillings to Mr. Jennings, which gave me a tidy profit. Since my weekly wages were just about £ 12, it was as if I had one extra payday each month. It was interesting that Mr. Jennings never met me or visited the property. I just sent him the rent, and everything went smoothly. I gave up the idea of car repairs, and I didn't spend much time seeking real estate sales, because I felt I needed the weekends for leisure activities.

One day I met a Czech man in the Bohemia restaurant. We talked about various things—where we were born, why we came to Australia, and what we were doing in Melbourne. He told me he was an electrical engineer, owned an appliance store, had married an Australian girl, and that they were expecting their first child. He further added he was looking for someone to help sell his appliances.

I listened for a while, not jumping at the opportunity too quickly, since I did not want to appear too anxious. After a short while, I asked him how he proposed to pay for someone's efforts to find customers for his merchandise. He said he would be willing to split the profit in half on each appliance, even if the salesman gave the customer a discount. This was agreeable. I asked him where his store was located, and when he gave me his card. I read, "Joseph J. Phillip: Radio, Electrical, Manufacturing, Sales and Service, 119 Gardenvale Rd., Gardenvale—which was a suburb of Melbourne. He suggested that I follow his truck to his store. At his store, Joe introduced me to his wife, who was nice-looking, although I have never seen a woman with so many freckles. After a few words with his wife, Joe showed me how a sale was handled when a customer entered into an installment contract for a purchase. However, he said that I wouldn't have to do that part, because he would take care of it after I brought in the customer. I told him that I would be glad to try to sell his merchandise. He gave me many different leaflets picturing refrigerators, radiograms, vitamizers (blenders), clock radios, and so forth. We agreed we'd be in touch.

On the way home, I tried to think of how to go about finding customers. I didn't think I would find many buyers for refrigerators, since few of the immigrants I knew owned their own homes. But there were so many other items to be offered, and those were a better possibility. How would I let the general public know that I could help them purchase these items at a discount? Advertise in the newspapers? I found that impractical; I had no shop. To list my telephone number would be unwise, because I worked during the weekdays. I had to find another way.

As usual, I went to the Bohemia restaurant on Sunday. Because the restaurant didn't have a parking lot, customers had to find parking space on the street, often a block away on a busy day. It just so happened that on this particular Sunday, I parked my car in front of a shop that sold children's clothes. I glanced at the window and saw a sign: "We make home visits, please call LA 8673 for an appointment."

I noticed there was a middle-aged lady behind a counter, not looking very busy. Suddenly I had an idea. What if I advertised my activities by way of leaflets, indicating the times I was available, listing this lady's telephone number? I could pay her some small amount weekly for taking the calls. Well, I had nothing to lose.

I walked in, and the lady politely asked me how she could help me. I told her immediately that I wasn't shopping for children's clothes, and presented my idea. She listened—somehow surprised with this unusual customer—studied my accent, and willingly agreed to my plan. I introduced myself, and she said that her name was Mrs. Johnson. She thought it over and agreed that 10 shillings a week would be her fee. I thought it was fair, thanked her, and informed her that in the very near future I would start advertising.

At this point, I had another task ahead of me. Who could prepare a suitable leaflet for me? I inquired here and there but had no luck. One day, however, I was lucky. I met an immigrant from Hungary, Laslo, who was an artist and photographer. We discussed the idea, and he agreed to prepare a sketch for me.

A few days later we met at the Bohemia. He showed me a rough sketch on which he had left space for my photo. I liked it, and he quoted a price of £6 for five hundred leaflets, which would take a few days to print. We made an appointment to meet again so that he could present the final sketch.

On the given date, Laslo showed me the finished product, which looked perfect. I ordered five hundred copies, and told him that if I exhausted the supply, I would reorder.

About three days later, Laslo called me and brought me the order. I was very pleased, and paid him £6. After he left, I immediately went to Mrs. Johnson to show her the leaflet. I gave her a little notebook in which she could keep track of interested callers.

I started to distribute my leaflets right away, and soon a few calls came in. When I called Mrs. Johnson, she gave me the names and addresses of the callers so I could make an appointment with them. I told the customers to go to department stores to look and decide what kind of appliance they needed, get the price, and come to see me, or I would go to their homes. I remember that some wanted refrigerators, while others wanted smaller appliances: clock radios, vitamizers, or radiograms. After they made their choice, I would automatically give them a ten-percent discount and split the additional profit with Joe. They were happy, Joe was happy, and everyone gained.

Some weeks I sold four items, some weeks more. Gradually, I became known, and some customers recommended me to their friends. In my place of work, I also promoted some sales during lunch hour. Joe took care of finances and deliveries, and seemed pleased that our system worked.

I will never forget one truly exceptional week. One lady, a Mrs. Smith, wanted me to come show her what I was selling. When I entered her home, there were nine children, all under six years of age. Obviously, she was operating a small day-care center.

I told her what I sold, gave her a few leaflets, and asked her to give some to the mothers when they came to pick up their children. We decided I would return at the end of the week, and arrive at a time when the mothers would be there.

When I went back, I had in my pockets a good supply of candy—fruit-type sugar candy, so the children wouldn't choke on it. When the mothers entered, I would pick up one child in my arms, give the child some candy, then would pick up another one and the next one. Soon, I distributed all the candy. I could see in the mothers' eyes that they liked my way with their children.

After a while, I started to ask the ladies if they had decided to purchase any of my items and to my great surprise, they had made some decisions. Some even ordered two items. My system with the children obviously helped, and together with other sales that week, I ended up selling nineteen items.

These activities—the renting of spaces in the small warehouse, the laundry for my friends in the Bohemia restaurant, and searching for appliance sales—took up most of my time after returning home from work. This, of course, meant it was rather difficult for me to schedule time to see Jean, or to join Jan and Henry on the tennis courts. Jean found it hard to accept my explanation about why I was too busy to see her.

Henry surprised Jan and myself one day with the news that he was leaving to accept a job in New South Wales, a neighboring province. He had taken a job with SMHEA (Snowy Mountain Hydro-Electric Authority) as a storeman, because his two-year contract with the government had been fulfilled. Although we were happy about his new job, his leaving was a great loss for Jan and me. We arranged a last game of tennis, a dinner after, and wished him good luck. Our separation was rather emotional, because we had worked together in Prague, and we had spent almost two enjoyable years together in Australia. After he left, I never saw him again. However, we kept in contact by correspondence. He wrote me that he married an Australian girl, and they had two children, a boy and a girl.

Jan's contractual obligations were to end in the latter part of 1952, but he decided to stay with the company as long as they could use his services. This was fine with me. At least the two of us would continue working in the same place.

Another Christmas arrived at the end of 1952, which meant my two-year contract with the Australian government was almost at an end. I still hadn't heard from the United States Consulate General about granting me a visa. It was frustrating for me, not knowing if or when that time would ever arrive.

On January 22, 1953, I received my "Certificate of Authority to Remain in Australia." I was now entitled to stay here indefinitely. Up until now, I'd been stateless, since my escape from communist-ruled Czechoslovakia automatically canceled my citizenship. Although I didn't intend to remain in Australia, this at least gave me a true residence.

It was a wonderful feeling to be wanted, just as if I had a new home. Jan had already received his certificate a few weeks before, and to celebrate, I invited him to the Bohemia restaurant where we had an excellent dinner together. When I told Jean about my certificate, she asked me to her parents' home for dinner, so I enjoyed a second celebration.

Now that I had fulfilled my contractual obligations to the government, I could have left for another job. But because Jan stayed on at NASCO, I decided to stay, too.

But my prolonged wait for the visa to emigrate to America was very irritating. So much time had gone by—first two years spent in Germany, and now two years in Australia. I was approaching my thirtieth birthday, not knowing what the future would hold. I constantly lectured myself to remain patient. Despite the long, tedious delay, I was optimistic that someday the visa would be issued.

One evening, when I was out with Jean, she told me about a family friend, Mr. Paris, who made candles. Since he was retiring and leaving Melbourne, he suggested that Jean could earn a little extra income by making candles, which he claimed was easy. He even offered to go to Jean's parents' home to show her the process. Jean agreed, and invited me to be present.

When Mr. Paris arrived, he brought in a couple of boxes with various items: a metal mold into which the melted wax was poured, a little bag of paraffin, the wicking, the pots, and an electric hot plate. Jean's parents suggested the garage for the demonstration.

I was very curious about the entire procedure, which indeed seemed quite simple. The paraffin went into the pot, which was placed on the hot plate. While the paraffin was heating, Mr. Paris prepared the metal mold with the wicking.

After the paraffin had melted, he poured it carefully into the mold and sat back to wait for the wax to cool. While it did, Mr. Paris showed us a box with bottles of various dies that could be used to color the candles.

Then it was time to remove the candles from the mold. For Jean, her father, and myself, the whole effortless procedure was a total surprise: the candles came out perfectly. Better yet, Mr. Paris said that except for the molds, the material was quite inexpensive.

Later that evening, after Mr. Paris left, I stayed on to find out the general consensus about the whole matter. Jean was interested in the idea of making candles on a part-time basis, and she asked me to join her as a partner. Her father offered us the use of his garage, and said he could make the steel molds at his machine shop. After some discussion, we decided to call our new business "Candlecraft."

It was a very unusual evening for all of us. I was involved in another new enterprise, another new experience. I wasn't sure whether I had made the right decision in becoming even more involved with Jean, but since it didn't require any large investment, I could at least look forward to making some additional income.

Within a short time, Jean's father brought into his garage a specially-designed rack that held seventy-two molds. Seventy-two candles could be poured at one time, a great time-saving device!

We bought boxes for the candles, and small labels bearing our company name. Little by little our business progressed. At first we produced only white candles, but we eventually worked our way to thirteen different colors. Because the demand for candles was small, we produced small quantities. Australia's warm climate meant that candles could only be used in cool places; otherwise, they would bend or even collapse. The business was not very successful, but we'd never expected to make a great deal of money.

On June 2, 1953, Queen Elizabeth was crowned in England. Not long after, we learned she was to visit Australia and New Zealand the following February. Now was the time to make patriotic candles—red, white, and blue—and sell them in boxes with our label and the royal crown on them.

When I learned the exact day of the Queen's visit to Melbourne, I joined thousands of Australians and other nationalities on the street where the motorcade was to pass. People were standing three and four deep for a chance to see the Queen. As she was driven by, I saw the Queen standing in an open car, waving to the crowds. At that time, royalty was very popular in Australia, and we sold many of our special patriotic candle sets. But since this was also the hottest time of the year in Australia, we postponed making any new candles until spring. I was just as well pleased with this decision, candle—making was not my favorite—or most profitable-enterprise.

Every car owner knows that cars do not run forever without some maintenance. My car, a 1939 Vauxhall, suddenly needed repairs; the shock absorbers and other parts were not working correctly. I happened to know a very good mechanic, Mr. Freiberk, a Czech acquaintance. He rented a small private garage in which he did general car repairs. But my job took several days, because he had a difficult time finding parts for such an old car. I felt as if I were without hands and legs when I had to use the bus or rely on my friends for transportation. Finally the car was repaired. The bill was very high, and it cost me almost three weeks' salary, but I considered it a small price to pay to have my independence again.

I had made a New Year's resolution to look for a change in my employment, but our patriotic candles had distracted me. Now I began looking at the want ads every day. I saw one ad for an expediter at the Commonwealth Aircraft Corporation. I had no idea what that meant, but I applied for the job anyway.

When the personnel officer finished looking over my application, he asked when I could start working. Elated and surprised, I told him I would like to give at least one week's notice to my present employer. He agreed and gave me a verification of my new job. I was curious about my mysterious new job as an expediter and asked him to show me where I would be working. We went into a large, noisy area, where numerous people seemed to be making aircraft components. After we passed through this section, we entered the office where I would work. I was introduced to a young man, Ken, whom I was replacing. At least here, the noise was minimal.

Many thoughts entered my mind after leaving the Commonwealth Aircraft Corporation. Should I change jobs, or should I continue with NASCO? Naturally, there were some pros and cons. What was very important was the higher salary, and I would be in an office instead of a large warehouse. This just about convinced me to make the change.

The following day, I gave one week's notice to NASCO. When I told Jan about it, I could tell that he was sad to see me leave; first he'd lost Henry, and now he was losing me, too. He would be the only Czech left among NASCO's one hundred workers. Nevertheless, he accepted my explanation and wished me good luck.

My next step was to go to the Personnel Office to give them the date of my final day at work. They agreed to prepare for me a note which would show my record of employment with the company.

While there, I said good bye to some nice friends, one of whom was my favorite blonde young lady, Connie McKenzie. Connie was married, but I found enough courage to give her a hug and kiss on the cheek.

When I went back to personnel to pick up the records I had requested, I asked to see Mr. O'Keefe. I had to say good-bye to this man who had been so kind to me. Mr. O'Keefe asked me why I was leaving. When I explained that I had found an office job at the Commonwealth Aircraft Corporation, he understood. I thanked him for giving me a job two years ago and we shook hands. Then I went to the warehouse to say good-bye to Eric.

It was a rather emotional day. I had mixed feelings, wondering if I had done the right thing. I had liked my job at NASCO. But now that I was free from the contract with the Commonwealth, I wanted to work in a real office.

Chapter 24

JOB NO. 5: COMMONWEALTH AIRCRAFT CORP.

On the way back from NASCO, I decided to stop at the nearby Commonwealth Aircraft Corporation. I went to the Personnel Department, where the young lady recognized me immediately. When I asked her if someone could show me around, she called Arthur Woods, the superintendent of the area where I was about to begin working. We shook hands, he asked me to follow him, and we went to my new office. I said hello to Ken, who was to show me the scope of the job. Then Mr. Woods and I went to the production line. There I met Norman, the foreman, to whom I would bring the required supplies necessary for assembling the canopy, ailerons, and flaps for Sabre jets. After this short tour, we returned to the Personnel Department, where I had to finalize some papers.

Ken gave me a brief talk about the corporation. This plant had been designed by and built with the assistance of the United States. The U.S. had sold Australia thirteen Sabre jets that were to be assembled here. Ken showed me a picture of one of the jets, which had the engine in the nose instead of underneath the wings.

Each jet's parts were listed in an assembly book, approximately one inch thick. There was a date on the front of the book by which the jet was supposed to be completed. I was surprised to see that two of the dates had already gone by. I didn't ask Ken why. I also didn't say anything about the pictures of half-naked women on the walls in his office.

As Ken's time was up at the end of the week, I tried to get as much information as I could. Actually, the job seemed to be very easy: just to make sure the parts for the assembly were on the assembly line, and not to hold up production. Before I left, Ken introduced me to the stockroom clerk, from whom parts were to be supplied and delivered.

On Monday of the following week, I was on my own. I had six assembly books on my desk, which represented six jets that had to be assembled by the dates shown. The first one was about half-completed.

I immediately went to see Norman to find out how everything was progressing. He shrugged his shoulders and said he was short of stainless steel bolts, lead weights for balancing the flaps, and some other items. This, of course, put me right to work. Making notes of everything he needed, I went to the stockroom clerk. Within a short time, I delivered the required parts to Norman, who appeared a little surprised to receive them so quickly. This first experience gave me a clue that it was important to be in close touch with Norman who was responsible for the assembling of these parts.

A few weeks went by. The first jet was completed. But five more were scheduled, and two of them were already behind schedule. During one of my visits with Norman, I noticed his cabinets were very empty. The system was that I had to go to the stock clerk for parts each time for each jet, and he had opened boxes for the various items needed for just one jet.

I had an idea. I took one of the assembly books and multiplied each required item by five. This would eliminate four extra trips to the stock room. Proceeding on my own, I went to the stockroom and gave the clerk the items list needed for five jets. Later that day, when he inquired why the quantities were so high, I told him production was behind schedule. I repeated this procedure time after time, and now Norman's cabinets were filling up with an ample supply of parts. What was the result? Production moved faster, and the men even had to work overtime. Within a few weeks, everything was on schedule.

When Arthur came to see me and asked me why the production was progressing so well, I explained my system. He shook hands with me and said, "George, that is an extraordinary idea. I am very pleased to have you with us. Thank you."

During my period of employment with this company, I didn't have much time to play tennis with Jan. At NASCO, we simply walked out from the warehouse and onto the courts. Now we had to set up the day and time. As Jan didn't have a phone or a car, I could only visit him. I also had to see Jean and take care of my other jobs. Thus, we played tennis less often, and with coming of the winter months-June, July, and August-weather conditions meant we had even fewer opportunities to play.

One day I received a letter from the U.S. Consulate General. My hands were shaking as I hesitantly opened it. My emigration number had come up! I still remember the words: "The United States Consulate General contemplates granting you a visa to emigrate to the United States of America. If you are interested, please detach the lower portion of this letter, sign it, and mail it to this office."

I read the letter again and again, and I don't think anyone could imagine the happiness I felt. My eyes were teary as I realized my dream was finally coming true. Instead of mailing the detached portion of the letter, I hopped into my car, and drove to the U.S. Consulate.

When I handed it to the secretary, I was informed that within a short time, I would be granted the visa to emigrate. I also was told that after I received my visa, I would have to leave Australia within three months. I thanked the secretary, feeling greatly elated, and left.

With this special news, many things were about to happen. I couldn't notify Jean, because she had just left for Tasmania on a two-week vacation. Now I had to find a way to break the news to her when she returned. I knew that she would not be very happy. At one point, when I had told her that I received a letter from my sponsors in America, she said, "Why do you want to go to the United States to join two old people? You will be under obligation to them for helping you. You will have to take care of them until their last days, and who knows whether or not they will even leave you their money?"

I often thought about Jean's words, but my mind had been made up a long time ago, and I was determined. Nothing could stop me from emigrating to that great country. It had always been my dream, and Jean's negativity wouldn't have any effect on that.

My next step was to inquire about a passenger ship going to America. Later I would have to dispose of my car, rent the storage house, sell my radio, and decide what to do about our candle business. My lifetime goal, however, was now in reach, and all of these things seemed trivial.

When I went to work the next day, I immediately told Jan my great news. He looked at me rather surprised and wondered why his own visa had not yet arrived, since he had landed in Australia before me. I had filed for emigration immediately after arriving in Hamburg, and perhaps that was the reason my visa had come before Jan's.

Two weeks passed, and Jean returned from Tasmania. When I saw her, I tried to find the words to break my news. This was very difficult. She had known from the start that I intended to go to the United States, but because of the long duration of our friendship, she probably hoped that I might change my mind, marry her, and remain in Australia.

On our next date, Jean sensed my moodiness, and asked what was the matter. With some hesitation, I told her that I had been notified by the American Consulate General that my visa was soon going to be issued for my emigration.

She looked at me, and I could see her eyes filling with tears. From her point of view, ours was not simply a friendship. I knew that, despite the fact that I had told her from the beginning that I wanted only to be her friend. She had said to me, "That's all that matters," in the car on the hill outside of Melbourne. Instead, she had fallen in love with me.

I could sense how much this news was hurting her. She repeated the argument she had used before: "I still can't understand why you would go to America and take on the responsibility of your sponsors in their old age. You will be tied down in some small town where they live, they will depend on your help, and God knows what your life will be."

I couldn't make a quick response. I remained silent, until gradually we changed the subject. Early in October 1954, I received my visa and the notification that I had to leave Australia within three months. I quickly made a list of all that I had to do and set up some priorities. Since my car was very old, and I knew it would be difficult to sell it. I decided to go more often to the Bohemia. If I spread the news that I was leaving, perhaps someone there would be interested in purchasing my car.

After several visits to the restaurant, I was pleasantly surprised. The owner introduced me to Mr. Hoch, a Czech, who had learned that I was emigrating and wanted to sell my car. I described the Vauxhall which was parked outside. We went out to look at the car, which had just been repainted and was running very well.

He inquired about the price. When I told him I couldn't sell it immediately since I needed it up until the last day before my departure, Mr. Hoch agreed to wait. For that reason, I quoted him the reasonable price of £200, but added I would like the money earlier to help pay for my ship fare.

We went back into the Bohemia to have dinner. During the meal, we discussed my rental place. Expressing an interest, Mr. Hoch asked to see the place.

The following weekend, I showed him the property, and told him the rent I paid each month and the amount of rental fees I collected. I said the price would be very reasonable, £60, and explained that the place had possibilities. At some future date, I suggested, the lot could be purchased, the house removed, and the land used for a business. After he agreed to the price, I explained all the details concerning the space and gave him the names and addresses of the renters. An arrangement was made that he would give me the money for both the car and the rental place as soon as I knew the amount of my fare from Sydney to the United States.

Because I knew that the fare was going to be expensive, I carefully delayed the transaction of the rental, trying to collect as much rent as I could up to the last day. Much to my surprise, Mr. Hoch didn't put any pressure on me. I felt very relieved and very lucky that the whole issue had been resolved, because the disposal of my car and property had been my greatest worries.

Now I had to sell my radio, cancel the collecting of my wash in the Bohemia, and cancel Mrs. Johnson's services as my phone representative to sell appliances.

I was extremely busy now, with very little free time to see Jean. But she was not as eager to go out as she once was-when she still had hope that I would marry her and remain in Australia. The situation was very difficult for both of us, and whenever we did get together, I saw the sadness in her eyes.

As far as my job was concerned, everything was going well. Production on the assembly line was on schedule, and within a few weeks, we would be completely caught up.

Among the frequent guests at the Bohemia was a Czech tailor, Stan. One day I asked if he would make me a suit. There were no shops in Melbourne at that time with ready-made suits; the weather was so warm most of the year that almost everyone wore casual clothing.

Stan agreed, and told me the name of a downtown store where I could buy the material. We decided to go there together to look at samples. Finally we chose a greenish one-very nice, but also very expensive, at £6 a yard. I needed three yards, which was a lot of money for me to pay. But because I was to arrive in America in cold weather, I felt I had to have a winter suit. Stan took my measurements and said the suit would be ready in two weeks.

Next I wrote to the Orient Lines in Sydney to book passage to the United States, inquiring as to the cost and the date of the ship's departure. At first, I thought I would ask Jean to help me with this, but I changed my mind. I wanted to avoid the issue as much as possible.

When I went to work and saw Jan, he immediately told me that he had also received a visa for America. I explained about writing to the Orient Lines to book passage, and he asked me to help him do the same, since his English was poor. I agreed and wrote them.

After several days, I received an answer from the Orient Lines which informed me about the date and the name of the ship, the Orsowa, which would leave Sydney for San Francisco on January 29, 1955. The cost was £623 which, converted to U.S. dollars, amounted to $1,370. I had known that it would be expensive, but this amount was a great shock, as it would make a huge dent in my savings. Nevertheless, I sent them a check immediately, and within a few days, received the ticket.

I was extremely busy now with preparations for the voyage. I only had a few weeks to get ready, and I had to liquidate quite a number of things. I decided to give my share of the candle business to Jean.

One night as I was driving home, it suddenly started raining very heavily. I saw a man walking on the sidewalk without an umbrella. I felt sorry for him, stopped, and offered him a ride. He only had a few blocks to go, only a couple of streets away from my rooming house. After he introduced himself as Lee Feiler, I mentioned my name and told him I was about to leave for America on the Orsowa.

Very surprised, he said that his good friend, Mrs. Schadek, would be on the same ship. She was a native Australian, who had lived in the United States for many years. He suggested I look her up on the ship. He added that she was an elderly lady, very friendly, who could give me some information about life in America. He also suggested that I contact his brother, Arthur, headwaiter at the Fisherman's Grotto No. 9 restaurant in San Francisco, who might be of some help to me.

When I saw Jan the next day after work, he rushed to give me his good news. He had received a letter from the Orient Lines about space available on the Orsowa, leaving the very same day as I. Traveling together would make the trip more enjoyable for both of us.

A few days before Christmas, the two Polish fellows in our rooming house told me they were interested in buying the house, which Mrs. Hall was considering selling. I immediately telephoned Mr. Weissman and recommended that he contact Mrs. Hall and ask her to list the house with his agency. Then I introduced the two Polish men to Mr. Weissman, who did indeed handle the sale. For brokering this deal, the two men gave me £10.

There were only a few days left before Christmas. Although I was leaving Australia, Jean invited me to be with her family. I accepted, but with an uneasy feeling, because I knew it would be a hard day for both of us.

Jean's sisters, her brother, and some of her nieces and nephews were there. I bought a large box of candy for the family and a pretty necklace for Jean. Despite the fact that Jean's family knew that I was leaving, they were very gracious, all wishing me good luck in the future. One of Jean's sisters asked her if she would miss me. Jean replied, "We were very good friends, and George was a wonderful lover." Then she turned around so we wouldn't see her tear-filled eyes.

I felt very uncomfortable. I just had to conquer my emotions somehow and stay calm. But it wasn't easy.

On New Year's Day, I decided to take Jan to Praha in downtown Melbourne.

It was traditional in my homeland to have pork on this special day. Therefore, we both ordered pork, dumplings, and sauerkraut. After the meal, Jan and I toasted one another, and our new future in the United States.

The new year 1955, started out on a very busy note. I had so many things to take care of after work.

Day by day, I had to notify my friends that I was leaving. Then I had to tell Joe, for whom I had been selling appliances.

Joe was very unhappy with my news. He said, "George, you should reconsider and stay. Television is coming to Australia, and that will be a tremendous business. You could have America right here. The sets will sell as soon as they come into my shop." I agreed with him, but of course, nothing could keep me from going to the United States.

I contacted Mr. Hoch to make the final arrangements about his payment for the rental property and the car. He agreed to give me the money the following week.

During the remaining days before my departure, I went for dinner to the Czech restaurant, Moravia. Among the diners was Bob Pribyl, a barber whom I knew very well. When I told him I was leaving soon for America, he told me he had also applied for emigration to the United States, as he wasn't happy with the Australian heat or the social life. After dinner, we wished each other good luck.

A day or two later, the tailor, notified me to come for a fitting. I asked him how soon the suit would be ready, and he said five days-which was cutting it rather close to my departure.

The time had also come for me to notify my employer, Commonwealth Aircraft Corporation, about my departure. I planned to take a train from Melbourne to Sydney on January 27, and I had to give a week's notice.

Somehow, all the arrangements were taken care of. Stan notified me that the suit was finished. It was a perfect fit. Stan assured me that the suit would not wrinkle in my suitcase—which was filling up rapidly with my many mementos.

Mr. Hoch gave me the money for both the car and the rental place. I told him that on January 27, I would pick him up and take him with me to the railroad station, where I would give him the keys to the car.

Finally, I had to make last arrangements with Jean. I didn't think that she'd want to come to the station, but to my surprise, she said she would. Jean told me that she would ask her father if she could borrow his Holden.

I went to the railroad station early and bought my ticket. As I was giving Mr. Hoch the keys to the car, Jean arrived, dressed in an attractive outfit. I introduced her to Mr. Hoch, who excused himself and left. Because he knew that Jean was my close friend, he most likely didn't want to watch us saying good-bye.

Jean reached into her small shopping bag, took out a small box, and handed it to me. She said that she had baked some cookies for me to eat on the train, because no food was available, and the stops were few and far apart on the long trip.

CHAPTER 25

Goodbye, Melbourne

AS WE STOOD ON THE PLATFORM, I HAD A LUMP IN MY THROAT. IT WAS HARD TO leave this nice person with whom I had shared so many good times for almost four years. It goes without saying that her eyes were wet. So were mine, and they are tearful even now as I am writing these lines. The memory of that time is deep. It was very difficult for both of us.

In a short while, the conductor was shouting, "All aboard" and now it was time for good-bye. I gave Jean a big hug and kiss, and lifted my suitcase and briefcase onto the train. In a few moments the train pulled out, and all that was left was just waving and waving until Jean disappeared.

The train cars had wooden benches, made out of slats and contoured to fit the body. It was warm in the morning, but it became very hot during the afternoon, even with all the windows open. I thought there would be many people on the train. To my great surprise, I was almost alone in the car.

As time dragged by, I thought back about my experiences in Australia, the knowledge that I had gained, and the skills and benefits I had gained from my various jobs. But now I was a wanderer again, going into the unknown. I kept thinking, "What lies ahead? Where must I start? What will I do?"

My head was spinning as I looked back-and looked forward. I had a great deal of curiosity about America. Well, I had to wait and see what happened when I got there, but I knew that it wouldn't be anything like my arrival at the refugee camps in Germany. Now I was on my way to a great country—a land of opportunity.

Chapter 26

SYDNEY

On January 28, 1955, I arrived in Sydney. Someone in Melbourne had told me about a Czechoslovak restaurant, Praha, not too far from the Sydney harbor. Because my luggage was quite heavy, my first order of business was to board the ship and leave my suitcase and briefcase in my cabin. Then I would look for the restaurant.

I proceeded to the harbor and entered the ship Orsowa, one of several belonging to the Orient Lines. I was eager to see my room, and to my great surprise, I found it much better than I expected: clean and quite spacious. A steward instructed me about the location of the dining rooms, the swimming pools, the dance floor.

The steward gave me the key to my room, and I put away my belongings. Then I set out to find the Praha. It wasn't too far away, and when I entered, there were not many guests. I ordered coffee and dessert. The manager was Czech, and because he wasn't busy, I chatted with him. Suddenly a couple came to my table, and I immediately recognized Mr. and Mrs. Obdrzalek, my former students on the Fairsea, whom I had taught English. Four years had passed, but their appearance hadn't changed. They told me how happy they were that they had attended my classes, and how much they appreciated learning English. This knowledge had helped Mr. Obdrzalek secure a job as a tool and dye maker.

I invited them to sit with me for a visit and meal. The Obdrzaleks said they had already eaten but would have a drink with me a little later—just now, they had to leave. Because this was a rather sentimental meeting, I agreed to wait for them to return, and they assured they would be back very soon. To pass the time, I ordered a schooner of beer (Schooner was the size of glass in which beer was served, approximately 12 ounces).

In a short while, the Obdrzaleks returned. Mr. Obdrzalek pulled out a small box from his pocket and handed it to me to open. In it was a silver bracelet with several charms hanging on it. These charms were of Australian animals, kangaroo, koala bear, platypus, kookaburra (an Australian kingfisher), and others. Mr. Obdrzalek told me that the bracelet was for my future wife, and that the gift was in appreciation for my teaching them English. I was very touched, and thanked them. We left wishing each other good health and the best in the future. I left the restaurant with a warm glow of gratification that my teaching had been so much appreciated.

Upon inquiry, I was told there was a large store, Johnson's, where I could buy a few things made of wool; Australia was famous for its wool production. There I purchased a very nice rug called a hunting blanket, a wool sweater, and two pairs of socks. These were the last purchases I made in Australia.

I still had some free time, so I decided to take my camera and walk towards the Sydney harbor bridge. When I arrived there, I asked a passer-by to take a picture of me. Then I proceeded to the ship.

On January 29, 1955, the Orsowa left for New Zealand. Now it was only a matter of three weeks until I put my feet down on the continent of America. My dream would finally come true after six years of anticipation.

As we were leaving the harbor, many relatives, friends, and onlookers were waving good-bye to the passengers standing by the ship's railing. Lots of ticker tape was thrown on the deck to express farewell. It was quite a sight to see the harbor and the coast line. The Sydney harbor bridge looked like a gate to the open sea. After a while, we were in the Pacific Ocean.

It was almost impossible to become acquainted with the entire ship during the first few days; it was just too large. But I noticed there was quite a difference in the appearance of the passengers as compared to those on the Fairsea. These passengers were nicely dressed, clean and more fashionable. There was a different mixture of people. Several children belonged to mothers who, I learned later, were "war brides" the wives of U.S. soldiers who had married them during World War II.

My friend, Jan was also sailing on the Orsowa. We sat next to each other in the dining room, but Jan spent most of his time playing shuffleboard, while I preferred to be in the swimming pool. I felt very content.

The weather was beautiful, and many people sat in the deck chairs and enjoyed the sunshine. On our first afternoon at sea, I sat in one of these chairs next to a war bride who had a son about ten years old and a daughter about twelve. I was puzzled when the daughter approached and said, "Hi, Mom." I had never heard that expression before, so I asked the children's mother about it. She explained, and we began a conversation. I felt a little pang when she told me that her name was Jean. She said that her husband had been a serviceman in Australia during the war.

Later that evening in the dining room, the man next to me said he was from Switzerland and was on his way to Colorado. I felt very sophisticated when I was able to respond that I was going to New Jersey.

The next morning was another nice day, and as I was standing on the deck leaning against the ship's rail watching the glittering ripples of the relatively calm Pacific Ocean, I began to reminisce. I had mixed emotions about leaving Australia, where life had been good to me, and where I had met so many wonderful people. But my cherished dream was to go to America, and not even Australia could hold me.

Our first stop of this twenty-one-day voyage was New Zealand.

CHAPTER 27

NEW ZEALAND

WE LANDED IN AUCKLAND ON A BEAUTIFUL DAY. WHEN I LEFT THE SHIP, I joined a group that was preparing to take a sightseeing trip. A bus and guide were provided by the Orient Lines.

While waiting for the bus, I noticed two men walking on the sidewalk, dressed alike: white shirts, dark pants, and large black hats. They were Maori, which the guide told us comprised sixteen percent of the New Zealand population.

In a few minutes, the bus arrived and we were on our way to see the New Zealand countryside. After a half-hour drive, we stopped at a restaurant in a mountainous area. While we drank a cup of tea and ate a biscuit and honey, we enjoyed a wonderful view.

After the refreshments, the guide suggested we form a half-circle so that we could hear her better. The guide was middle-aged, very pleasant, and quite professional. She spoke about New Zealand, telling us that it was comprised of three main islands. She said that the country was the scene of volcanic activity. The guide explained that the capital is Wellington, but that the largest city is Auckland. She also told us that New Zealand produced wheat, oats and barley. The country exported gold, silver, and coal, as well as wool, butter, fish, cheese, lamb, beef, apples and timber. The guide rather proudly said that New Zealand's exports exceeded its imports.

Although the country looked quite green, we learned that there was skiing in the highest elevations, mainly on Mount Cook.

The guide told us that executive power rested with a governor. There was the University of New Zealand, with several branch colleges. New Zealand has its own army, and those forces had distinguished themselves in World War II.

After the guide's talk, we boarded the bus and returned to Auckland. The trip had been quite interesting and educational. We thanked our guide and returned to the ship.

CHAPTER 28

FIJI

ON FEBRUARY 3, WE ARRIVED AT THE PORT OF SUVA IN THE FIJI ISLANDS. Tugboats pulled us in, and the ship was docked at a large and spacious pier. Just as in New Zealand, there was free time to go ashore and sightsee.

When we left the ship and entered the port area, there was a tall native watching the passengers. Someone next to me said "Isn't he wearing an unusual uniform?" We immediately were informed that this was a Fiji policeman. He wore black and white skirt with a half-diamond design. When I approached him, I inquired if I could take his picture, and he agreed. Then I noticed his very bushy hair—about six inches high, thick and charcoal gray. I asked if I could touch his hair on top. It looked so rough, but felt smooth.

I couldn't help but talk about this policeman with a man who was walking next to me. He said that the police were the highest paid people on the island, and that the British kept a strong force in Fiji, which was part of the Commonwealth.

It was a beautiful warm day. The doors of shops and even business offices were wide open. I noticed an Export/Import Company, and walked in to inquire if anyone there happened to be a stamp collector. A gentleman seated at the front desk said he was a collector, and began to look in his drawer. In a few minutes, he gave me an envelope containing several stamps. I asked for his address and told him that I would send him some stamps from the United States.

Not far from the outskirts of Suva were native huts that had been designated for sightseeing. A number of people headed that way, and I joined them. There was a wide path along the Rewa River, and for the first time in my life, I saw how bananas grew on bushy trees. What an experience! I loved it!

After a bit, we reached the native huts, which all looked alike. There was one hut underneath some very high palm trees. I looked up to the top of these palms and saw coconuts still in their shells. Underneath the palm nearest to the hut, there was a wide cloth, forming a large square. On it was sign reading "Please do not enter this area." Next to this squared-off patch, there was another hut that had no sign in front.

When I entered this hut with some other people, a native woman welcomed us. She spoke English, and I complemented her on her neatness. The floor was heavily laden with branches from the palm trees. In the middle was a wide double bed, and I commented, "The bed looks very nice, it must be comfortable." The woman smiled and replied, "This bed is only for guests. I sleep on the floor." She pointed to the branches from the palm trees. I was a little taken aback.

Before we left, I asked her why the sign outside read, "Please do not enter this area." She didn't answer immediately, and I noticed that her eyes filled with tears. In a few seconds, she said, "Two weeks ago I lost my eight-year-old son. A coconut fell on his head and hit him so hard that a couple of days later he died." She was weeping. I didn't want to ask any more questions, so I just expressed my sympathy. We all looked at each other, and without any discussion, we left her some Australian money. After a few minutes we walked back to the ship.

After dinner every night, there was a dance. I noticed some well-dressed passengers at the dance and learned that they were from the first-class. They were allowed to come to the second-class section, but we were not allowed to go to the first-class section. A remark was made that the first class passengers were snobbish, but that there was more fun in the second-class.

Although the passengers on the ship were very friendly, it was rather difficult for single men to ask ladies to dance since they usually wee with their husbands. The exception was the war brides who had gone to Australia to visit relatives and were now returning to their homes in the United States. Two of these ladies, Jean and Martha, were friendly. I'd already met Jean and her two children on deck. Martha did not seem to lack for company because she always had some gentleman sitting next to her at dinner.

On February 4 we left Fiji and were on our way to Hawaii. It was supposed to take a number of days, and in spite of the fact that the ship was large, it was difficult to pass the time. I swam and played shuffleboard with Jan, but even so, there was still a lot of free hours. Occasionally I would go to the bar for a drink. Drinks were very inexpensive, and that kept the bartenders busy.

I was impressed with the fine weather we had: no rain, a calm ocean, and a beautiful sky. The deck of the ship was always crowded, and since we saw the same people every day, we enjoyed many friendly conversations. One day an elderly gentleman said to me, "I can't find one person on this ship who would give me an argument." He didn't look drunk, but I had no idea what kind of argument he was looking for, so I couldn't give him an argument either!

On February 6 we crossed the equator. There was special entertainment that night: a masquerade party, costumes, and judges to give out prizes. One fellow dressed as a hobo. He sat on the floor wearing a small rucksack, a black hat, and shabby clothes. People danced around him all evening, but he wouldn't move an inch. He won first prize.

The next day, we had February 6 again, thus gaining an extra day. That surprised some of the passengers, but I expected it as I had the same experience on the Indian Ocean during my trip from Germany to Australia.

Gradually we were all getting "Hawaiian Fever," as the ship drew closer to the islands. There were some 130 of these islands, although most were uninhabited. I couldn't understand why there didn't seem to be any Hawaiians on board. Possibly they were in first-class.

Chapter 29

HAWAII

On February 10, the Orsowa landed at the port of Honolulu. It was a beautiful day, and everyone was excited to visit this famous island that was pictured in magazines all over the world. Now we could see it with our own eyes.

When the ship had docked, we heard music coming from the large pier area. There were four musicians playing welcoming Hawaiian songs, and several pretty Hawaiian girls, all dressed in grass skirts. They wore beautiful leis around their necks, made from real flowers. The girls started to distribute dozens and dozens of these beautiful leis, draping them around the necks of the passengers. Then the girls started to perform hula-hula dances. Everyone was happy, smiling and clapping hands. What a wonderful greeting to the Hawaiian islands!

During lunch, six of us whose destination was the United States decided to hire a taxi to go sightseeing. We would be in Hawaii for two days, so we had plenty of time.

When we left the ship, one could notice a difference between British Commonwealth countries and what we saw here. In Hawaii steering wheels were on the left, while the cars were large and came in all kinds of models and colors. The cars in Australia, New Zealand, and Fiji were small with their steering wheels on the right.

The six of us found a taxi-a beautiful Cadillac—and couldn't believe that a Cadillac would be used for a taxi. The driver agreed to take us on a tour around the island. The first stop was a high mountain area. Near the plateau, we could see an unusual waterfall. Its water was drawn upward by a strong wind and fell back down like rain. I called it an upside-down waterfall.

Our next stop was the banana fields, which were spectacular. We bought a few of the bananas, and agreed we'd never tasted anything so good.

Then we stopped to see the sugarcane fields, which were just being harvested. Our driver explained that before the men began to cut the cane with machetes, a fire would be started along one side of the field to burn dry leaves, spiders, spider webs, and snakes. Only then would the men come in and do the cutting.

Our next visit was to the Dole pineapple fields, which spread on acres and acres of land. We saw a truck pulling very wide equipment, designed to pick the pineapples off the bushes. Behind this wide machinery, were men dressed in leather clothes and wearing leather gloves to pick up the pineapples that had been missed by the machinery. The reason for all the leather clothes was that the bushes were covered with needle-like points.

We drove on to the Dole plant, where we saw the pineapples being unloaded onto conveyor belts. There they would be peeled, the core would be removed, and the fruit would go into a slicing machine. The employees were dressed in long, white coats and had designated jobs like slicing, chucking, crushing, canning, and packaging. Our driver said that the company employed approximately 6,500 people during the peak season. At the exit to the Dole factory were huge glasses of pineapple juice, and visitors were welcome to drink as much as they wanted. We drank a glass or two, which tasted every bit as delicious as the bananas.

It was getting late in the afternoon, but the driver suggested that we should stop at a restaurant for a cup of coffee—and see the beautifully-carved totem poles that the restaurant owner sold. We drank the coffee, but decided the totem poles were too awkward to lug onto the ship!

After all these stops, we finally returned to the pier. It was a pleasant, but educational tour, and we were delighted when the driver charged us only forty dollars for our ninety-six mile trip.

After dinner on the ship, Jan and I went downtown to the main promenade area. As we walked along, we saw a large group of people who were acting like fans at some game. Bewildered, we approached the crowd and saw a box that was showing a baseball game. It was my first glimpse of a television set.

Jan and I spotted a quaint-looking restaurant, and decided to have a drink. We sat at a table next to a narrow canal that was surrounded by tropical plants. It was unusual sight-something I had never seen in any other restaurant. It was a very enjoyable evening for both of us.

After dinner, no dance was scheduled as it was expected the passengers would return to town to see the night life. I stayed on the ship as I had a day full of events and sat in the lobby, spoke to same passengers who were also going to the U.S.A.

The next day after breakfast, Jan and I decided to go for a walk around Honolulu.. We stopped in a store and bought some colorful shirts and shorts, decorated with flowers. Then we walked on to the famous Waikiki beach. But it was a disappointment. The beach was small, with coarse, gray sand. It couldn't compare to Australian beaches, which were miles and miles long, and made up of sand like fine flour. Jan and I didn't go in the water, because we wanted to see as much of Honolulu as possible before our departure from Hawaii.

During that afternoon departure, many people gathered on the dock. The group of musicians who had welcomed us the previous day arrived again to say "aloha" which means both hello and good-bye.

The ship's rail was crowded, and I was fortunate to have a good spot from which to watch the hula dancers. Suddenly I heard someone on the dock calling my name, "Mr. Knava, Mr. Knava!" and waving his hand. He was one of the students to whom I had taught English on the Fairsea. I was allowed to leave the ship for a moment to speak to him, and I asked an elderly lady standing next to me to reserve my place until I returned.

The young man had been one of my best students. Now he explained that, thanks to me, his English was so fluent that he'd been able to get a job in Honolulu. I was happy that I'd had this opportunity to see him again.

When I returned to the ship, the elderly lady had kept my spot for me. I thanked her and introduced myself. She said, "So nice to meet you, my name is Schadek." Stunned, I repeated her name, "You are Mrs. Schadek?" When she looked puzzled at my surprise, I explained, "Lee Feiler told me that you would be on this ship and that I should get in touch with you."

Mrs. Schadek asked how I knew Lee, and I told her about giving him a ride in Melbourne one rainy night when I saw him without an umbrella.

My conversation with Mrs. Schadek was interrupted as the musicians began playing that Hawaiian tune, "Now is the hour..." People on the pier were shouting and throwing ticker tape as the ship slowly pulled away. We were on our way to British Columbia.

Because we hadn't had an opportunity to really talk, Mrs. Schadek invited me to see her in the lobby of the first-class section. Now we had time to become acquainted. I learned that Mrs. Schadek was born in Australia but had married an American, her husband was a retired carpenter and builder. Then Mrs. Schadek asked me where I was going to settle in the United States. I told her that eventually I would be living in New Jersey, but that first I wanted to stay in California for a while. I explained that I had some money in a New York bank, and that I had sent an airmail letter to transfer $200 to the Bank of America in San Francisco. I was hoping by the time we landed there, the money would be waiting for me, and I could find a room somewhere.

When Mrs. Schadek heard this, she gave me her card and told me that after we arrived in San Francisco, I should immediately get a taxi and come to her house. I couldn't believe that this lady would welcome a total stranger in her home. I thanked her, and after another hour of chatting, I went back to the second-class section.

In the lounge I saw Jean, one of the war brides. She told me how bored she was, and asked me to sit down with her for a while. Her two young children were running around the ship, while Martha, the other war bride, was off with one of her gentleman friends. Jean was interested in my background. She said that she'd never met anyone from Czechoslovakia but because of the war in Europe, she had read about my country in the newspapers. By now it was almost dinner time, and Jean asked if I would sit with her and her two children so we could continue our conversation.

After we finished our dinner, Jean invited me to her cabin. I was rather hesitant, but also somewhat curious to see what the ship's family quarters looked like. It turned out her cabin was very small, with a bunk bed for the children and a single bed for Jean. I sat down on the bed and continued my story. After a while, Jean tucked the kids in and I finished telling her about my experience in Czechoslovakia and Germany.

Suddenly Jean left her chair and came to sit next to me on the bed. I could sense that she would like to have a little romance with me. And we almost did-until something odd and unexpected happened.
There was a quiet knock on the door. Then, before Jean could even answer, the door opened a crack and a man's hand appeared, holding a bowl of French fries. Without saying a word, Jean quickly went over and took the bowl. The door closed.

I was rather shocked, concluding that Jean must be involved with a man who worked in the ship's kitchen. I looked at her, she blushed-and offered me some French fries. I did not take any, because I just wanted to get out of there. I wished Jean good night, and I left.

The next morning everything was back to normal. I met Jan at our usual table for breakfast. He'd seen me dining with Jean the night before, and looked at me questioningly, with a little smile. I told him that Jean had wanted to hear the rest of my story, but because of the presence of the children, nothing happened.

In the afternoon I went to get a haircut. I had overheard two fellows saying that haircuts in the United States cost $5. I needed one, so I went to the ship's barber shop. There was quite a long line waiting—apparently everyone had heard about expensive American haircuts—but at least when I finally got in, it only cost $1.50.

Later I visited Mrs. Schadek again. We discussed various subjects. I mentioned that Leo Feiler had suggested that I look up his brother,

Arthur, who worked as a headwaiter. He thought that he might help me to get some kind of job there. Mrs. Schadek was a wonderful listener, but I wanted to know something about her, too. I tried to find out about her likes and dislikes. I asked if she liked tea or coffee. She said she preferred tea, and very seldom drank coffee, but that Mr. Schadek liked coffee better than tea. She told me that her husband had difficulty walking, which was why he had retired. She said they were childless. Mrs. Schadek volunteered that her first name was Daphne-I never heard that name before.

After a while I ran out of questions so I decided to leave. Mrs. Schadek asked me to come see her again when we arrived in British Columbia.

We were approaching the Canadian waters near Vancouver, where the sea was surrounded by beautiful wooded hills. There were also numerous picturesque islands. I couldn't understand how so many healthy trees could grow on those islands, since all around them was saltwater.

Luckily, a teacher from the area overheard me admiring the trees and wondering what kind they were. He told me that most of them were Douglas fir or spruce, and explained that because they were so abundant, forestry was a principal industry. He said that the country was also rich in minerals. He also pointed out that because the western part of Vancouver Island was so full of inlets, most transportation was done by ferries.

Before the ship reached Vancouver harbor, he and I had dinner together. He had told me so many fascinating details about British Columbia, so now it was my turn to tell him about Czechoslovakia. After dinner I thanked him for his educational talk and said good-bye.

That night I tossed and turned, realizing that tomorrow morning I would actually be on North American soil.

CHAPTER 30

BRITISH COLUMBIA

ON FEBRUARY 13, WE ARRIVED IN VANCOUVER HARBOR, WHERE WE HAD A couple of days to sightsee.

On that first morning, Mrs. Schadek asked me a favor. She said that there was a well-known company called Safeway in Vancouver, which sold Red Rose tea. Since she was unable to buy that brand in San Francisco, she wanted me to get her a couple of boxes here. I knew that Mrs. Schadek had poor circulation in one leg and apparently didn't get around much better than her husband—so I was glad to help. Vancouver had the heaviest traffic I'd ever seen, with five lanes going in both directions. I hoped I wouldn't have to try to cross the street to get to a Safeway store. But I was lucky. I saw a sign for the supermarket-on my side of the street. When I went inside, I was amazed at all the merchandise. It seemed to take me forever to find the tea. I bought Mrs. Schadek her Red Rose, and purchased razor blades and some chocolate bars for myself.

I went back to the ship, and told Mrs. Schadek about my surprise at the size of the supermarket. She smiled and said, "You will see more and larger ones in the United States."

We talked a bit about San Francisco: what I would do after disembarking and where I would stay. I said that my only chance for a job was to contact Arthur Feiler, Lee's brother—but that I didn't know what to do about living quarters. Mrs. Schadek solved that problem by offering me a room in their home. She said that since they had no children, there was plenty of space. What a relief!

On February 15, we left Vancouver and were on our way to San Francisco. I hadn't gone sightseeing in Vancouver, because there were no arrangements made for a guided tour. However, I'd heard so much about the ferry system that I went to see how it worked. I had visualized a pontoon-type platform being pulled by some kind of mechanism, but the Vancouver ferries were quite modern, almost like floating buses, heated in the winter and provided with seats. Still, I wished I could have seen more than the ferry system. As we left the harbor, I took one last look at this picturesque area surrounded by its beautiful wooded inlets.

When we were out in the open sea again, I told Jan about my decision to stay in San Francisco for a while. I also told him about Mrs. Schadek's offer to let me stay with them, and about my intention to find a job. He was a little surprised, because he'd thought we would continue on to the Zacks' in New Jersey, who had also sponsored Jan. He told me that he intended to join them right away.

I took some time to organize my luggage for the custom inspection. I was a little worried about my stamp collection, fearing that I might have to pay some custom fee-and my money reserve was down to $10.00. I had some empty envelopes, so I took a lot of stamps out of their albums and put them loosely in the envelopes.

After I finished all this rearranging, I spent some time with Jan. As we were approaching San Francisco, I paid a final visit to Mrs. Schadek, and told her that I would come to her home by taxi, after clearing customs. She agreed and informed me that her husband would be meeting her.

And now it was almost time for the biggest moment of my life.

PART III

UNITED STATES

Chapter 31

SAN FRANCISCO

On February 17, 1955, my dream was finally fulfilled. Just the view of San Francisco from the ship gave me the realization that all my long years of waiting were over.

When we left the ship, we were asked to go to the aisle that showed the first letter of our last name. There was a long platform with all the letters of the alphabet, indicating where to stand for customs inspection.

I was only fourth in line and was very nervous about the inspection. I had one large piece of luggage and my briefcase. In both I had my postage stamp collection, mixed in with various belongings. But my fears didn't materialize, because I wasn't asked to open either piece. Now I was on my way to the exit—to the land of freedom and opportunity.

I will never forget that wonderful feeling when I took my first step out of the building downtown on Market Street. I stood there for a moment with tears in my eyes. It is almost impossible to describe my emotion.

I hailed a taxi and asked the driver to take me to 1562 Hayes Street, the home of Mr. and Mrs. Schadek. I had no idea how far away the Schadeks lived. The taxi driver did not go straight in one direction; after three or four blocks, he turned left, soon after he turned right, then left again and then right again. Finally, he stopped. When I asked him the fare, he said $6.50. I was dismayed. I had only $10, so after paying him, I was left with $3.50.

I rang the bell, and in a moment, Mr. Schadek spoke to me from an upstairs window. He said, "I'll be right down." When he opened the front door, I introduced myself. When I walked in, Mrs. Schadek welcomed me. It was reassuring to see her again, even after such a short time.

When I told her that the taxi driver charged me $6.50, she almost screamed, "What? It shouldn't have been more than $3 at most." She knew right away that the driver had realized I was a foreigner and "taken me for a ride." She was furious, but there was nothing we could do about it. After we'd exhausted that subject, Mrs. Schadek asked if I wanted to make a cup of tea. We opened the Red Rose that I had bought for her in Vancouver.

We chatted a bit, then Mrs. Schadek told me I would be staying in their spare room upstairs. She added, "Take your luggage up, make yourself comfortable, and then have dinner with us." I couldn't believe how hospitable these people were to me, a total stranger.

I told the Schadeks I would go to the Bank of America first thing in the morning. Then, as Lee Feiler had suggested, I planned to look up his brother, Arthur, at the Fisherman's Grotto restaurant. Lee had thought I might be able to find a job there. Mr. Schadek said he would see me at breakfast, because he was an early riser except—during baseball season, when he would watch the game until the end. Before going to bed, I thanked the Schadeks for their generous hospitality.

It was wonderful to sleep in a bed in a house after twenty-one days on the ship. There was only one drawback: the smoke from their cigarettes. I had noticed on the ship that Mrs. Schadek always had a cigarette in her hand. And her husband, it seemed, smoked just as much as she did. Although I closed the door and opened the window, it was some time before the room cleared of smoke. Nevertheless, I fell asleep and had a good night's rest.

In the morning, I had something new for breakfast: cereal with a banana and milk, which I liked very much. As soon as I finished eating, I said good-bye to Mr. Schadek and took a trolley to the Bank of America. Unfortunately, my money hadn't arrived yet. I had almost no cash—just enough for trolley fare. Fortunately, as I wasn't too far from the Fisherman's Grotto, I could walk there.

When I arrived at the restaurant, I understood where it got its name. On the outside, there was a life-sized fisherman mounted on the edge of the roof holding a fishing pole. On the line a fish was hanging, as if it had just been caught.

I asked at the door if I could speak to Mr. Arthur Feiler, the headwaiter. To my great relief, he showed up immediately. I told him I had just arrived from Melbourne, where I had met his brother after picking him up in a rainstorm. I explained that Lee had given me this address with the hope that Art could help me find a job.

He told me to wait a minute and walked to the back of the restaurant. When Art returned, he told me that Al, who owned the restaurant with his brother, said that the only work available was as dishwasher and kitchen cleaner on the third shift, from 2:00 A.M. until 10:00 A.M. Art explained a Chinese man had just quit the job that morning.

Well, here I was with no money in my pocket, so I took it. Since I had no idea about employment possibilities in San Francisco, I was grateful to have found this job so quickly. Thanking Art, I told him I would write to Lee about his help.

It was a pleasant day, and I walked all the way back to the Schadeks' home. I told them I had found a job, but that my money had not yet arrived. With her usual instinctive kindness, Mrs. Schadek handed me a $20 bill and said, "Take this, because I don't like to see you without any cash. When you get your money, you can return it." I hesitated, feeling I was already somewhat of a burden to them. But as it was a loan, I finally accepted it.

When I told the Schadeks more details about my job, Mrs. Schadek seemed a bit horrified. "You took a job as a dishwasher on the third shift?" I said that I had no other choice, since it was the only position available.

While we were having tea and pastry, I asked Mrs. Schadek if we could look in the want ads. But after scanning the newspaper, we were disappointed at the lack of prospects.

I felt fidgety; it was difficult for me to pass the time without being active. When I noticed some ashes from Mrs. Schadek's cigarettes next to her chair, she accepted my offer to vacuum the room. When I finished, Mr.

Schadek showed me his huge garage behind the house, which he thought could be converted into a nice apartment. He reminded me that he was a builder, and suggested that we work on it together. It sounded promising. However, I had just arrived in America, and I didn't want to make such a commitment until I knew what the future held. Thanking him for his offer, I told him I would think about it. I felt so grateful to these people, who were treating me like a son.

After supper, I asked Mrs. Schadek if she had some stationery so I could write to my sisters and brothers in Czechoslovakia, just to let them know I had arrived safely in the United States. She handed me a pad and some envelopes, and I excused myself and went upstairs to do my correspondence before it was time to go to work.

Shortly before midnight, I took a trolley and went downtown. I was early for work, but I wanted someone to show me the ropes. But when I entered the restaurant and walked back to the kitchen, there wasn't anyone there to ask about the job. I wandered around and saw Al in his office. He didn't notice me at first, so I sat down. Finally, he looked up and stared at me rather blankly. I reminded him that I had been hired for the job that began at 2:00 A.M., and I was hoping someone would tell me what to do. Al said that the dishwasher on the previous shift was sick, but that he would show me around and explain my duties. He added that the chef who came at 4:00 A.M. would tell me more. Al pointed out the equipment I needed: rubber gloves, broom, detergent, hoses for washing the floor.

Now, it was time to start clean-up.

I didn't know where to begin, because the kitchen was a real mess. I didn't want to slip and fall on the greasy latticed floor, I decided to wash it with hot water and stack the slats in the corner to dry—while I scraped pieces of fish, crabs, prawns, and noodles off the floor and into a large bucket. Little by little I made some headway, until I could finally put the lattice slats back down on the wet floor. Then I started to wash some huge pots that were piled in the large sink. They were extremely smelly after containing seafood, pasta, chili sauce, soup, ketchup, and vegetables. Some of the pots were so deep that I could hardly reach the bottom. What a job! But at least the kitchen looked more like a kitchen.

At 4:00 A.M. the chef came in, and I introduced myself. He told me his name, which I couldn't understand. His English was very poor, and from his accent, I guessed he was either French or Italian. His first order was, "Clean the oven with steel wool. Be sure to go with the grain, up and down only." Next he asked me to take a flat top—a vehicle on four wheels, with a top the size of a door—and go to the supply room to pick up ten gallon-sized ketchup containers and some large cans of chili sauce, stewed tomatoes, and mustard. When I returned, he showed me how to open the cans and where to dump them.

The next order of business was to bring in bags of potatoes, onions, celery, carrots, cabbage, cauliflower, and jars of pickles. He started to fill large bowls with the vegetables, one after another. Then he began to slice bacon and ham, while I had to take care of the waste to make space for him to work. As he chopped this and that, very quickly, I thought he was going to lose one of his fingers.

At 6:00 A.M. breakfast orders began to come in. The kitchen became extremely hot, and smelled of fried foods. I cleaned up empty cans, jars, trays, and dirty utensils, whatever was accumulating. When things finally slowed down, the chef made a late breakfast for both of us: eggs sunny-side up, bacon, toast with jelly, and coffee.

I was glad when it was over at ten o'clock. I changed clothes, said good-bye, and left. Wow! What a job! I was tired, but I walked to the Bank of America to see if my money had arrived. It wasn't there, so I took a trolley and went home.

When I arrived at the Schadeks, they asked me about my job and had a good laugh when they heard my list of duties. I told them I had checked with the bank, but the money had not yet arrived. Mrs. Schadek offered me a cookie and a cup of tea, but I wasn't hungry, so I excused myself, went upstairs, had a shower, and then slept all afternoon.

When I awoke, I shaved, and joined the Schadeks, who had invited me for dinner. I asked Mrs. Schadek which company operated the trolley buses. After she told me that it was the Municipal Railways, I phoned them to inquire when the last trolley would stop at Hayes Street. When they informed me that it would be 1:00 A.M., I was very pleased, since I had decided not to go to work as early as the previous night.

At 12:50, as I was closing my window and ready to leave, the trolley went by. I was surprised to see it, but I still thought there would be another one at 1:00 o'clock. I went out to the stop, waited and waited. After a half hour, when no trolley arrived, I went back to the house and phoned Fisherman's Grotto to tell Al that the Municipal Railways had given me the wrong information.

Very understanding, he said, "Take the night off. But be sure to call my brother, Mike, in the morning and explain."

In the morning, I called Mike to tell him what had happened. But he wasn't as understanding as his brother. He said, "Sorry, George, we can't have undependable employees here. Come by in the morning for your money."

Well, as fast as I had gotten the job, just as fast I lost it. Here I was unemployed again. In the morning. I went to collect my wages. I remember I received exactly $11.35: my first salary in America.

I walked to the Bank of America again. This time the money was there, and they gave me a passbook that would enable me to make deposits or withdrawals.

When I arrived home, I told Mrs. Schadek the bad news about the loss of my job, and the good news that my money had arrived. I returned the $20 loan, and thanked her for the favor. Then she told me that she had cut out a want ad for an opening that Sears Roebuck had in their garden center, not too far away, I decided to go there immediately.

Following Mrs. Schadek's directions, I went to the personnel department of Sears Roebuck and asked a young lady about the opening. She told me to go to the garden center and talk to the man in charge. There I saw a tall, large, black man, who said he was the manager. I showed him the clipping, but he told me that the job was already taken.

On my way home, I somehow got lost and asked a man in a pickup for directions to 1562 Hayes Street. He said he was going that way and to "hop in." I never heard that expression before, but it sounded friendly.

After a few moments, he asked me where I was from—obviously he had detected my accent—and I replied from Czechoslovakia. He said that he knew someone from Czechoslovakia, and tried to pronounce a name that sounded like Mr. Binis. I corrected him and said, Mr. Benesh? He agreed that was the name, and told me that Mr. Benesh owned some kind of factory downtown on Mission Street. I explained that I was looking for a job, and he encouraged me to go there. Just then we pulled up in front of 1562 Hayes Street. He let me out, wished me luck, and I thanked him.

The Schadeks were disappointed at my news about the garden center, but they cheered up when I told them about Mr. Benesh. After our usual cup of tea, I left to go to his factory.

It was still early in the morning. Taking my overalls with me just in case I got a job, I went by downtown trolley, then walked along Mission Street looking for the factory. After a couple of blocks. I saw a sign, "Fritzi of California," on a large building. I went in to inquire and saw a sign that said, "Office."

I knocked at the door, and a nice-looking woman asked if she could be of some help. I told her I was looking for a factory in the area owned by a Mr. Benesh. She smiled and said, "This is it." I was pleasantly surprised that I had found the place so quickly. I asked her if Mr. Benesh was Czech. She looked at me with a rather long stare and asked me why I wanted to know. I replied that I was Czech, had just arrived in the United States, and was looking for a job. She told me that she was Fritzi Benesh, and would go to her husband's office to inquire if he wanted to see me. Well, now I knew where the name of the company had come from.

Within a minute or two, she returned and asked me to come in. I wanted to speak Czech to him at first, but decided against it in order to show him that I knew English. I introduced myself, and Mr. Benesh told me to sit down. He asked me when I had left Czechoslovakia and where I had been since then, but he didn't volunteer anything about himself. I only inquired when he came to the U.S.A. When he replied in 1939, I guessed he was probably Jewish, and his wife's name, Fritzi, was a Jewish name. When we finished our chat, Mr. Benesh welcomed me to America, wished me luck, and asked me to see Mr. Hoffman downstairs, who would tell me if a job was available. Thanking him, I told him how pleased I was to meet him. On the way out, I repeated the same words to Mrs. Benesh.

When I went downstairs, I entered a large room with a few employees. Everyone was busy. I asked the first person I saw if I could speak with Mr. Hoffman. When he appeared, I informed him that Mr. Benesh had sent me to see if he could use my help. Mr. Hoffman, a man about sixty, rubbed his chin, looked around the large room, and said, "When can you start?" I replied, "I have my overalls with me and can start at once."

My job would be to make up cardboard boxes, Mr. Hoffman explained. Nick would show me around. In a short while, a tall man introduced himself as Nick. When I informed him that I came from Czechoslovakia, he said he was from Yugoslavia. Because we had something in common, I felt he would help me. Nick showed me around what he called the sorting room, where thousands of blouses, skirts, and dresses were sorted and shipped all over America.

Nick told me that Mr. Benesh designed the clothes. He took me upstairs into a cutting room, where there was a long table—about fifty feet long and five feet wide—on which were layers and layers of material spread full length. Between each layer was a paper that came off a huge roll, and above was an overhead saber saw that the cutter guided over the patterns. A stack about three inches high was cut per pattern into thousands of pieces.

These pieces were picked up by Chinese people, who took them home and sewed them together into blouses, skirts, or dresses. These were subsequently placed on a freight elevator, brought downstairs into the sorting room, and from there were shipped out.

After we made our tour, we came back into the area where I had to make up boxes for shipping. Nick showed me how to make one and from then on, I was on my own. Although it was something new for me, it was very simple.

When I finished making about two dozen boxes, Mr. Hoffman sent me to help Nick fill orders from various customers, such as department stores. It was something to see. Nick would say, "George, get this order," and it would cover one gross of blouses, size 34, one gross of size 36, one gross of size 38, then some skirts in sizes 10, 14, 16, 18, and so forth. Next I had to pack them—which was the easiest thing for me to do, since I learned how to pack in the NASCO warehouse.

I was bounced from one task to another, like a boy Friday. Sometimes I was sent upstairs to help pack smaller orders, consisting of more expensive blouses or skirts. There I worked with three ladies whose job was to check these expensive items for imperfections: accidental oil spots or missing buttons. If any article of clothing was found to be defective, it was put in a large box and sold to the employees.

I noticed that Lydia—one of the three ladies—had seen a beautiful blouse that appealed to her. She dropped a little oil on the tail of the blouse and then put it aside, but not in the box with the other rejects. When Mr. Hoffman came in, she told him that there was a blouse with an oil spot and asked if she could buy it. He never even looked at it, just quoted her a price of one dollar.

The time of the year plays a large role in the clothing business, because there is a lull before the next season's merchandise is needed. Of course, that had a great impact on part-time employees, of which I was one. Thus, after nine weeks, I was laid off. I thanked Mr. Benesh for the job, even though it hadn't lasted very long.

When I went home to the Schadeks, I reported that I was unemployed again. They shook their heads and couldn't believe that a steady job was so extremely hard to find. But the area had no industry of any great size, except for Bethlehem Steel Company, which was miles away, near San Jose.

I asked Mrs. Schadek if she would be kind enough to watch the want ads for openings. Had I known that my position at "Fritzi of California" would only last a few weeks, I would have been looking for another job.

In most major cities throughout the United States, there were and still are numerous Czechoslovakian immigrants. In all of these cities, the immigrants formed Sokol clubs, the name of the popular gymnastic organization in Czechoslovakia. These clubs either constructed their own buildings or rented halls, depending on how large their membership was. In Cleveland, there were so many members that they had nine buildings.

Since I had joined a Sokol club when I was five years old, I was delighted to learn about the Friday meetings at the Sokol Club on 239 Page Street, where gymnasts and various guests and friends met to spend a pleasant evening together. The club had been founded by immigrants who had come to San Francisco here many years ago. They—and their descendants—had remained true to their Czech heritage and kept their Czech culture and customs.

After I lost my job at Fritzi of California, I walked up and down Market Street hoping I might see a "Help Wanted" sign, but had no luck. I tried the market at the Petrini Plaza where I bought my groceries. I asked the manager if they needed help in the produce department or elsewhere, but he told me there were no vacancies.

So the following Friday, I went to the Sokol Club to take my mind off my job worries. I arrived early and had the opportunity to meet Mr. and Mrs. Chlup, the managers of the club. We talked for a short while, then Mr. Chlup took me to the balcony from where I could watch the gymnasts. The hall reminded me of the one in my home town, where I had attended exercise classes every week.

After about an hour, I went to the restaurant. I had just ordered a glass of wine when a man approached me, said his name was Fred Divisek, and asked if this was my first time at the club. I introduced myself and inquired if he spoke Czech. He replied in my native language—music to my ears—that he was of Czech descent, and had been born in the Chicago area. Fred wanted to know about my background, so I told him that I had recently come from Australia. When he asked where I was working, I replied that I just lost my job at "Fritzi of California," and was looking for another one.

A little while later, Fred introduced me to two ladies, Mrs. Marie Smallwood and her sister, Irene Lasek. Mrs. Smallwood was in the real estate business, and Fred asked her if she knew of any jobs. She replied that she didn't know of anything permanent, but said she needed someone to work on a house she was trying to sell. The fence was leaning over a neighbor's property, and he was complaining. She gave me her card and said to call her if I didn't find anything.

The next morning I phoned Mrs. Smallwood to inform her that I would work on her fence. Since she lived only a few blocks away from the Schadeks, she volunteered to pick me up.

The house was downtown, in a rather hilly area not too far from the cable car terminal. We walked to the back of the house where she showed me the fence. It was a solid fence, with four strong posts about half the size of telephone poles. I could see that someone had started to dig a short trench and had left the pick and shovel lying on the ground. Mrs. Smallwood told me that she had hired a man, but he'd quit on the first day. I asked her what the pay would be, and she said one dollar an hour. I wasn't too happy to hear such a low rate—that was probably why the man had quit!—and hesitated before giving her an answer. I finally decided to follow a Czech saying, "It's better to have a sparrow in the hand than a dove on the roof." I told her that I would take the job and start at once.

I had come prepared with my overalls and work gloves. Because of my experience setting telephone poles at PMG, I knew exactly what I had to do, only here I would have less sophisticated equipment. In Australia, we had turn buckles, wire rope, and eyebolt connectors, and steel rods. For anchors, we'd used eucalyptus logs eight by eight inches square and four feet long.

To do this job, I needed four solid pieces of wood to use as anchors and some strong wire. I prepared the holes for the anchors, about three feet deep, and made narrow trenches for the wire. The stony ground was not easy to work in, but I managed to dig into it. Then I also had to dig out the dirt around the poles, so they could straighten up without cracking.

In about five hours, I had these preparations done. When it was time for me to leave, I walked to the cable car terminal and took a trolley to the terminal near Market Street. From there, I walked home to the Schadeks.

When Mr. and Mrs. Schadek asked me where I had been, I told them the story about my new job. I described the task to Mr. Schadek. When I told him I had to get strong pieces of wood for anchors and strong tie wire, he offered me all kinds of wood and wire that he had in a building in his backyard. Kindhearted as always, he offered me kielbasa and rye bread for lunch.

When I finished my snack, we went out back, where there was plenty of material that I could use—even a saw. "This is perfect," I said. Since Mr. Schadek was curious about my project, he offered to load all the supplies into his car and take me to the house for my second day on the job. What a nice guy he was!

The next morning I could hardly get up. My body was sore and aching, because I wasn't used to digging with a heavy pick and shoveling out those deep holes. However, the work had to be done. Mr. Schadek and I drove to the house. When I showed him my project, he examined it for a moment and agreed with my plan. After telling me to "take it easy," Mr. Schadek left.

From that moment on, it was only a matter of how long it took to do the job. I made wire loops, with one end around the posts, and the other around the anchors. Then I started at the first post. I put the anchor in the hole, dropped heavy stones on top of it, and packed the dirt as hard as possible. Taking a piece of smaller wood, I placed it in the center of the loop and twisted the wire until the post was standing up straight. To make each post and the entire fence vertical, this process had to be done slowly at every post. By late Sunday afternoon, the job was completed and the fence no longer leaned over the neighbor's property.

Mr. Schadek was eager to learn the result of my labors. Proudly, I informed him that it looked very well. Then I phoned Mrs. Smallwood to notify her that the job was finished. She was surprised that I worked the entire weekend. When she asked me how much she owed me, I quoted eighteen dollars for my labor and twenty dollars for Mr. Schadek's materials. She thanked me and said she would send me a check.

So now I was at loose ends again. I decided to go for a walk in the nearby Golden Gate Park. On my way there, I noticed a variety store named Odenthall's, with a sign in the window, "Room for Rent." I continued my walk, thinking about that sign. I had been at the Schadeks for weeks, and I felt I should move.

I went back to inquire about the room. A tall man, who introduced himself as Mr. Odenthall, came to the door. He called his wife to show me a very large, bright room, facing the street, with a double bed and a small gas heater. Following her, she showed me a bathroom and a large kitchen that I could share with the man in the next room. The rent was $27.50 a month. She would provide clean bed sheets weekly, electricity and hot water.

As the price was very reasonable, I agreed to take it at once. After I paid her, she gave me the keys, one to the room and one to the house. Clean sheets would be left for me on the banister railing every Monday, and I would place the used ones in a large basket nearby.

Upon my return to the Schadeks, I told them I had rented a room from Mrs. Odenthall. According to Mrs. Schadek, the Odenthalls were very nice people whom they had known for years. But she said they would miss me, since they'd come to think of me as a son. I was very pleased to hear those kind words. I assured them that if they needed any help, I would always be available and that I would visit them often. As a matter of fact, I would stop by the next morning to check the want ads.

It was hard for me to leave those wonderful people. I thanked Mrs. Schadek for all her kindness, and I gave her a hug and a kiss on the cheek. I shook hands with Mr. Schadek and thanked him as well. A few minutes later, as I opened the door at the Odenthalls, here I was, at a different house, with a different address—which meant I would have to notify my relatives and friends all over again!

The next morning, I visited Mrs. Schadek to look at the want ads. Unfortunately, there was nothing. When she asked me how my first night was, I told her I slept like a log, but I still felt exhausted after all the digging. As usual, we had tea and some pastry. If she needed anything, I told her she should not hesitate to call me at the Odenthalls.

Next I went to the Petrini Plaza market to do some grocery shopping. I had a cabinet to use as a tiny pantry. Everything about my room was nice, but I felt a little lonesome.

At the Schadeks, I always had someone with whom to talk. Here I was more isolated. I kept busy by taking care of my change-of-address letters to my relatives, and somehow the hours went by.

Later in the afternoon, while I was still writing letters, Mrs. Odenthall knocked at my door to inform me that Mrs. Schadek had phoned to say she would like to see me. When I got to the Schadeks, they told me Mrs. Smallwood had left my check and wanted me to call her. When I did, she asked me if I could come to her house.

As soon as I arrived, Mrs. Smallwood introduced her husband, James. She thanked me for doing an excellent job on the fence. And now, another job was offered! Mrs. Smallwood had bought a condemned restaurant that she'd decided to remodel into a sculptor's studio. She asked for my help in cleaning it. The salary would again be one dollar an hour, she would provide all the necessary supplies, and she had hired a carpenter, Mr. Chlup, to work with me.

I wasn't too enthused about undertaking a cleaning job in some old restaurant, but beggars can't be choosers, so I accepted. We agreed that Mrs. Smallwood would pick me up at 8:30 A.M., and on the way, we would stop at a hardware store to buy some materials for the job.

After we finished our agreement, Mrs. Smallwood's sister, Irene Lasek, came in. Now the conversation changed. I was asked many questions: where I was born, where I was during World War II, and why I had come to the U.S.A. It was late evening by the time I left.

In the morning, Mrs. Smallwood and I stopped at a hardware store and bought rubber gloves, trisodium phosphate, a couple of buckets, sponges, brushes, and a few other items. Then we drove to the restaurant, which was very dark, very dirty, and very greasy. The ceiling was peeling, and the walls were filthy.

Mrs. Smallwood asked me to wash the ceiling and all the walls with the TSP. Mr. Chlup would bring scaffolding and rope to help me arrange a platform, because the ceiling was quite high. She would return in the afternoon to see how the work was progressing.

It looked as if I had my work cut out for me. I took the materials out of the boxes and looked at the directions on the package of trisodium phosphate. After mixing it with the proper amount of water, I put on rubber gloves. With a sponge, I washed a section of one wall. It seemed to look all right. When the carpenter arrived in the afternoon, I had part of one wall clean as high as I could reach.

Mr. Chlup brought paint, ladders, scaffolding, all kinds of wood, rags, and several tools. With the wood, he had to design and build steps, a platform, and shelves for displaying the sculpture. He asked if I could start cleaning the ceiling and the back wall, so he could do all the woodworking there. After he helped me to erect the scaffolding, I started to clean the ceiling.

It was very messy job; the ceiling had to be scraped with a putty knife to get rid of the scaly paint, and then washed with TSP. The liquid ran down into my arm pits, because I was using both hands alternatively. The rubber gloves were disintegrating from the chemical liquid, and my neck soon was aching from constantly looking up.

This had been going on for hours when Mrs. Smallwood came to check on the work. I had quite a bit done by then, and she seemed pleased. She told me that her friend Barbara Hertz, who was a famous sculptress in San Francisco, was going to use the place as a studio. She added that after Mr. Chlup completed the platform, an opening for a door would be cut through the concrete retaining wall, and that from there, steps would lead down into a garden.

Soon after Mrs. Smallwood left, I decided I'd had enough for the day. I locked up and couldn't wait to get home, since I was sticky, sweaty, and soaked from the TSP.

The first thing I did when I arrived at the Odenthalls was to get into the shower and soak my shirt to get rid of the chemical. Then I scrubbed every inch of my body and washed my hair. I suddenly realized I was ravenous, so I heated up a can of chicken noodle soup, and ate it with a buttered roll. Still hungry, I made a hamburger and had it with ketchup on rye bread, followed by coffee and a Danish. I remembered my oldest sister Marie's words. "If you have to work hard, you have to eat well." I decided Marie had been right. After supper, I went to the Petrini Plaza market to buy a thermos. I planned to make sandwiches for lunches and take coffee and pastry with me. That would help make the hard days a little more bearable.

I took the trolley in the morning and began work at 8:00 o'clock. Soon Mr. Chlup arrived, and he started in on his project. Since I was making the floor wet by my tasks and he was adding sawdust with his, it really looked messy.

The worst part of the job was the section of the ceiling and the wall where the restaurant's stove had been. Those areas were so greasy that I had to go over them twice or even three times.

When Mrs. Smallwood came to check on us, she seemed disappointed at our lack of progress. I explained to her the difficulty of the job because of the greasy ceiling and wall area. Then Mr. Chlup pointed out that his part required a lot of measuring and cutting before the actual assembling could begin. Before she left, Mrs. Smallwood asked if I could work overtime—one hour in the morning and two hours in the evening.

But on Friday, I worked only until 6:00 P.M. I wanted to go to the Sokol Club, my only form of entertainment. When I arrived, Fred Divisek was there with his wife and Irene, Mrs. Smallwood's sister. They asked me to join them. Irene had already told them about job I was doing for her sister, so I launched into a description of all the difficulties that were involved in the work. Irene explained that her sister played cards every day with Barbara Hertz, the sculptress, who undoubtedly was pushing for the studio to be finished.

Fred asked me if I had a driver's license. When I told him I had my military license from Czechoslovakia, which I thought was valid all over the world, he said, "That's not true. You have to get a driver's test here from the Department of Motor Vehicles. I'll loan you my station wagon when you go to take the test." Fred offered to let me drive his car Sunday afternoon, so I'd be prepared for the test. I asked Irene what kind of car she drove. She replied that she had neither a car nor a license; the Diviseks always brought her to the club. Fred wondered how I managed without a car. I replied that I was saving money to buy one, hopefully soon.

Fred picked me up Sunday. To my relief—and his—I had no problem driving the station wagon. He assured me I would pass the test, but suggested I apply soon, because it might take a long time to get an appointment.

On Monday I was back on the job. After three days my washing job was finished. Now I had to scrub the floor, pick up the sawdust that had adhered to the wet areas, and help Mr. Chlup stack the unused wood.

On Wednesday Mrs. Smallwood came again to inspect our work. This time she was much happier, and said that now she could have a contractor make the opening in the concrete wall. I told her I could do it, because I'd had a lot of experience in Australia opening sidewalk trenches for laying underground telephone cables. She looked at me with a great deal of surprise "You must be joking. What else can you do?" I replied that I'd had about two dozen different jobs before this one. All I would need for the opening were a compressor and jackhammer, which her husband, who was a plumber, could rent. Mrs. Smallwood said she would talk to him about it.

I was curious as to what the garden was like on the other side of the concrete retaining wall, and Mrs. Smallwood offered to drive me there. I couldn't believe it was necessary to drive to what was essentially the building's back yard, but when I saw it, I understood. The retaining wall had been ordered by the city to protect guests in the restaurant, Mrs. Smallwood explained, and that caused the peculiar division of the property.

When we entered the garden, it was full of yellow flowers—as if it had a yellow floor—and at the side there was a large lattice structure on which roses were climbing. The roses were pretty, but full of dead branches and leaves, as if they'd been unattended for a long time. I mentioned that I could help with them, since pruning and grafting had been my hobby in Czechoslovakia. Mrs. Smallwood said she would think about it, but first we must finish the studio.

The next morning the compressor and jackhammer that Mr. Smallwood had rented were delivered. The renting company installed the equipment in the designated place, and the delivery man showed me how to start the compressor. Luckily, it was similar to the one that I had used in Australia.

Mr. Chlup and I marked the wall where the opening had to be made. Now I had to do the job—which wasn't easy, due to the vibration, the dust, the noise, and the fact that the jackhammer had to be used in a horizontal position. It was very hard on my arms, and I had to wear a mask and goggles. It took quite some time before the opening was finished and ready for Mr. Chlup to install the door.

While Mr. Chlup was working on the installation, I cleaned up the pieces of concrete, then dug out a space behind the cavity for the concrete steps. Luckily, there were no large boulders, and I could manage with a pick and shovel. When I finished, we made some forms for the steps out of scrap wood.

The next day Mr. Chlup brought several bags of concrete and a wheelbarrow in which we prepared the mix. It was very hard work, especially carrying the mix in buckets to fill the forms for the steps. However, we managed. I smoothed the surfaces, then let the concrete dry.

By the end of the week, the restaurant had begun to look like a studio. The forms from the steps were removed, the concrete pieces and excess wood were hauled away, and now the place was ready to be painted. When Mrs. Smallwood gave me my second week's pay, I jokingly asked her if I could paint the studio. To my surprise, she agreed, so I confidently said I would use white since the area was rather dark. I told her that by Sunday night it would all be done, except for the woodwork, which was a job for Mr. Chlup. She said that Mr. Smallwood would deliver the paint, brushes, rollers, and other necessary items early Saturday morning. Mr. Chlup agreed to let me use his scaffolding and ladders.

On Friday I went to the club as usual. I needed to get away from that messy and dusty job and be in a different atmosphere. Fred Divisek was there, and we sat together. During our conversation, Fred mentioned that he was a partner in the Rowland Music Company and played for the San Francisco Symphony Orchestra. But before I'd had a chance to learn more about his music career, he inquired about my progress with the remodeling of the restaurant. I told him that now we would have to call it the studio, since it was finished except for painting. He asked me when I was planning to go for my driving test. I replied that as soon as I finished the painting, I would have time to take the test.

Early the next day, I prepared the scaffolding in the far end of the studio, so that the section around the door and veranda would be done before Mr. Chlup started on the woodwork. At nine o'clock, Mr. Smallwood arrived with the supplies, and I was ready to start. The most difficult part was the ceiling and the high areas of the wall. I had to cover the floor, section by section, to catch the dripping paint. But by the end of the day, I had the whole ceiling and about one-third of the rear area completed.

On Sunday, I started to paint the walls, which were a lot easier than the ceiling. By late afternoon, I was finished. When I returned home, I called Mrs. Smallwood to tell her that my portion of the painting was done, and that in the morning I would wash the windows. She was thrilled, and thanked me for sacrificing my weekend.

After supper, I decided to visit Mr. and Mrs. Schadek who were happy to see me after such a long time. When they inquired about my job status, I told them about my latest one, but said that after Monday, I would be unemployed. Mrs. Schadek offered to continue watching the want ads for me. She complained about the pain in her leg and said the doctor had prescribed stronger medication. He was concerned about some purple discoloration, which was a sign that her poor circulation was getting worse. I was sorry about her problems, and wished I could help. After more conversation, I asked Mrs. Schadek if I could use the phone.

I called Fred and told him that I intended to go to the Department of Motor Vehicles to make an appointment for the driving test. He said any day would be fine with him. I thanked him, and thanked Mrs. Schadek for the use of her phone. Because of her bad leg, she asked me to make tea. When she inquired about my relatives, I reported that I had been so tired that I hadn't even written them.

In the morning, I took some cleaning spray, paper towels, and a sponge. I was ready to finish this awful job. The windows and even the doors were dirty from all the dust, so it took me a long time. When Mr. Chlup came to paint the woodwork, he was pleasantly surprised to see that my part was completed. He smiled and said, "George, you have your head screwed on right."

Mr. Smallwood came in to do the plumbing, and asked me to help him. I also helped Mr. Chlup disassemble the scaffolding. Then, finally, the job was done. I gave Mr. Smallwood an account of the hours I had worked, my new address, and the telephone number of Mrs. Odenthall, where a message could be left for me. I shook hands with him and Mr. Chlup, and left. Mission accomplished—but here I was unemployed again.

The next day I went to the Department of Motor Vehicles, and was given an appointment for Thursday, at 9:00 A.M. I went to Mrs. Schadek's house and phoned Fred about the appointment. While Mrs. Schadek and

I had tea, she gloomily informed me that there were no jobs in the want ads.

On Wednesday, I wrote a few letters and enjoyed some much-needed rest.

Fred stopped by Thursday morning, and gave me the key to his station wagon. I went to the DMV, and took the test. An officer sat next to me and directed me to drive around, left and right, through some stop signs and back. When we returned to the station, he said everything went well, and I passed but he couldn't give me one hundred percent because I had rested my left elbow on the door. Well, I learned something again: no one is one hundred percent.

After the test, Fred took me home and said he had talked to Mr. Rowland about giving me a job. I should go there in the morning to inquire about it. I was very surprised and relieved. Maybe I wasn't going to be unemployed, after all!

CHAPTER 32

JOB AT ROWLAND MUSIC CO.

I HAD NO IDEA WHAT KIND OF JOB I MIGHT HAVE AT THE ROWLAND MUSIC CO. When I entered, Fred introduced me to Mr. Rowland, who was tall, good-looking and much younger than Fred.

The store was not very large and not very well-organized. The building was old and needed painting on both the outside and the inside. Mr. Rowland took me upstairs, where he had some tools and spraying equipment. He showed me a small piano that I was supposed to refinish, and gave me a few instructions. I had never done this kind of work before. I stripped off the paint, sanded the piano, and sprayed it with the first coat. Later that day I gave it a final coat.

My next job was to open boxes of musical instruments and place them in the stock room. A few of these were held out to be displayed in the front window, and I did my best to find a place for them among some other instruments that were already there. But no matter how I arranged them, I didn't like the outcome. They were all on a flat floor and sitting on white paper. I tried to think of some way to improve the presentation.

When I went to the stock room to put away the empty boxes, I suddenly had an idea. Those boxes could be arranged in the front window, with the instruments displayed on top of them. But the boxes would somehow have to be covered. Now I had another idea. I had noticed that upstairs there was velour curtain hanging on some kind of traverse rod, which at some point had probably been used to divide the room. The color was perfect, sky blue. I went downstairs and told Fred what I had in mind. He hesitated for a moment, then asked me to speak to Mr. Rowland, who agreed to my plan. I took several boxes down to match them with the instruments. Then I carried down the curtain, which was surprisingly heavy.

I started to place the boxes in a staggered arrangement: the tallest boxes were placed in the back, with the smaller boxes at different levels in front. Then I covered them with that beautiful velour curtain, making folds between the boxes. I placed the instruments on top of the boxes, including some small items such as harmonicas, mutes, mouthpieces, etc. It looked quite nice, but I still was not satisfied.

Something had to be done with the background. I asked Mr. Rowland if he had some peg-board with which to make a wall in the middle. I would devise a gate through that, so instruments could be taken out and changes could be made to the display. He liked the idea, called his supply house, and had the material delivered that same day. Luckily, there was a saw, a drill, and other tools I needed already on the premises.

I measured everything, cut the peg-board to the correct size, made some framing, hung the gate on hinges. When it was all finished, I painted everything white. I thought it looked very well with the blue velour, and invited the staff to give their opinion. They were all delighted. With a smile, Mr. Rowland said, "George, well done! I don't think we've ever had such a nice arrangement in this window. Thank you."

Unfortunately—beautiful display notwithstanding—there was not enough business to keep me occupied. Fred told me that Mr. Rowland was thinking of selling the business and would have to let me go. But he gave me the name of a friend, the owner of the Viking Food Company, and said he'd arranged for me to get a job there. Once again, I had reason to be grateful to Fred. At least I wouldn't have to tell the Schadeks I was unemployed again!

CHAPTER 33

THE VIKING FOOD COMPANY

I WENT STRAIGHT FROM MY MOST RECENT JOB TO THE VIKING FOOD COMPANY shop in downtown San Francisco, where I asked to see Walter, the manager.

I introduced myself to Walter, who told me to report at 2:00 A.M. I was to work on the third shift making sandwiches until 10:00 A.M. I was rather shocked; I hadn't realized that Viking was open twenty-four hours a day. But of course, I needed the job. I walked around to look at the place. In addition to the food preparation area, there was a small restaurant that sold sandwiches and drinks.

The next morning, I reported to work a little before two o'clock, and to my great surprise, Walter was there. He showed me around and introduced me to three other workers, two ladies and a man, named Art, who was supposed to teach me the job. Art himself was responsible for bringing in all kind of supplies.

Within a few minutes, I heard an announcement on the intercom, "seventy-five liverwurst on rye." Art pointed out where to get the bread, and put a keg of pickles and a large pot of mustard next to my work area. The name of the bread was "Langendorf," which I will never forget as long as I live. The bread was on a flattop cart with casters so it could be moved around easily.

Now came the time to make those seventy-five sandwiches of liverwurst on rye. Art showed me how to break a loaf quickly, take five slices in each hand and spread fifteen of them in line, five deep. This, of course, made seventy-five. He picked up a four-inch paint brush, dipped it into the large pot of mustard, and demonstrated how to brush the mustard on them. Finally he stacked the liverwurst and the pickles on half of the slice, then put the other slices on top—and we had seventy-five sandwiches. He took a long butcher knife and cut them from corner to corner, and that was it. I had put them all on a huge tray and give it to one of the ladies at the far end of the counter, who packaged the sandwiches in wax paper. Then the other lady ironed the edges of wax paper to seal them. This finished the operation, and they were now ready to be picked up in the morning by van drivers, who would deliver them to vending machines located in nearby businesses.

The next announcement on the intercom was, "one hundred ham and cheese," and the process repeated itself. I was so busy that I didn't even have time to eat one. But I didn't see any of the workers eat the sandwiches, either, which helped me to hold off. Maybe they knew something I didn't.

Soon the van drivers returned, and I noticed that they brought back sandwiches that had not been sold the previous day. These sandwiches were left in our work area, where one of the ladies marked the edges with a steel point that left no visible mark. After these returned sandwiches were invisibly "branded," they were put on trays and carried into the restaurant area, where they were displayed behind glass to be sold. No one knew that they were not fresh. These had to be sold first, before any new sandwiches were made for the restaurant.

Well, here I was, "a sandwich—making expert"—another contribution to my previous experiences. How great! Despite all my education in Czechoslovakia, I was bouncing from one ridiculous job to another. Did I come to America to be a sandwich-maker, a show-window arranger, a pick-and-shovel man, a jackhammer operator, a ladies' apparel sorter-and-shipper? What a career! But I tried not to worry, because I felt sure that one of these mornings the sun would appear on the horizon, and a better job would come along. I was in the U.S.A., where there were so many opportunities to build a bright future. My current weekly pay was $43 after deductions—this certainly was not too promising for a bright future—but I was determined to save every penny I could. I was an optimist, and I knew somehow, someday, I would be able to use my education, to find a wife, to raise a family.

At the end of my second week at the Viking Food Company, Walter gave me my paycheck and said, "Sorry, George, I can't keep you because you're too slow. I need someone more experienced. I wish you good luck."

Here I was without a job again.

I went to a nearby Bank of America to deposit my check, as I was trying to build up my savings, and from each paycheck, I managed to save some money.

Of course, I didn't know where my next paycheck would come from.

CHAPTER 34

RECORDAK CORP.

NOW, I HAD A FAMILIAR WORRY: TO SEARCH FOR A NEW JOB.

I went to Mr. and Mrs. Schadek's house to tell them my sad news. They were very sympathetic. Mrs. Schadek said, "It's all for the best, George, because that job was not for a man of your talents. Don't worry, something else will turn up in the near future." Mr. Schadek added, "George, these things happen in life and you have to learn to take disappointments."

It was a bright morning. I wasn't exactly in a singing mood and all kinds of thoughts were popping into my mind as to what I should do. Since it was Friday, I planned to go to the Sokol Club to see my friends, maybe they could cheer me up.

When I walked into the refreshment room of the club that evening, I saw some familiar faces. However, it was not unusual that every Friday some new members would come to have a drink and a visit. Prices for drinks were much lower than anywhere else in the city. A bottle of wine cost seventy-nine cents.

As I looked around the room, I noticed an unfamiliar face, obviously a visitor, who was talking to some of the members. I went to greet them and had a few words with them in Czech.

A friend introduced me to the stranger whose name was Jack Pilersky. I invited Jack to have a drink with me. After a glass of wine, we had quite a long conversation. He had worked for the Eastman Kodak

Company in Prague a number of years ago, then later worked for the same company in New York. At the present time, he was employed by a Kodak subsidiary, the Recordak Corporation, which was located at 350 Mission Street in San Francisco.

When he asked me where I worked, I replied I had just lost my job that very day and was now looking for another one. Jack inquired about my education and previous employment. It took quite a long time to explain my varied work experiences, but he listened patiently.

Little by little, the members were leaving as it was getting late. I had spent the entire evening talking with Jack, who thanked me for the wine. He said they were quite busy at Recordak, so he would ask his supervisor if there was some sort of job for me. To my great surprise, Jack invited me to have breakfast with him and his wife at their home on Sunday morning. He lived very near me, across the street from the Golden Gate Park.

The next day, Saturday, I visited Mr. and Mrs. Schadek to look at the want ads. Unfortunately, there were none available. When I told the Schadeks about Jack's offer to help, they wished me good luck.

On Sunday I went to the home of Jack and Marie Pilersky, both of whom were from Czechoslovakia. Mrs. Pilersky prepared a delicious breakfast of scrambled eggs, bacon, toast and coffee, followed by homemade pastry. Before I left, Jack gave me their telephone number and asked me to call him Monday night. I thanked them for the very nice breakfast and for a most enjoyable visit,.

I had been informed at the club about the frequent concerts in the Golden Gate Park, where the San Francisco Symphony Orchestra performed without charge. To end the day I went there. I was looking for enjoyment, and thought I might meet some nice girl—but had no luck.

Monday night I called Jack from the Schadeks. I had doubtful feelings that anything positive would come from my call, because so many times before, I had heard those words, "I'll let you know," when people were trying to be polite. This time I was very surprised. Jack told me he had spoken with his manager, Joe Cavanaugh, who wanted to interview me the next day. It looked promising, Jack said, because they were very busy.

I was so surprised! I thanked him and said I'd be there. Mr. and Mrs. Schadek were very pleased to hear this hopeful news.

On Tuesday, I went to see Joe Cavanaugh at 9:00 A.M. He asked me to sit down, and we had a long conversation. He was a very pleasant man, about forty-five years old, who said he was originally from Flushing. New York. Joe asked me when I could start working, told me my wages, and explained I would be an assistant to Eddie, the maintenance man in the laboratory.

We went to the lab, where Joe introduced me to Eddie. I still couldn't quite believe that I had found a job so quickly. Eddie said I could start the next morning. "Bring some work clothes," he said, because I would be mixing chemicals for developing film. I was extremely happy, thanked him, and we shook hands.

Before I left, I inquired about where Jack worked. Eddie asked a secretary to take me to Jack's area in the parts and tool department, which was like a huge cage. I told Jack about the job and thanked him with tears in my eyes; I was just overwhelmed that there were so many kind people who were willing to help me. Jack smiled and said, "Now there are three Czechs here." The third Czech was a friend of his, Frank Holubar, who was employed in the darkroom.

Curious, I asked Jack why he worked in this cage. He explained that he issued all kinds of expensive items that were kept under lock and key. Employees had to sign for any of these items that they borrowed for a job. After this short conversation, I thanked Jack again and asked him to extend my best regards to his wife.

I couldn't wait to tell my good news to Mr. and Mrs. Schadek, who were elated. Then I went home to prepare for the next day. I checked my overalls to be sure they were clean. During my discussion with Jack, he told me there was a room where coffee was available, but that it would be a good idea to bring a sandwich for lunch, since Recordak didn't have any vending machines. After my experience at Viking, I was just as well pleased with that news!

The next day I left early and took the trolley downtown. I wanted to be on time, but found it took me only about twenty minutes to reach work. When I arrived, no one was there, and the laboratory door was closed. I waited, and at 7:30 Eddie showed up. He led me through the lab and turned on all kinds of switches, including one that took care of the air conditioning, and a special pump that purified the air.

Of course, everything was totally new to me, and Eddie had to show me one phase after another. My first order of business was to clean the rubber wheels on the racks: four with eight wheels in the developer, four with eight wheels in the hypo, and four with eight wheels in the water tanks. The rollers had to be absolutely clean of anything that would scratch the 16 mm film. Eddie said we would develop and process ninety thousand feet of film a day. My other task was to mix the developer and hypo, each in thousand-liter tanks.

After a few days, all this was just routine and repetitious, not requiring a full eight hours. During the extra time, Frank Holubar, the third Czech employee, taught me how to make facsimiles in the darkroom. This was done by projecting light through a lens above the film onto sensitized paper, which was first dipped into developer, then hypo, then dried outside of the darkroom on a huge heated drum.

Eddie was a young fellow, twenty-four years old, and very handy. He'd been trained in the New York laboratory and then transferred to San Francisco. He was married but had no children. Eddie confided that he had a problem because his wife didn't like to live so far from New York, where her family was. This worried Eddie, because he liked his job and liked San Francisco.

Our maintenance shop had all possible tools one could think of. Eddie built a table saw for cutting wood and showed me how to use it. On occasion we had to do some plumbing, with either stainless steel or copper tubing, to prevent any possibility of rust. We also did some electrical work—conduit installations to protect the wiring from chemicals, and relocating fluorescent light fixtures wherever they were needed. We even installed floor tiles and oiled the film—handling equipment.

I knew that California occasionally had earthquakes, but I couldn't imagine such a thing—until I experienced one for myself in 1956. I had just finished mixing one thousand liters of hypo in a large stainless steel tank on the ground floor, from which it was transferred by pump into another, almost ceiling high tank that rested on a strong steel structure. Just as the pumping was finished, the building began to shake: the hypo was splashing out of the tank onto the concrete floor, the fluorescent fixtures were swaying, and tools and other equipment were falling on the floor. As I read somewhere that one should stand in a door or in the corner of a room during an earthquake, I immediately rushed to the doorway. When it ended after several seconds, I ran into the film-processing area to see if any help was needed. Luckily, there was no noticeable damage except for a two-inch crack down the entire length of the wall. The film-processing machine was running and two operators were still attending it, but the rest of the employees had stopped work and were looking at each other in a daze.

After a while, things went back to normal. Now I knew something about an earthquake, even if nothing serious had happened. I had to mop up the hypo, then put everything that had fallen to the floor back in place. The employees were still talking about it for several days later, expecting some aftershocks. Luckily, none came along.

I liked my job in spite of the fact that it had nothing to do with my college education. It was very diversified; every day something new came along, and either Eddie or I had to take care of it. Eddie strictly did maintenance, but I went from one job to another, wherever help was needed-mostly in the darkroom. I didn't mind as I had a chance to work overtime, even on Saturdays, and earned good money. One day when Marie Pollock, the secretary, came to my work area to pick up my time card, she said, "George, Mr. Cavanaugh told me that if he had ten employees like you, he could send many others home." Well, it was nice to hear that, but I took the compliment with some reservation. I did think about it, however, and began to look around to see how the others worked.

Many of the employees smoked, and while smoking, the work naturally slowed down or even stopped. Perhaps that was a factor, since I didn't smoke. I couldn't anyway, because I was around film a lot, and in the darkroom, smoking was not allowed. If anyone watched me they could see I was constantly working, and that most likely gave the boss a favorable impression. Marie's statement, gave me a certain assurance that my job was safe.

One day Frank Holubar came to my workshop and said that he and his wife, who was also Czech, would like me to come for dinner on Sunday. They had two daughters, Eva and Helena who both spoke Czech. During our conversation Sunday evening, Frank told me that years ago, he had worked in the Czech Embassy in Vienna. Mrs. Holubar prepared an excellent meal. Much to my surprise, as I was about to leave, she handed me a box that contained a homemade cake. It was very kind of her. I thanked her for it and for the delicious dinner. Before I left, I gave each girl a silver dollar.

One day, when I was visiting Mr. and Mrs. Schadek, they had a guest, Mr. Cunningham. He was from England, was retired, and was making a tour of the United States. He had bought a car, a 1948 DeSoto. Now he wanted to sell it and fly back to England.

Since I was interested in buying a car, he showed it to me and told me the price was three hundred dollars. Mr. Schadek said it was a good buy and suggested I take it for a short spin. The car had fluid drive. When it went into motion, one had to lift his foot off the peddle to allow the automatic to engage in second gear. After that it was fully automatic. I offered Mr. Cunningham two hundred and fifty dollars. After some hesitation, we settled the deal for two hundred and seventy-five dollars. The next day I paid him, and now I was the proud owner of a car that seemed as large as a ship. What a difference from the 1939 Vauxhall convertible I had owned in Australia!

Several months had gone by since my arrival in San Francisco. Soon after I had arrived there, I sent letters and postcards to my relatives in Czechoslovakia, to my former boss in England, and to some friends in Melbourne, because several of them wanted to come to America. If they decided to come to San Francisco, I offered to meet them and assist them in any way I could.

Soon some began to arrive. They needed sponsors who could give them an Affidavit of Support and a certificate of accommodation, just as I had to have. I couldn't help them in that respect, but they managed to receive help from various churches and from relatives. However, I did help one Czech, Josef Richter, a butcher, as I knew he wouldn't have any problem finding a job. The papers cost me the lawyer's fee of fifteen dollars, which Josef repaid me after he arrived.

One day when I went home, I was very surprised to see my very good friend, Bob Pribyl, with whom I used to sit in the Czechoslovak restaurant, Praha, in Melbourne. He explained he had purchased an airline ticket at a very reasonable price from someone who couldn't leave Melbourne, and that he hadn't had time to notify me.

Bob was an excellent barber, but he could barely make himself understood in English. But for his trade, English was not that essential. In Melbourne, he worked in a very exclusive barbershop, where he made a good salary and excellent tips. He also was a very good cook.

Because I lived in a room, I couldn't offer Bob overnight lodging; so I decided to take him to Mr. and Mrs. Schadek, hoping that they would help. My idea met with success. Mrs. Schadek was impressed that he knew how to cook, since both she and her husband had difficulty walking. Bob was now all settled, and I was happy that this arrangement was made. When I told Bob about the Sokol Club, he agreed to go with me one evening.

During the Friday sessions, different guests would often come with the regular members. This particular Friday, two pretty girls were there that I had never seen before. Mrs. Chlup, the restaurant manager, told me that they were from Toronto.

As they were sitting alone, Bob and I decided to welcome them. We introduced ourselves and asked if we could join them. Drahomira was Czech, and Margaret was English. Drahomira spoke English very well, and did most of the talking. She said they were in San Francisco on vacation, and were staying at a hotel downtown near Gary Street. We had a very nice evening, exchanging stories about our travels. During our conversation, I asked the girls how they liked Toronto. It turned out that they were not exactly happy there, and were undecided as to where to settle. That's the reason they had taken this trip to California. This was welcome news to me, since Drahomira—Mira—interested me very much from the first glance. But Bob was not exactly the right person for Margaret, as he was forty-three and she was twenty-five. Still, we could make a foursome.

As the weekend was coming, I asked the girls if they would like to go on a ride with Bob and me to the Napa Valley, across the Golden Gate bridge. I knew it was warmer there, and we could enjoy the swimming pools. When they accepted, I drove them to their hotel and said we would see them the next morning.

CHAPTER 35

SAN FRANCISCO
LATER MONTHS

THE NEXT DAY WAS PLEASANT, ALTHOUGH THE SUN WAS HIDDEN BEHIND WHAT is known as the "traveling fog" over the city. It is not actually fog, but a huge cloud that blocks the sun, mostly during the summer months of June and July.

We went across the Golden Gate bridge and after a few miles were in a sunny area. Soon we reached the Napa Valley and the swimming pools. There were many people there, and surprisingly enough, even members of our club. None of us had brought bathing suits, but we had a couple of blankets to sit on while enjoying the sun and watching the swimmers. That evening, we drove back to San Francisco and ate at a large cafeteria.

On Sunday I invited the girls and Bob to take a trip to Mt. Tamalpais, on the other side of the bay. It was one of the highest of the local mountains, with a long winding road. When we reached the top, it seemed as if we could touch the clouds. The view was beautiful, and we were fortunate to have good weather.

When we returned to San Francisco, we went to the same cafeteria, and because Bob didn't have a job, I was the host. Then we drove to Golden Gate Park, where we took a nice walk to end the day. I told the girls I would call them during the week to make plans.

Monday morning Joe Cavanaugh asked Eddie and me if we could

paint the laboratory and do an extensive cleanup, because some visitor was coming from the company headquarters in Rochester, New York. Since I was too busy to go out with the girls during the week, I decided to see them on Friday at the club.

When I entered the club on Friday, I saw only Margaret, who was talking to one of the members named Nelson. She told me that Mira was in the gym playing volleyball. I went to the balcony and observed that she was a good player. After the game, I asked Mira about the weekend, but she said that she'd decided to go to Vancouver to visit a friend. I offered to drive Mira back to her hotel, but she had already accepted a ride with Nelson and Margaret.

Well, George, I said to myself, this looks like another episode that has collapsed. I thought I might have become more interested in Mira, but her leaving for Vancouver put an end to it.

The following week the big shot from Rochester arrived, and Eddie and I were introduced to him. He seemed pleased with the appearance of the place. With him was our director, Mr. Spalteholz, who was in charge of Kodak's western region. Mr. Spalteholz liked me, and called me "Cookie," because every time he saw me in the coffee room, I was eating a cookie with my coffee.

One day he asked me several questions about my past experiences, and when I mentioned I knew how to prune trees, he said he was looking for someone to prune his sycamores. I offered to look at them and see what I could do. He lived in Redwood City, and the following Sunday I went there with my tools. He had three large sycamore trees that badly needed pruning. It was fortunate I arrived early in the morning, because I could finish the job in one day. I had my thermos of coffee, and guess what else? Cookies, of course! I had them with my coffee when I took a break.

When I was finished, I knocked at the door to ask if I could wash my hands. I didn't see any lady, and assumed that Mr. Spalteholz was either a widower or divorced. As I was coming out of the bathroom, a little dog snapped at me when I bent down to pet him. Then he bit me in the palm of my hand. His master apologized, and offered to take me to a doctor for a rabies shot. I declined because the bite was so small. Mr. Spalteholz gave me a bandage and inquired as to how much he owed me-but since he was the director, I said there would be no charge.

The next day he came into my lab and gave me a check for $15 and a small box. Guess what was in the box! Cookies! They were delicious, and he said he had baked them himself. That was an unusual treat for me-cookies from the director. Mr. Spalteholz even offered me a job as manager of the Phoenix branch. I was very much surprised and pleased, but I declined because I had heard it was extremely hot in Arizona, and I had enough heat in Australia. I think Mr. Spalteholz worried that, with my educational background, I could do better than work as a maintenance man, and he was trying to help me get ahead.

One day my supervisor, Joe Cavanaugh, told me that Eddie's wife had finally convinced him to return to New York. Joe offered me Eddie's job, and with a great deal of surprise and pride, I accepted and thanked him. I was confident that I could do it, since I did most of the actual work while Eddie walked around, looked at machines, and appeared busy.

There was a little party for Eddie, and he was presented a cake and a gift. We all wished him well. I knew he wasn't happy about leaving, but he'd always known that eventually his wife would insist on the move.

The day after Eddie left, a very important pump, designed to purify air through water, was not working to satisfaction. Joe decided to order a new one. When it arrived, he asked me if I thought I could install it. I looked it over, and saw that it primarily involved a lot of copper tubing and making sweat joints.

I agreed to do the job, and Joe told me that it had to be done over the weekend so that production could resume on Monday. He was happy that I accepted, and said he would help me. I didn't need help as far as assembling was concerned, but I needed assistance to hold the pieces of pipe while I made the sweat joints. We progressed quite well, and in twenty-three hours the pump was installed. We only needed an electrician to put in a certain type of heater, and that completed the job.

On Monday, I started the pump, and it went fine for a while, then stopped. We looked for leaks in the water supply or air supply, but everything was in order. Finally, we decided to call the electrician, who admitted he had put in the wrong heater. He came back, installed another size, and everything was fine. Joe and I were quite proud, since we had saved the company much money by not hiring a contractor to work on a weekend.

Because some customers ordered several copies of one-hundred-foot reels of 16mm film, an employee had to rewind each reel to run it on a special projector. To eliminate this extra rewinding, I designed and made a rig that could run indefinitely. The only thing that had to be done was to watch for the splice and record the number of times the splice went through. This method would save a lot of time.

I was extremely busy and had lost contact with the girls. I'd even missed several sessions at the club, but I finally went one Friday evening. Bob had found a job at a barbers' school, where apprentice barbers were taught. I saw only Margaret at the club, and asked Mrs. Chlup, the manager, where Mira was. She told me that Mira hadn't yet returned from Vancouver.

Margaret was dating Nelson, a Czech refugee who now lived in the U.S.A. Mrs. Chlup knew I had become fond of Mira, and advised me to go to Vancouver. But that wasn't possible, so somehow, I had to put her out of my mind. I kept busy at work and received a salary increase.

Shortly before Christmas, Bob surprised me by announcing that he was returning to Australia because the U.S. requirements to become a barber were too stringent. He would have to go to school and pass exams about the human head before his license would be issued, and Bob realized his English just wasn't good enough. Mr. and Mrs. Schadek were sad about losing him; he had become like a son, cooking and doing all their chores.

I had another surprise. I received a card from Mira in Vancouver wishing me a Merry Christmas and a Happy New Year-but with no return address. I took it as no more than a little "thank you" for the rides and hospitality I had given her and Margaret.

Yet another surprise was that Margaret had become engaged to Nelson. Now the chapter on both girls was just about closed. One can't win all the time, but life had to go on.

I had no plans for Christmas. However, I didn't think I should spend the holidays at the Schadeks. I was still very busy and hardly had enough time to write Christmas cards to my relatives and my friends.

Nevertheless, the last Friday before Christmas, I went to the club and found Fred and Ann Divisek there. With them were two ladies: Irene Lasek, Mrs. Smallwood's sister, and Mrs. Marie Vogl, who was from Czechoslovakia. Mrs. Vogl came from the town of Skutec, where she'd had a business selling linen, lingerie, shirts, and tablecloths. We had a nice evening with the Diviseks, and I offered Irene and Mrs. Vogl a ride home. Fred and Ann also invited the three of us to spend Christmas with them.

We had a very pleasant Christmas—my first in the U.S.A., so it was one that I will never forget. The Diviseks had two children: Karen, who was about 9 years old, and Jimmy, who was 7. The children added to the joyful festivities. Fred and Ann invited us all again to spend New Year's Eve and New Year's Day with them. It was difficult for the Diviseks to find a baby-sitter, so they always celebrated the holidays at home. We spent the evening playing cards.

After the holidays, everything went back to normal, except for the fact that I was beginning to see Irene more often. She would invite me to her apartment, because we both liked music and she had many records. We enjoyed each other's company and sometimes went sightseeing, watching the sea lions on the little island by Cliff House, and driving to the other side of the bay across the Golden Gate bridge.

One day Irene suggested that we visit her mother, who lived in Santa Ana with another of Irene's sisters, Elsie, and her husband Clyde. Her mother was totally deaf, and Irene told me, the only way to have a conversation was for her to read lips.

We started our trip very early in the morning in order to return the same day. In the vicinity of Santa Ana, there were many trees filled with oranges, and hundreds of oranges on the ground, wasted. It almost broke my heart, because as it brought back memories of when my sister would bring home one orange a week, and what a treat it was. Here they were rotting on the ground. What a shame!

Elsie and Clyde were very friendly and hospitable. They wanted to hear about my experiences in Czechoslovakia, and we had a very pleasant day with them.

I would occasionally go for a walk to the nearby Golden Gate park, especially when there was a concert. These were especially enjoyable to me, because Fred Divisek was a drummer with the San Francisco Symphony Orchestra. Better yet, there was no admission to these concerts, because they were organized by the city. One day I was caught off guard. The president of the club, Joe Malek, saw me in the audience and-without warning me-went to the microphone and asked me to welcome any Czech immigrants who were there. I certainly wasn't prepared, but I couldn't disappoint him. So I simply said, "Thank you, brother president, for giving me this opportunity to stand in front of this wonderful audience. I would like to welcome all of you as I am one of you. Also, I want to thank all our sponsors who helped us come to this wonderful country of freedom. Without them we wouldn't be here. Thank you."

That was my quick, impromptu speech for which I received much applause. On the stage near the band were some ladies in Czech, Moravian, and Slovak national costumes. I learned the day had been organized as "Czechoslovak Day," and just by chance, I happened to be there.

At one of the club meetings, it was decided we would present a play, The Niece. I was given the part of the bridegroom who was courting the aunt's niece. Mrs. Vogl was chosen to play the aunt, and Ann Divisek, the niece. There was a loveseat on the stage on which I was supposed to become better acquainted with the niece. After some persuasion, the aunt agreed to the marriage. This was the first play given by the club and was a great success. The gym hall was packed, and we received a wonderful ovation.

Once in a while, I would write to my sponsors, my "aunt" and "uncle" in New Jersey. When they replied, they invariably always asked when I was coming to see them or even to settle there. I always found some excuse to postpone my visit, because I wanted to see more of California, and because I needed to save more money before making a cross-country trip.

I found a postcard in my mail one day, written by my aunt. It was sent to me from a festival they had attended. After a few words of greeting, there were five signatures: Anna Zack, Joseph Zack, Tessie Sytar, Joseph Sytar, and Jo Ann Sytar, (friends of the Zacks.) I was puzzled by the name, Jo Ann, because I had never heard the name before. When I answered to thank my aunt for the card, I inquired about her friends, Joseph, Tessie, and Jo Ann.

When Mrs. Zack replied, she wrote that Jo Ann was the daughter of Mr. and Mrs. Sytar, and that her name was abbreviated from Josephine Ann. In my next letter, I asked my aunt to send me the Sytars' address. When the reply came, I wrote a note to Jo Ann, asking her to thank her parents for their greetings, and requesting that she write me something about herself.

Several days later, Jo Ann replied that she was a model at a very exclusive store, Bergdorf Goodman on Fifth Avenue, and that she lived with her parents in New York City in a building with the name "Sokol." I knew the building must be similar to many all over the United States where Czech immigrants had settled and built Sokol halls with apartments.

This, of course, led to more frequent exchanges of correspondence as I wanted to learn Jo Ann's age, if she had a boyfriend, and if she could speak or at least understand Czech. She replied that she was about my age, she spoke Czech fluently, she was not engaged-but she didn't answer my question as to whether she had a boyfriend. I guessed she most likely did, but because she continued to write me, I also assumed she didn't have a serious relationship with anyone. We exchanged several letters as pen pals, but as I was so busy working overtime, I didn't write as often as she did. Thus, the letter exchange was one letter from me to two or three from Jo Ann. She complained a little about this, but she continued to write me about her activities and her family. I asked her for her phone number because I was curious to both hear her voice and hear her speak Czech.

To my astonishment, she spoke Czech very fluently and had a nice voice. That made me more interested in her, but the only problem was she was becoming slightly annoyed at my laxity in replying to her letters and not phoning her enough. Then she began to write less frequently, and that worried me since I wanted to keep in contact.

I told Fred and Ann Divisek about my pen pal, and they advised me that the only way to resolve this was to go to New York and meet her in person. I thought about their idea, but I must confess that I thought it would be more advantageous if I could find some Czech-speaking girl in or near San Francisco. Once in a while I did meet a girl whose parents were Czech immigrants, but the girl was either too young or too old. It really was not easy to find a girl with an age close to mine who could speak and understand Czech.

When I learned there was a Yugoslav church in San Francisco, I decided to attend one of the Sunday masses. I understood some of the Yugoslav language and thought I might meet some prospect there. In front of the church, there were about forty people. No one spoke to me, and no one seemed interested in greeting a stranger. Therefore, I went home.

At the club, I met a Czech who had lived in England, married a very attractive English girl, and eventually emigrated to the United States. He took me over to introduce me to his wife who was sitting at a table alone, knitting. At adjacent tables were other guests, Czech-speaking, laughing and having a good time. I sat down with my countryman and struck up a conversation in English with his wife. She said that she understood why her husband wanted to go to the Czech club to chat in his native language, but that it was boring for her because she was unable to understand it. This example gave me an idea what my life would be like if I married a woman who didn't speak Czech.

Since I'd had no luck in San Francisco, I decided I wanted to meet Jo Ann in person. I was receiving letters from her often, even though I didn't answer every one. She was patient, and I surmised that she, and perhaps even her parents, were encouraging her to meet a Czech who might be a possible husband. I decided to spend more time corresponding and on occasion would call her.

I thought of going to New York during my summer vacation, and had been saving money for the trip. Frankly, I was becoming lonesome; in spite of the fact that I had some good friends, it was time for me to settle down. It had been seven years since my escape, and I was still stateless. By crossing the Czech-German border, I had automatically lost my Czech citizenship. I was not a German citizen, even though I lived there for two years, and wasn't an Australian citizen after having lived there for four years. I'd lived in America for a little over one year and needed four more to become a U.S. citizen.

I felt frustrated and uneasy. I longed to find the right partner and start to live a normal married life. And I continued to read the want ads, hoping to find a desk job rather than continue as a maintenance worker.

One day I saw an ad that described taking a course to obtain a real estate license. I decided to attend the evening classes.

Because I had been a real estate salesman and had a real estate license in Australia, the course was not too difficult. I passed it and received a California license. I was glad to have it, but like my previous experience, I found that it required too much time on the weekends. I felt I needed time off for other activities on weekends, so I didn't take advantage of my license.

Several months had passed since my friend, Bob, had returned to Australia. One day when I went to visit Mr. and Mrs. Schadek, I was astonished to find Bob there. He explained that upon his return to Australia, he went to a soccer game in Melbourne and encountered some Czech friends. One had said, "America is only for smart people," and that's all Bob had to hear. So here he was back, in the good old U.S.A. again. I could hardly believe a remark like that would prompt someone like Bob to return-but he did!

He explained that he had taken an English course in Melbourne and had studied the U.S. requirements for obtaining a barber's license. Now in San Francisco, he attended night classes and had finally received his license. He worked in a very exclusive hotel and was making an excellent salary.

A few weeks later, Bob phoned to tell me that Mrs. Schadek had been hospitalized because she had lost almost all feeling in her left leg. I visited Mr. Schadek, who said that the doctors thought his wife's leg should be amputated, but she had refused. I was very worried about her condition.

Our club made plans to go to a Czech festival the following weekend in Scio, Oregon, a small town near Portland, where Bohemian settlers had kept Czech traditions dating back to early in the century. They had built a club building with a restaurant and a large gym for physical fitness exercises and sports. They also arranged competition between various clubs, and ours had been invited to participate.

In addition to the athletes, older people went as spectators. I traveled there with three of our members. We left on Friday and drove almost all night. The next day the restaurant served a traditional Czech dinner: pork, dumplings and sauerkraut. Everyone had a wonderful time at the festival. A band played Czech songs, and we all sang and danced.

During that weekend, I met an elderly couple, Mr. and Mrs. Pokorny, who were also from San Francisco. They asked me if I would help with the driving on their return trip, since Mrs. Pokorny didn't drive. We started back about two o'clock Sunday afternoon. The Pokornys' car was very comfortable, and we had an enjoyable conversation.

As we were driving through the town of Eureka, I had to watch the winding road very carefully. About a couple of miles beyond the town, I noticed lights blinking behind me: the police! Then I heard the siren and stopped. An officer asked for my driver's license and said that in Eureka, I had driven 35 miles an hour in a 25-mile-zone. We all agreed we had never seen such a sign. But we lost the argument, and he issued me a ticket to appear in court on Monday.

I explained I couldn't return, and suggested that I pay him the fine of $10, which he could give to the court. He agreed. Because I was driving, I paid the fine instead of Mr. Pokorny—although I thought that since I was doing him a favor by driving his car, he should have offered to pay it. My salary then was only $75 a week, so for me $10 was quite a lot. I remembered that in Eureka, I had seen a police car parked in the center of town, and realized it was probably a speed trap to catch out-of-towners. It also entered my mind that he probably never turned in the money. After I returned to San Francisco, I thought I should write to the judge of the Eureka court, but I dismissed the idea and chalked it up to experience.

When I got back to my rooming house late that night, I had a phone call from Bob, informing me that Mrs. Schadek had passed away. She had died on Friday, and was buried the same day. I immediately went to see Mr. Schadek to express my condolences.

After that, I visited Mr. Schadek often, because I felt sorry about the loss of his wife. I thought if he talked about her, it would somehow ease his sorrow. I also watched baseball with him, and noticed that before the game, someone would always sing the U.S. national anthem. After so many games, I finally learned the melody and the words. Bob was still living there, and one day, I noticed he had packed many of Mrs. Schadek's clothes to send to his relatives in Czechoslovakia. I had thought of asking Mr. Schadek for some of his wife's clothes, because I knew my relatives could use them—but now I dropped the idea.

As summer approached, many activities were being planned by Sokol clubs all over the U.S.A. I learned that another festival was going to take place at the Los Angeles Sokol Club. As I wanted to see Hollywood, I lost no time in asking Fred and Ann Divisek to go with me. They agreed without any hesitation. Fred said they had some very good friends there, and this would give them an opportunity for a visit. Irene also decided to go along.

Fred took his station wagon loaded with food, drinks, and sleeping bags for the children. Our first stop was Fresno, which was about halfway. We then drove on to Hollywood, which was a little disappointing; it was not the glamorous city I'd envisioned.

Fred and Ann had phoned their friends before our departure. They now gave us a warm welcome in their large, beautiful home in a nearby suburb. They had prepared a delicious dinner, and soft background music made the visit very special. We had intended to stay at a motel, but they insisted we stay with them, since they had many rooms.

The next day we attended the dinner at the Sokol Club. Afterwards there was a calisthenic exhibition and a "Beseda," which is the national dance of Czechoslovakia and similar to square dancing. Four couples, wearing beautiful colorful costumes, dance to the music. The performance was well-organized, and the evening was most enjoyable.

The next time I went to the club, I was surprised to see my longtime friend, Jan Kriz. He told me after visiting our common sponsors, the

Zacks, he had gone to Ohio, but didn't like it there. Then he had returned to California, settled in nearby San Mateo, and found a job with United Airlines as a parts-distribution man. He said he had discovered another club, The International Club, located in downtown San Francisco. Jan invited me to meet him there the following Friday.

For me, the evening was a dud, and I wondered why Jan liked the place. There was a guitarist playing, but no dance floor. I realized The International Club was not for me, and left.

This experience prompted me to make an important decision. With summer around the corner, I decided to make arrangements to visit Jo Ann in New York. Our correspondence had dwindled, and my telephone calls were few and far between. I wrote and asked when it would be convenient for me to come. She had told me she usually took a long summer vacation with her parents, who had a house on a lake in Connecticut.

It didn't take long for Jo Ann to reply. She suggested I should come the first week in August. She would make a hotel reservation for me, and I could meet her in the restaurant located in the Sokol building. I replied that while I was there, I would like to visit my sponsors, the Zacks, in New Jersey. It was arranged that I would visit them during the first three days after my arrival, when Jo Ann would be in Easthampton, modeling at a fashion show. Then, we would meet in New York again, and go to Connecticut and spend some time with her parents.

This itinerary sounded wonderful, and I booked a flight on TWA. When I told my friend, Jack Pilersky, about my travel arrangements, he said he would give me one dollar to buy flight insurance-and that I should name him as beneficiary. Then, in the event the plane crashed, he would receive a big payoff. I must have looked horrified, because Jack said he was just kidding, and claimed that he was really throwing away his dollar because flights were so safe. But I didn't think it was a very funny joke. I had never flown before, and I must admit that it gave me goose bumps.

Before my flight, I wrote to my aunt and uncle and said that I would soon be visiting them. They were now living in a small town, Washington, New Jersey, not too far from the Delaware River Water Gap.

I boarded the plane at International Airport with mixed feelings: excitement and fear. I couldn't believe that the plane would stay in the air for nine hours without refueling. I was really very relieved when we landed safely in New York.

Jo Ann had sent me instructions on how to get to my hotel, which was near her apartment in a building named Red Sokol Hall. She had arranged for us to meet at a restaurant in another building, called Blue Sokol Hall, a couple of blocks away.

Finally, the moment arrived. I found the restaurant and took a table. In a few minutes, a woman came in, wearing a black dress with a stole around her shoulders. She was slim, with blond hair, and was absolutely beautiful. She came towards me. I stood up, and tentatively said, "Jo Ann?" She smiled and nodded her head. Now I knew why she was a model! I fell in love with her at first sight.

I asked her if she would like a drink, but she said the restaurant was full of smoke and suggested that we leave.

While we were walking and talking, we passed a movie theater where The King and I was playing. Since Jo Ann had heard it was a good movie, we decided to see it. Actually, it was a most welcome idea, it was an extremely hot day. To make matters worse, I was wearing my wool suit from Australia. The air-conditioning was even more wonderful than the movie!

The next day Jo Ann had to go to Easthampton to model for Bergdorf Goodman. She told me to take a bus at the Port Authority for my visit with the Zacks. After three days in New Jersey, I would return to New York, where we would meet at Altman's Jewelry Store at 3:30 P.M. We happened to be standing in front of that store after the movie, yet I wondered why she had chosen that particular spot. Perhaps she thought I should buy her some jewelry or an engagement ring?

Everything seemed different in New York. People always seemed to be rushing, and the extreme heat bothered me. I went along with the plans Jo Ann had made, because she had been born in the city and knew it very well.

We took a taxi to Bergdorf Goodman, where she modeled in the

Knitwear Department. She was also a sales clerk, and on Saturdays, did bookkeeping. After she showed me around the store, it was time for dinner. We strolled for a few blocks on Fifth Avenue until we came to a French restaurant, very elegant. We had a delicious meal with wine. It was expensive, but I had worked hard and this was my vacation.

The days were long at that time of the year, and Jo Ann wanted me to see as many places in New York as possible. We went to the United Nations, and walked around the building, which was glittering at sunset.

The next day I took a bus from Port Authority to visit my aunt and uncle in Washington, New Jersey. My uncle was at the bus stop, waiting for me. I recognized him easily, even though it had been eight years since I had seen the Zacks in Prague. Now they were both over sixty-five and had retired.

Washington was a very attractive town, clean, with little industry. The Zacks lived in a pleasant home at the center of town. When I entered, my aunt gave me a warm welcome, and I smelled a lovely aroma coming from the kitchen. Shortly after, Aunt served a delicious dinner of roast pork, dumplings, sauerkraut, and apple sauce-the traditional national meal in Czechoslovakia.

After dinner, Uncle showed me some of the town. When we returned, Aunt said she had arranged for us to visit their friends, Mr. and Mrs. Pospisil who lived nearby in Stroudsburg. On the way, we stopped to have a view of the Delaware Water Gap, a beautiful sight.

Stroudsburg was even smaller than Washington, but a nice town. Even though we'd had a huge dinner, Mrs. Pospisil served us cold cuts with beer, and then coffee with homemade "kolace," a well-known pastry in Czechoslovakia. Mrs. Pospisil said they had two sons. One was married and lived in New York City. But the other son, a test pilot, had been killed during a flight when his plane crashed. His widow, of Czech parentage, was left with two sons, ages seven and five. She lived with her mother, and Mrs. Pospisil said they expected us for a visit.

When we arrived there, their daughter-in-law, was outside with her sons. We were introduced, and somehow I wasn't even surprised to hear that her name was Jean. She was attractive, slender, rather short, and spoke Czech very well. We conversed for a while, and she told me that she worked in town as a saleslady. She asked me how I liked California, and added that she'd always wanted to live there.

It was obvious that my aunt and uncle were playing the role of matchmakers. I sensed it and tried not to be negative. However, I had just met Jo Ann, and in three days we were planning to visit her parents in Connecticut. I had no time to stay in New Jersey and get to know Jean. I felt sorry for her because she was too young to be a widow, and she seemed to be a very nice woman. But all things considered, I couldn't get involved. So when we left, I wished Jean all the best, but didn't promise any further contact.

When we returned to the Zacks, we had plenty of time to talk: about what happened in Czechoslovakia after the communist takeover, my travels around the world, my relatives, and my life in San Francisco. My aunt told me that they had met the Pospisils years ago at the Red Sokol Hall, and discovered that she and Mrs. Pospisil both came from Mnichovo Hradiste in Bohemia. At the same time, they learned that Jo Ann's father had been born and raised there, and thus they all became close friends.

When it was time for bed, my aunt asked what I would like for breakfast and offered me a wide choice: fruit, cereal, or bacon and eggs. What a wonderful variety for a bachelor! At breakfast the following day, Aunt asked me the question I'd been expecting: how I liked Jean. I answered that I thought she was a very nice person. As I knew they wanted to make a match, I explained the arrangements I had made with Jo Ann to meet her parents-and hoped the subject of Jean was now closed.

After breakfast, my aunt showed me the house with its beautiful paintings, crystal, and fine china. Then she surprised me by saying that if I married Jean, I would have a ready-made family. She added that Jo Ann was thirty-five years old, and to have children at that age would be difficult. I listened but made no comment.

My uncle saved the day by asking me if I would like to see his garden. He had a lot of vegetables and a nice shed, equipped with a workbench and a number of well-organized tools. He told me that he had a helper named Patek, a black man, whom he had taught to speak Czech.

We spent quite a long while in the garden, talking about different methods of planting, watering, and the use of insecticides.

The morning went by so quickly that we didn't realize it was time to eat. When we went back inside, I could smell the same delicious aroma as the night before. Aunt said that she hoped I wouldn't mind eating leftovers, and I quickly assured her there was nothing I'd like better.

After this excellent meal, Uncle suggested that we go for a ride so he could show me some of the area. He pointed out the site of the Sokol festivals, and mentioned that was where they'd sent me the postcard last fall. We stopped for ice cream and returned home. The ride had been very enjoyable, and I felt as though I was really on vacation.

I asked my aunt if she had saved the postage stamps from the letters I'd sent them from Hamburg. I used special stamps, the kind that cost normal postage plus a few Pfenning extra, for the so-called "Nothilfe"-meaning help to rebuild Germany. She brought me a small envelope and noticed my disappointment when I saw only a few stamps inside it. My aunt explained that the mailman had constantly asked for the stamps, so she had given him some. Well, what was done, was done.

She then added that I had sent them some money from Germany to save for me. I remembered I had sent them thirty-five dollars, out of which some deductions had to be made: fifteen dollars for the Affidavit of Support that they had mailed to me in Germany, and two dollars for ties that I had requested. There was about eighteen dollars left, but I told them it didn't matter.

My only disappointment with the Zacks came while I was in the D.P. Camp Zoo, where there had been a great food shortage. Many other refugees were getting Care packages from their relatives or sponsors in the United States, but I never received one. Even after I had written the Zacks about the camp's meager food, my aunt and uncle only replied that they wanted me near them during their old age. It gave me a negative feeling toward them, and that is the reason that when I landed in San Francisco, I wasn't in any hurry to join them. I decided to stay on the West Coast for a while to see California and survey the possibilities for my future there. I knew that once I left California for the East, I might never return. Now that I was visiting the Zacks, I guessed they felt rather guilty or uneasy and were trying to make amends. Well, it was all water over the dam and I held no grudge against them.

I asked aunt and uncle their impression of my friend, Jan Kriz, who had visited them. They looked at each other. I gathered from their expression it wasn't too good. It simply didn't work out, and he left. I knew Jan very well, he was a decent man, I said, a very good friend and an excellent worker. I'm not sure if I changed their minds.

After breakfast the next day, the time had come for me to say goodbye to my aunt and uncle. I had no idea when I would be back. I could see that they didn't want me to leave, that they wanted to have someone around for their old age. I could also see that it wouldn't work out.

My uncle drove me to the bus station, and the Pospisils—with Jean and her two sons—were there to see me off. I thanked them again for their hospitality. When I waved to them out of the bus window, my uncle said, "Why don't you just grab these boys!?" That remark certainly underscored that both the Zacks and Pospisils had planned to match me up with Jean.

When I arrived in New York, I registered at the same hotel, since it was familiar. Then I walked to Altman Jewelry Store to meet Jo Ann as we had arranged. I asked her if she wanted to look at some jewelry and I said I would like to buy her a pair of earrings. She chose a nice pair and thanked me.

We went for a walk and Jo Ann told me that the fashion show was very successful, and she described the exclusive homes in Easthampton. Our next subject was the trip to Connecticut the next day. It was decided that I would pick her up by taxi at her apartment, and we would go to Grand Central Station to take the train.

Jo Ann suggested we go to a Czech restaurant for dinner. She ordered pork, dumplings and sauerkraut. Since I had eaten so much of that at the Zacks, I chose viennerschnitzel, potato salad, and beer. After dinner, Jo Ann told me about a nearby store that sold Czech products. Jo Ann said that she never went to visit her parents in Connecticut unless she brought them something from that store.

We went there and bought some salami, some hot dogs called "parky," and some "jaternice"—sausage similar to kielbasa. I was worried about taking all this food to Connecticut in such hot weather, but Jo Ann explained she used a cold pack that she kept in the freezer of her refrigerator.

The next morning we were off. Our destination was Springfield, Massachusetts, from where we would take a bus to Stafford Springs, Connecticut. At 7:30 we boarded the train, and were fortunate to have window seats from which we could see the countryside. For Jo Ann, who had traveled this route many times, the trip wasn't anything new, but for me it was an entirely different matter. I was now over three thousand miles away from San Francisco, and I immediately noticed the difference in scenery. There were many maple, oak, and pine trees, which made the East much greener than California, where the hills were brown.

At the onset of our trip, Jo Ann decided to inform me about the background of her family. Her father, Joseph Sytar, who was born in Czechoslovakia, decided at the age of fourteen to become a tailor. He went to Leipzig, Germany, where he received his apprenticeship as a ladies' garment tailor and designer. Later he lived in Paris, where he worked for eleven years. During World War I, Joseph was drafted into the French Legion, and after the war ended in 1918, he returned to the newly-formed Czechoslovakia. While in the army, the soldiers were told that upon returning home, they would be given jobs by the government. Joseph applied for a job as a policeman. When the recruiting officer saw him, he was informed that at five feet, six inches tall, he was too short. Her father was a rather hot-tempered man and told the officer, "I wasn't too short to fight in the war, but now I am too short to be a policeman." He went home and told this story to his mother, and said he was leaving for America. His mother tried to dissuade him, but in vain. Joseph came to the U.S.A. in 1919. He had been corresponding with a friend, Lanka, who also was a tailor. When they met in New York, Lanka introduced him to his boss, Mainbocher, a famous couturier on Fifth Avenue. Before the interview, Joseph had said to Lanka, "I cannot see your employer as I haven't any suit to wear, and I can't speak one work of English." Lanka said the suit didn't matter, and that since Mainbocher was French, they could speak in French.

Joseph applied for the job, was accepted, and received two weeks wages in advance so that he could buy himself a suit. He was employed as a ladies' garment fitter, designer, and tailor. He made suits for many famous women: the actress, Marlene Dietrich, and the Duchess of Windsor, the wife of the former King Edward.

One day the Duchess of Windsor was being fitted for a suit. Joseph approached her husband and asked him, how he would like to have it fitted. The Duke replied, "Joseph, you are the fitter, you do it how you think it should be done, and so it will stay."

Joseph retired in 1952 at the age of sixty-six. He and Mrs. Sytar now lived in their recently-purchased home in Staffordville, Connecticut, five miles from Stafford Springs. The town was once very popular as a health spa, and people would come for the water there. Jo Ann said that many years ago, even the Indians liked to drink the water from the many springs.

Jo Ann's mother had been born in Malkov Drahenicky in Southern Bohemia, Czechoslovakia, the daughter of a farmer. She had come to America in 1911 at the age of sixteen, and worked first as a domestic, then later as a cook for the well-known Czech painter, Nadherny, in New York City. She and Joseph were married in 1920 and Jo Ann had arrived a year later. Their son, Jaroslav, called Jerry, was born in 1924.

Jerry was an excellent student. When World War II began, he volunteered at the age of seventeen and served in the army for almost four years. He was in the D-Day invasion and had won five battle stars. After his parents moved to Connecticut, Jerry decided to join them in Staffordville, where he worked in the local textile mills.

When we arrived in Springfield, Massachusetts, we took a bus to Stafford Springs, where Jerry was waiting to drive us to their home, five miles away. This drive was the most beautiful scenery of the entire trip.

When we arrived, Jo Ann's parents came to greet us, and she formally introduced me. I immediately commented on the lovely spot where their house was located. Then we sat down on the porch that offered a magnificent view of Staffordville Lake. Jo Ann and her mother served afternoon coffee and peach pie which her mother, an excellent baker and cook, had prepared.

When we finished, we went down to the lake for a swim. I could see Mrs. Sytar on the porch watching us. I think she was wondering what kind of a man Jo Ann had brought. She knew that we had been corresponding and phoning each other, but now meeting me in person was the test.

At one edge of the lake was a wooden rowboat that Jo Ann had named The Queen Mary. We decided to wait until the next day to go rowing. Instead, I stretched out on a blanket, and Jo Ann went up to the house to talk to her parents. I had an idea that she wanted to hear their comments about their guest.

In a short time, she returned. The sun had disappeared, and we enjoyed the peaceful atmosphere. The property was simply beautiful. Jo Ann's parents had certainly chosen an ideal retirement place.

Suddenly the bell on the porch rang to inform us that supper was ready. Jo Ann's mother had prepared sauerbraten with dumplings and a very tasty gravy. As usual, beer was served with the delicious meal, which was followed by dessert and coffee.

I felt slightly uneasy at being treated like a king. After all, I was a total stranger to them-just Jo Ann's pen pal. But to hear Czech spoken made me feel as if I were at home.

Later in the evening, Jo Ann's mother showed me the bedroom upstairs where I would sleep. Jerry and his father also had their rooms upstairs, while the mother and Jo Ann slept downstairs, where it was much cooler. I was very surprised at the number of rooms: four bedrooms, a living room, a dining room, a kitchen, a full bathroom, a large porch, and a half-bathroom in the basement.

The following day, I awoke late, at about nine o'clock. It must have been the country air, because I slept like a log. Everyone said it was to be expected after the long trip the day before. Mrs. Sytar offered either pancakes or eggs, I selected the pancakes, and they were delicious. After breakfast, we took a walk along the road, called Lakeshore Boulevard. The many pine trees gave the area its name, Land O'Pines.

There were about forty-three cottages on the lake, which was considered a summer resort. Some of them were owned by affluent people who lived there only in summer, but others had winterized these cottages to be able to live there year-round.

It was such a beautiful day that we decided to go for a boat ride to Snake Island, about a half-mile away. We had a swim, then took a blanket and sunglasses and boarded The Queen Mary. We landed at the little island, which was a lovely spot. I tied the boat to a nearby small tree and spread out the blanket to enjoy a sun. I told Jo Ann how much I was enjoying the visit and how pretty she was. Neither of us had worn a watch but we could judge the time by the sun. When it was fairly low, we decided to return. We had a pleasant and romantic afternoon.

When we returned, we had a chat with Jo Ann's parents and a cold drink. I asked Mr. Sytar how he had happened to find this splendid place. He explained that they used to vacation here, because his wife's sisters and brothers lived in the area. The oldest brother, Matthew, had arrived in the U.S.A. first, early in the twentieth century, and had married the daughter of Mr. Hak, a wealthy button factory owner. Mr. Hak needed workers, and because of the poverty in Bohemia, Matthew had sent money to his siblings to come to America.

We exchanged stories about our different experiences, always speaking Czech. I admired how well both Jo Ann and Jerry spoke the language. The reason was obvious: they had learned Czech in their childhood and spoke it only with their parents. In fact, when Jo Ann and Jerry began school, they barely knew English. I sensed that Jo Ann's parents were interested in me because of the language. It was only natural they preferred to have a Czech son-in-law.

The following day after breakfast, Jerry had to take his father shopping in Stafford Springs. I accompanied them to see the town. The first stop was the Central Package store on Main Street, where Mr. Sytar bought his Bohemian beer. The next stop, the A & P, was the family's favorite grocery store, because the manager was a friend. On our way back, Jerry suggested that we stop at the Hyde Villa restaurant, located in a small village called Hydeville. The owner, William Kunhardt, served us beer and spoke Czech quite well.

Back at the house, we decided to go swimming. Towards evening, when it was cooler, we went for a boat ride.

I was having such a wonderful time with people who didn't know me, so I felt rather uneasy about not contributing something. Therefore, the next day, I asked Mr. Sytar if I could help by doing some work around the property. Since the grass needed cutting, I mowed it, both in the front and back of the house. It took quite some time, because the property was large. Mr. Sytar seemed very appreciative of my effort.

We were very fortunate to have excellent weather. As a matter of fact, everything about my first vacation in America was absolutely perfect. However, it was coming to an end.

As I was leaving early on Sunday evening, we had to return to New York on Saturday. With only one day left, I knew I had to reach some conclusion about my future relationship with Jo Ann. Up to this point, I had faced many serious situations in my life, but this was one of the most difficult. Although we had corresponded for about nine months, we really didn't know each other well enough-as far as character, habits, and life style were concerned-to make such an important decision as marriage. Well, we were both old enough to know what life was all about; therefore, I was going to take a chance. I decided to propose to Jo Ann when we went for another boat ride. When I asked her if she would marry me, she replied, "Yes." We sealed it with a kiss. Now there were two matters to take care of: to ask Jo Ann's father for her hand in marriage, and to buy an engagement ring in New York on Saturday.

In a short while, we returned to the cottage. When I walked into the kitchen, Mrs. Sytar asked me, "Well, George, is it going to happen?" I had such a lump in my throat that I just I nodded my head. I could see in her smiling eyes great happiness. One parent down, one to go.

Jo Ann's father was sitting alone on the porch. I steeled up my courage and went out to join him. There I took a deep breath and said, "Mr. Sytar, Jo Ann and I have decided to get married. Would you trust me to take care of her? Could I ask you for her hand?" He smiled and agreed,

"I hope you will be very happy. She is a very good girl." We shook hands. My "ordeal" was over.

I didn't know if Jo Ann was listening around the corner, but in a few minutes, she joined us on the porch. After I told her that her father had agreed to our marriage, I gave her a hug and kiss. Moments later, her mother entered. I hugged and kissed her, too.

The mood in the house was suddenly festive. Mrs. Sytar fixed coffee and served us peach pie. Then we went for a swim.

After a while, a little bell rang to summon us back to the house. On the porch, the table was beautifully set, the candles lit, and there was an expensive bottle of wine that Jerry had brought to celebrate our engagement. Mrs. Sytar had prepared a delicious dinner of viennerschnitzel and potato salad, one of my favorite dishes. Jerry congratulated us and opened the bottle of wine to propose a toast. It was a wonderful dinner and a magical evening.

Before retiring, I told Mrs. Sytar I would buy Jo Ann an engagement ring in New York. Later, I would like to invite Jo Ann to the West Coast. I told her something about my life in San Francisco: the Sokol club meetings every Friday, my very good friends, the climate, the concerts in Golden Gate Park. Although she listened patiently, I could see in her face a sign of sadness. It was easy to understand, because California was a long distance away. How often could she see her daughter? Not a word was uttered, but I could feel her thoughts.

In the morning, we gathered for breakfast and prepared to leave. I thanked both parents for their hospitality with handshakes and hugs. As we walked to Jerry's car, I repeated again what a spectacular place they had, and how memorable my visit had been. This was all said somewhat emotionally, since I knew I wouldn't see them again until the wedding.

In approximately forty minutes, we arrived at the bus station in Springfield and told Jerry good-bye. When we waved to him from the train, that former war hero saluted us.

During the return trip, Jo Ann and I talked about our plans in New York. I asked Jo Ann if she knew of a good jewelry store. After our arrival, we found a nice variety of rings at a store she knew. The rings were marked with prices anywhere from two hundred dollars up into thousands.

Jo Ann said she liked a one-karat diamond priced at five hundred dollars. Well, this was all fine, except for the fact I didn't have that much money left; I hadn't planned on buying such an expensive ring! In front of the salesman, I pulled out my wallet and counted all the money-except for two hundred dollars that I kept in a "secret compartment," for emergency use.

Of course, Jo Ann didn't know about my emergency money, and I decided to keep it that way. Therefore, she thought I had only the $435 I had just counted out-which, by the way-seemed like a grand sum to me. I put the money slowly back in my wallet and suggested she choose a lower-priced ring. After she looked and looked, she said that was the only one she liked. We started to leave.

We were almost at the door when we heard the salesman say, "Just a minute, please come back." We walked back. He asked Jo Ann if that was the only ring she liked. She nodded. Then he asked me if I wanted to buy it for her. I said yes, but that I didn't have enough money for it. Much to my surprise, he said, "All right, you may have it. But remember the ring is worth a great deal more. Have it appraised at the shop on the other side of the street."

I bought the ring, and we walked across the street. The appraiser said, "It's worth more than six hundred dollars. Do you want to sell it?" Of course we didn't.

We decided to celebrate at the same Czech restaurant where we'd eaten the previous week. We ordered pork, dumplings, and sauerkraut dinner. While we were eating, some people came in that Jo Ann knew. When she told them the good news about our engagement, they heartily congratulated us.

After dinner, Jo Ann invited me to see her apartment on the fifth floor. There was no elevator in this old, massive building, and I wondered how her parents could have lived there for so many years. I asked, and Jo Ann explained that they'd been young when they moved in.

The building was at the end of the quiet street, there was little traffic, and the rent was forty-three dollars a month. That was why Jo Ann had remained there after her parents moved to Staffordville. I wasn't convinced. It still seemed very inconvenient to live in a fifth-floor apartment with no elevator.

When we entered her apartment, everything appeared neat and clean. In Czechoslovakia, it was and still is customary for one to take off one's shoes upon entering an apartment or a house. The owners offer their guests slippers, which are located in the foyer or hall. There were no slippers, but I still removed my shoes and stayed in my socks. Jo Ann said it wasn't necessary, but I liked the custom.

Jo Ann showed me the apartment, which consisted of a kitchen, living room, two bedrooms, and a small room, that she called "the ironing room." We sat on the couch in the living room and talked about our plans for the future. When I asked Jo Ann if she would visit San Francisco later in the year to see if she liked it, she agreed.

Minutes later, Jo Ann reached in her handbag and took out the little jewelry box with the ring in it. She put it on and thanked me with a kiss. We decided to celebrate with a bottle of wine. We touched glasses and wished each other a happy future. Jo Ann suggested that in the morning, she would call a taxi and pick me up at my hotel. That way we could spend a bit more time together.

The next morning we made the long trip to the airport. When the driver wished me a safe flight, the word, "safe," reminded me of Jack Pilersky, who had given me a dollar to buy insurance in case the plane crashed. I told Jo Ann the story.

Jo Ann stayed with me until I checked my luggage. Then it was the emotional moment when we had to say good-bye. We hugged each other tightly, and I told her I would write often.

I still had thirty minutes before boarding the plane so I went to a shop and bought some souvenirs: post cards, T-shirts, and a small bronze Statue of Liberty-to keep as a symbol of my own liberty.

And then I was on the plane. The flight seemed endless. I thumbed through the magazines and tried to doze off.

When we passed about the halfway mark, I decided to go for a walk in the aisle to stretch my legs. After a few trips back and forth, I noticed that the stewardesses were resting in their cabin behind the pilot's area. Because there was no door, I started to chat with them. When one stewardess detected my accent and learned that I was from Czechoslovakia, she mentioned that her grandmother had come from there. She was interested in hearing about my experiences in Europe, Australia, and now San Francisco, so that helped pass the time. Finally, we landed.

When I entered my apartment, I noticed that the sink-which always had a stained bottom-was now clean. That was a mystery, because I had scrubbed the sink often, but the stains wouldn't go away. There was a knock on my door, and it was Mrs. Korn, the woman who had the adjacent apartment to mine. She greeted me and asked how I liked my sink which she had cleaned by using bleach. I told her it was nice to know my apartment had been so well taken care of even when I was three thousand miles away!

That night, before I fell asleep, I thought about what had happened during my vacation. The realization that I was now committed to marry a girl I hardly knew frightened me. The trip had also cost me most of my savings, so now I would have to start all over again.

The next day at work I teased Jack that he'd been out of luck: my plane didn't crash. We both had a good laugh. Then I told him about my engagement. He was very surprised, but congratulated me. Soon the news spread, and I was the butt of lots of kidding and jokes.

During my visit with Mr. Schadek the following day, I informed him of my engagement. He seemed both pleased for me, and sad for himself. He told me how much he missed the companionship of his wife which was easy to understand. Then he smiled, said this was supposed to be a happy occasion, and offered me a glass of wine.

After returning home, I called Fred and Ann Divisek to tell them about Jo Ann. Like everyone else, they were surprised.

I was looking forward to Friday night at the Sokol Club. Sometimes I met long-time members who had actually helped to rebuild the club after the 1906 earthquake! There were often interesting people there. Because the club didn't charge any dues, the largest source of revenue was the fees from different organizations who rented the hall for dances or meetings.

That Friday, I saw several unfamiliar faces and asked Mrs. Chlup, the manager, about them. She said they were members of the Lodge of the Czechoslovak Society of America, a nationwide fraternal organization with headquarters in Chicago. This year they were holding their annual meeting at our club.

One of its older members, Antonin Kohoutek, sat with me and explained the history of the Lodge. He said that he was an underwriter for the Czechoslovak Society, the oldest insurance company in the U.S.A. It had been founded in 1854, when three corn growers made an agreement that if a calamity destroyed one of their corn crops, the other two would share their own crops.

This fraternal group gradually grew larger and larger, spread into other states, and eventually established their headquarters in Chicago. He recommended that I should join, take out an endowment policy, and after several years, I would have earned enough interest on my capital, that I could buy a home or a car. Antonin filled out the forms for me that night-and I am still a member.

One evening Fred and Ann Divisek invited me for dinner to hear all the news about my trip. Their advice was that I invite Jo Ann to San Francisco as soon as possible. They both felt it was high time I got married. I confided that the great distance between California and Connecticut really worried me, because I knew how close Jo Ann and her mother were. Ann said she'd been in the same situation when she and Fred married but that a wife must live where her husband earns his livelihood.

It sounded convincing, but I nevertheless knew it would be very important for Jo Ann to like San Francisco. The Diviseks listened very patiently and said a lot of encouraging things. When I was with them, I felt as if I were in my second home. By the time I left that night, I had decided to ask Jo Ann for a visit around Christmas.

She didn't reply as soon as I expected. Finally, a lengthy letter arrived in which she explained that her boss hadn't wanted her to take a vacation during the busiest season of the year. Jo Ann insisted and threatened to resign. After much squabbling, the boss relented and she was given the two weeks. Obviously, he didn't want to lose someone who was a model, salesperson, and bookkeeper!

Jo Ann wrote she would arrive on Saturday, the week before Christmas. I reserved a room for her at the Hotel York, on the third floor and facing the street, so she would have a nice view of downtown San Francisco. When I asked the ladies at work where I could buy a Christmas gift for Jo Ann, they suggested Gumps near Union Square. I went there and bought a pair of jade earrings, which I hoped she would like.

Finally the day of Jo Ann's arrival came. The plane was supposed to land at the International Airport at 8:30 P.M. But when I called TWA to confirm the time, they informed me there was a two-hour delay. As I was busily trying to spruce up my apartment, the delay didn't bother me.

When I phoned again, I was told the plane had been redirected to Las Vegas, where a different plane would pick up the passengers. Now the arrival time was 2:30 A.M. At this point, I was beginning to worry. After a short nap, I called the airport, which confirmed that the plane would land at 2:30. Of course there was hardly any traffic at that hour, so I reached the airport in a few minutes and waited, brooding about this unfortunate start to Jo Ann's vacation.

Finally Jo Ann appeared. When she claimed her luggage, she found one piece damaged, which was just about the last straw. On our drive to her hotel, she told me the first plane had dropped hundreds of feet over the Rockies in some kind of air pocket, had lost one engine, and had made an emergency landing at Las Vegas. I felt terribly about this unpromising beginning to her visit. At the hotel, I asked her to call me in the morning after she had a good rest.

This was all rather upsetting, but I managed to sleep until ten o'clock. I phoned the Diviseks to tell them Jo Ann had arrived. Since they were anxious to meet her, they invited us for dinner.

Finally, Jo Ann called me about 1:30 that afternoon. She apologized for such a disruptive night and accepted the dinner invitation from the Diviseks. Before we went to their home, I showed Jo Ann some of the city.

The drive to Twin Peaks on this clear day gave a spectacular view of the city and its surrounding areas. She was fascinated by the cable cars, a familiar sight in San Francisco.

Jo Ann received a very warm welcome at the Diviseks. The children had already decorated their Christmas tree and were delighted with the candy I gave them. Then Jo Ann told us about her trip. Since this had been her first flight, she was very frightened during the emergency landing. She admitted she had asked a young man in the next seat to her to hold her. Later, after they landed safely, she apologized to him. I couldn't help commenting that if I were in such a situation and a pretty girl asked me to hold her, I wouldn't have hesitated. We all had a good laugh. I could sense that the Diviseks liked Jo Ann.

On our way back to the York Hotel, I asked Jo Ann if she would like to take a long drive on Wednesday to see Hollywood. On the same trip, she could visit her cousins in Pacific Palisades. I still had one week's vacation left, and Joe agreed I could split it.

It was a rather difficult task to plan entertainment, meals, trips, and job around Jo Ann's visit. Fortunately, because of the holidays, I had to be at work for only five days out of her two-week stay.

When I returned home from work on Monday, I phoned Jo Ann that I would pick her up at seven o'clock for dinner. I took her to a well-known restaurant, Omar Kyham, which had an extraordinary atmosphere and even more extraordinary food.

Jo Ann informed me that she had gone to the TWA offices during the day to complain about her damaged luggage. When they gave her nine dollars compensation, she told them that she would never fly TWA again.

When I asked Jo Ann what she planned for the next day, she said she had a surprise phone call from Ann Divisek, who suggested they go shopping together. So that took care of Tuesday. As for Wednesday, I suggested that we start very early to avoid the traffic and have brunch on the way. I would take a thermos of coffee and some pastry for a snack. We decided to leave at 6:00 A.M., because it would take approximately seven hours to get to Pacific Palisades.

George's lovely wife Jo Ann Sytar. Her photo from Bergdorf Goodman on Fifth Avenue in New York.

Above: Mr. and Mrs. Schadek who helped George so much.

Right: The Schadek's house on 1562 Hayes Street in San Francisco.

By the bar with George's friend from Hamburg, Mr. Nevrly, who flew over from New York to visit George.

Reading U.S. magazines, America was so new to George.

George playing billiards at Sokol Hall in San Francisco.

Mr. and Mrs. Chlup who were the managers of Sokol Hall at 239 Page Street in San Francisco.

Above: George with his first car in America, a 1948 DeSoto with fluid drive.

Below: George designed and made this rig which took 100 feet of 16 mm film. It was used for making extra copies of reels without rewinding.

Above: Sokol Club President Joe Malek asked George to welcome immigrants to America at Czechoslovak day in Golden Gate Park's concert in San Francisco.
Below: George's wonderful friends (left to right): Fred Divisek, Mrs. Vogl, Ann Divisek and Irene Lasek.

Above: Jo Ann Knava in her wedding gown on June 8, 1957.

Right: George in men's uniform at Scio's Festival.

Above: Left to right: Joseph Sytar, Jo Ann Knava and Tessie Sytar.

Below: Jo Ann's parents' house in Staffordville, CT.

After making these plans, we took a short ride to Fisherman's Wharf, so Jo Ann could see where I started my career in San Francisco as a dishwasher. The next stop was the pier where my ship had landed; then the exact spot where I had first put my foot down on American soil.

As arranged, I picked up Jo Ann on Wednesday morning at 6:00 A.M. We decided to take the quicker route, Highway 99, which was inland. Then we would return on Route 101, Elamino Real, the scenic route. It was a pleasant drive in my heavy, spacious car, which averaged seventy miles an hour on the three-lane road.

When we reached Fresno, we stopped at a restaurant for breakfast. According to the road atlas, the distance between San Francisco and Los Angeles was almost four hundred miles, so we still had a long way to go. But the weather was perfect, and we were enjoying our time together.

We arrived in Pacific Palisades early that afternoon. Jo Ann and her cousins had a joyous reunion, since they hadn't seen each other for a long time. They showed us their beautiful home and nicely-landscaped property.

After our visit, we decided to see the famous Malibu Beach and drive through Beverly Hills to look at the expensive homes. Then we drove to Hollywood, where Jo Ann was as disappointed as I had been.

On our return via the coastal road, our first stop was Santa Barbara, a beautiful city with palm trees and much greenery. Our next stop was San Luis Obispo, where we had a meal. It was another fine day and we had a lovely drive to Carmel, where I bought Jo Ann a scarf.

In Monterey, I decided to make a short trip to Fort Ord, a military camp, where soldiers were trained to speak foreign languages. When I entered the office to inquire if Czech was taught, I was told that not only was the language itself taught, but that the soldiers learned to sing songs in Czech. The officer gave me the name of the choral director. This gave me an idea. I would suggest to the president of our Sokol Club, Josef Malek, that we invite the group to perform.

When we left Fort Ord, we were near a beautiful marina in Monterey Bay. We heard that Pebble Beach and Cypress Point were very picturesque. We turned back a few miles to see these two places. At Cypress Point, I took a picture of the famous old cypress tree, which gave the place its name.

We continued on to Santa Cruz, where the beach was gray sand that was full of sea weed. We decided that the water was too cold for a swim. I told Jo Ann that I had been spoiled by the white sand of the Australian beaches.

The next stop was San Jose. Then we headed back to San Francisco. Before taking Jo Ann to the hotel, I showed her the building where I worked. Since I had to be at my job the next day, I said I would pick her up for dinner. After that we would go to the Sokol Club, which Jo Ann was anxious to see since I'd often told her about it in my letters.

Friday evening, we decided to go to Chinatown, perhaps the most well-known section of San Francisco. We had an excellent dinner of shrimp chow mein and special Chinese tea, which we both enjoyed.

At the Sokol Club, I saw two brothers, Eric and Felix Lenhart, whose large contributions to the club helped keep it solvent. Eric was in real estate, and Felix owned a ladies' dress shop in Berkeley, on the other side of the Bay. Both were unmarried, semi-retired Czechs who had left Czechoslovakia before the Nazi takeover in 1939. After I introduced Jo Ann to them, the brothers invited us to join them for a glass of wine. They were astonished when Jo Ann spoke to them in fluent Czech. When I mentioned I had to work the next day, Eric offered to show Jo Ann some interesting sections of San Francisco that she hadn't yet seen.

On the way back to Jo Ann's hotel, I asked her impression of the club. She replied that she liked the friendly atmosphere, and could see why I liked going there every Friday. We agreed to go to the Mark Hopkins Hotel for dinner the next evening, since the restaurant on the twenty-second floor had a magnificent view of the city.

After a lovely evening in that exclusive restaurant, I realized that we had already covered one week of Jo Ann's vacation. The following week would be Christmas.

The next morning, I was awakened by the phone. It was Jack Pilersky, who said that he and his wife would like to invite us for lunch at their new home in San Mateo, about twenty-five miles from San Francisco. This was welcome indeed, since I wanted to show Jo Ann some of the suburbs.

We received a warm welcome at the Pilerskys, and again Jo Ann was complimented on speaking Czech so well. After a tour of the house, we had a wonderful meal, and I complimented Mrs. Pilersky on being an excellent cook. Later we went into the backyard, which was full of beautiful flowers. Because the Pilerskys didn't have any children, gardening was one of their hobbies. Jack also liked to work with wood, and asked me for suggestions about what kind of structure he should make for the back entrance, which became very hot from the sun. He gave me a piece of paper and a pencil, and I designed a lattice arch to be mounted to the back of the house. It would be a perfect place to plant climbing roses, or ivy. After I figured out how much lumber Jack would need, I offered to come some weekend to help build it.

We had afternoon coffee and a homemade pastry called kolace. We felt as if we were back in Staffordville, since Jo Ann's mother had baked the same pastry. I still really didn't know whether or not Jo Ann knew how to cook, but I would find out later!

We thanked the Pilerskys for their generous hospitality and left. Part of the afternoon remained, so I made a little detour and drove by Mr. Spalteholz's house to show it to Jo Ann. I had a very good reason for this, because I wanted to give her an idea that someday we might like to own a home in that area. I told her that I had sold real estate in Australia, and that I could see the potential here. One could buy a house, clean it, fix it up, paint it, sell it, and then buy another one and do the same. By upgrading, one could finally have enough money to buy a dream house.

I drove back by a different route to enjoy the scenery. When we reached the city, Jo Ann asked me to stop by her hotel so she could change her dress. Then we went to dinner at the Fairmont Hotel, one of the most elegant spots in the city. When we got there, we went to the La Ronde Bar, which moved very slowly in clockwise rotation. It was a novel idea, and the bar attracted many patrons.

Before we entered the dining room, we browsed around and looked at the different displays in the hotel's swanky shops. Everything about the Fairmont was extraordinary.

For dinner we both ordered veal cutlet, which is similar to the Czech, viennerschnitzel. After our delicious meal, we sat in the lobby to enjoy the luxurious atmosphere and to discuss our plans. I had to work only a half-day on Monday, because that afternoon, there would be a company party. I had off Tuesday, Christmas Day, and Wednesday. Then I would be on the job Thursday and Friday—my last two work days in 1956.

Chapter 36

CHRISTMAS 1956

The Diviseks had invited us to spend Christmas Eve with them, so I gave Jo Ann some money to buy gifts for the children, a scarf for Ann, and a tie for Fred. I considered it our good fortune to have both Christmas and New Year's invitations from the Diviseks, since it spared me trying to figure what we would do on those two special holidays.

On Monday morning we all worked in the lab, but one could feel the Christmas mood growing. In the afternoon, production stopped, food and drinks were served, and Christmas carols were played and sung. It was a joyful atmosphere with many handshakes and hugs.

When I arrived home and phoned Jo Ann, she said she had done the shopping, and I told her that I would pick her up at 6:00 o'clock. As I was ready earlier than I expected, I went to visit Mr. Schadek. I knew he wouldn't have a very merry Christmas or a happy New Year, because he would be thinking of his wife. He was pleased to see me. He asked me why I hadn't come by for such a long time. I explained that my fiancee was here, and that I had been showing her the sights.

When Jo Ann and I arrived at the Diviseks, they greeted us warmly. Their home was beautifully decorated, and Jo Ann placed our gifts under their lovely Christmas tree.

Soon after our arrival, Ann served the dinner of viennerschnitzel and potato salad. She knew it was one of my favorite meals, and I was touched by her thoughtfulness. Because Fred's hobby was photography, he took many pictures.

After dinner, the children passed out the gifts. I was given two pairs of socks and a wallet. Jo Ann received a beautiful woolen scarf, which would be most welcome in the cold weather of New York City. The children were very happy with their toys. Fred liked the tie I gave him, and the tie clip from Jo Ann. Ann received a scarf from me and a pair of earrings from Jo Ann. After the distribution of gifts, I asked Fred to play a few Christmas carols on the piano. Later we cracked walnuts, a Czech custom.

While we chatted, the children played with their new toys. But it was getting late, so Jo Ann and I said good night. After all, we would soon be back for Christmas day!

This would be my second Christmas in the United States, and it was difficult for me to adjust to the American customs. Here Santa Claus gives gifts to children on Christmas, whereas in Czechoslovakia on St. Nicholas Day—December 6—children hang two stockings in their windows, and that is the night that Santa fills them. Parents put in chocolates, pencils, a few small toys, and a couple pieces of coal. The candy and toys are gifts from Santa as a reward for being good. The coal represents bad deeds during the year, and the children are told that if they behave the following year, St. Nicholas will not put in any coal.

The larger, more expensive gifts are given to children on Christmas Eve, and they are explained as gifts from Jesus. It is quite common that when friends send Christmas cards, they add the expression, "I hope you have a rich Jesus." That may sound a bit greedy or even sacrilegious, but it is part of Czech culture and has been so for centuries. The Three Wise Men's Day, called Epiphany here in the United States, is also celebrated on January 6 in Czechoslovakia.

When I was a young boy, three persons, dressed as the Kings, would walk from house to house. They sang a carol, "We three Kings are coming to you from a long distance to wish you happiness and health in the future." During the singing, one would come to the door and write in chalk K + M + B—meaning Kaspar, Melichior, and Baltazar. I will never forget that wonderful tradition.

On Tuesday, I picked up Jo Ann at her hotel at noon, and we went again to the Diviseks. Jo Ann brought a box of candy, and I had purchased a bottle of wine. Ann prepared another scrumptious Czech meal—pork, dumplings and sauerkraut. She really made us feel at home, and she did it with such obvious pleasure. I could see that she loved Jo Ann as if she were her sister, and everything was so natural between them. She was simply wonderful, and so was Fred. And they have remained so. I am still in touch with them after forty years. Their hospitality was as generous as the day before, and everyone was happy: talking, drinking, and eating. Fred liked to tease me, trying to Americanize me and correcting my English. I couldn't learn all the Christmas carols at once, because there were so many. But I loved to sing, and gave it a good try.

This happy evening had to come to an end. We couldn't thank them enough for such a wonderful Christmas. But when we left, I saw that Jo Ann was crying, and I realized that she must be thinking of her family back in Connecticut. This was the first time in her life that she was away from them at Christmas.

The next day I decided to take Jo Ann for more sightseeing. We stopped at Cliff House, which was at the edge of the Pacific. There was an enchanting view, not only of the ocean, but of a huge rock on which many sea lions were climbing, then jumping off into the water. It was very entertaining to watch them from the huge restaurant windows of Cliff House.

After brunch, we drove to Presidio Park and the surrounding area. At one point in the bay, we could see Alcatraz, which at that time was a prison for the worst criminals in America.

To complete our day, we went to dinner at Fisherman's Grotto, where I had my first job. I didn't have good memories of it, but I knew the food was delicious, especially the huge fried prawns. We enjoyed our meal and the decor, which featured all kinds of carved fish on the walls. We took our time and stayed there for quite a while.

Since I had to work the next two days, Jo Ann told me that she was going shopping for gifts for her family.

We were very busy at work the first day after Christmas. The holidays had slowed down production, and Joe asked me to work overtime to catch up. I didn't get home until almost 9:00 P.M. When I phoned Jo

Ann, we decided that it was too late to go out for dinner; especially since I had to work the next day. Jo Ann told me that she had received a phone call from Eric Lenhart that day, and that he had taken her for a ride to show her more of the city. I teased her a little, and asked her if she wanted to switch to him from me. She laughed, and said Eric wanted her to find him a Czech-speaking girl in New York.

I told Jo Ann that I would pick her up for dinner the next evening, and then we would go to the club again.

We went to dinner at the St. Francis Drake Hotel. It was quite nice, with a beautiful atmosphere and fabulous lobby. Afterwards, we found the Club unusually crowded. Eric and Felix Lenhart were there, and invited us to sit with them and another couple, Mr. and Mrs. Ludwig Salz, who were Czech immigrants. The conversation was in Czech, of course. When Mr. and Mrs. Salz learned that Jo Ann had been born in New York City, they marveled at her knowledge of the language.

Mrs. Salz inquired about how I had come to America, so I gave her the highlights of my journey. Then she invited us to their home for dinner the next evening, so they could hear the complete story. Mr. Salz told me that he'd had a brick factory in Stod, in the Black Forest near the German border. When the Communists took the factory in 1948, he and his wife had escaped across the border.

The next morning, I picked up Jo Ann and suggested that we go over the longest bridge in the U.S.A., the Oakland bridge, which had an eight-and-one-half mile span. From there we drove to the University of California at Berkeley, which had a large and beautifully-landscaped campus. It was a magnificent day for a drive, but we had to go back because of the dinner commitment.

Mr. and Mrs. Salz had also invited Eric and Felix. We had hors d'oeuvres and drinks, then Mrs. Salz served a delicious sauerbraten dinner. After we had coffee, we were invited to sit in the living room so that everyone could hear more of my story. After I finished, I asked Mr. and Mrs. Salz to tell us their own experiences, which they did. Mr. Salz said that when the Communists had seized their brick factory, early in 1948, it was not too difficult to cross the border. Refugees were leaving on trucks by the hundreds of thousands. As I well knew, a year later the Communists placed barbed wire obstacles and police stations around the border, and threatened to jail or shoot anyone that tried to escape.

Despite our exchange of grim tales, we had a most enjoyable evening.

On the way back to the hotel, I informed Jo Ann that Ann Divisek had invited us to go with them to Redwood City the next day to visit her brother, George Borovicka and his wife, Mabel. Jo Ann quickly agreed, since she loved Ann and Fred.

The next morning we went to the Diviseks, then the four of us took off for Redwood City, which was about thirty miles away. During the trip, Ann told us that her brother had served in Africa during the war, and had fought against the famous German general, Erwin Rommel. Ann said that George was very entertaining, whereas Mabel was very quiet.

When we arrived, the children rushed to greet their Uncle George. We were invited in and met Mabel, a slender blonde. George immediately offered us a drink. Because Mabel didn't speak Czech, the conversation was in English. They asked Jo Ann and me several questions.

I didn't want to go into my stories at length, and I made them as brief as possible. When I asked George about his experiences, he mostly talked about girls—all of whom he called "Bunny." Since he was a very good—looking guy, there had probably been many "Bunnies" in his life.

I didn't want to seem rude by conversing only with George, so I asked Mabel a few questions. She said she'd been born in Montana, although her parents were from Norway. I told her that one of my very good friends, Vlastik Kopyta, had emigrated from Hamburg to Tonsgerg and she knew the city.

The day went by quickly, and it was time to head back. Just before we left, Ann and Mabel had a lengthy discussion in the kitchen. In the car, we learned that Mabel had confided some worrisome news: George had recently seen a heart specialist because he wasn't feeling well.

When we arrived at the Diviseks' home, we didn't accept their invitation to come in, since we would be with them the next evening to celebrate New Year's Eve. I asked Jo Ann where she would like to go for our last dinner alone together. She suggested Fisherman's Grotto, explaining that seafood restaurants in New York just didn't have the same atmosphere. I thought back to scrubbing that kitchen floor-caked with prawns and noodles—but decided not to tell Jo Ann that she didn't know the half of it!

After the meal, I decided that we should discuss our wedding plans. I asked if she would choose the most suitable place and date. Jo Ann looked as if she was going to cry, then said, "I thought you'd never ask. I was getting nervous about our engagement, almost thinking that you wanted to call it off. Why did you wait so long?" I explained that I had first wanted to show her San Francisco, to make sure she would be happy living there after our marriage. Jo Ann replied that she liked San Francisco very much, but admitted that one worry was preying on her mind: Her parents would be very sad to have her so far away. However, Jo Ann said we could spend our vacations with them every summer.

After a long discussion on that subject, we finally set the wedding date—June 8, 1957. Jo Ann suggested that we be married at the Jan Hus Presbyterian Church in New York City. We drank a toast to that, and both felt very happy that it was settled.

I felt that a large hurdle had been crossed. We knew so little about each other, and, to say the least, our engagement had been hasty. But setting the wedding date was the final step. I took Jo Ann back to her hotel and sealed our decision with a kiss.

The next morning I picked her up and we drove to my apartment, so that Jo Ann could see where we would be living. I was relieved when it passed inspection! The apartment was small, with a living room, bedroom, kitchen, and bathroom, but Jo Ann was impressed with the large walk-in closet.

It was almost noon, so I asked Jo Ann where we should go for lunch. I explained that there weren't many restaurants nearby, and we would have to go downtown. Or, there was another possibility: I could make her "a professional sandwich" the kind I had made at Viking Foods. Jo Ann laughed and said she wanted to see what kind of a chef I was. I'd anticipated this might happen, and had gone shopping for groceries that morning. I offered pastrami on rye, ham and cheese on rye, or bacon and eggs. Jo Ann chose the pastrami, while I decided to have the ham and cheese.

Within a few minutes, the sandwiches were prepared. They tasted delicious, and Jo Ann smiled and acknowledged that I was a good "cook." After lunch, I played some of my records to create a happy atmosphere. We spent an enjoyable afternoon together.

Later I took Jo Ann to her hotel to change clothes for the evening. I bought some liquor for the party and picked her up at 7:00 P.M.

We received our usual warm welcome when we arrived at the Diviseks. Fred offered us drinks while Ann finished preparing a very tasty Czech meal of viennerschnitzel and potato salad.

After dinner we had coffee and dessert and awaited the arrival of 1957. Jo Ann was happy, but I could see some sadness in her eyes. She told me that my special friends, the Diviseks, were now her friends as well, so in addition to missing me, she would miss them, too. Since over five months would pass until we saw each other again, it would be lonesome for both of us.

After a few more drinks, midnight arrived. We all touched glasses and wished each other a happy, healthy New Year. We left soon after because Jo Ann had to get up early for her flight.

In the morning, we drove to the airport. Jo Ann had to board her flight thirty minutes before the plane left, so we didn't have much time to say good-bye.

On my return home, I felt better about what I had thought was a hasty decision in New York. Her visit to San Francisco helped erase my fears about marrying someone I hardly knew. I realized that our mutual Czech background, language, and culture would help us to have a successful life together. She and my Czech friends enjoyed each other's company. Jo Ann understood my interest in the Sokol Club, as she had the same interest in the New York Sokol Club. And she liked San Francisco, where I wanted to stay because of my excellent position with Recordak. All in all, I felt elated she had come. Now more plans could be made for our future.

Alone in my apartment, I tried to recapture my feelings about the seventeen days that Jo Ann was in San Francisco. I couldn't believe what we'd accomplished in such a relatively short time: all the traveling, all the visiting, sightseeing, and becoming better acquainted.

I couldn't wait to hear the Diviseks' opinion of Jo Ann. When 1 called them, Ann could only say complimentary things, telling me how fortunate I was to have found such a lovely girl. She also added that she liked Jo Ann as if she were her own sister, and was looking forward to the day when we would return after our wedding in June. Fred felt the same way.

I thanked her and Fred from the bottom of my heart for their hospitality and generosity, especially at Christmas and New Year's. Ann acknowledged my thanks and said they were very happy to have had our company, because it made the holidays more pleasurable for them. I felt very optimistic when I got off the phone, certain that 1957 would be the most wonderful year of my life.

CHAPTER 37

POST-VISIT TIME

LIFE RETURNED TO NORMAL—EXCEPT THAT MY FINANCES WERE VERY DEPLETED. From this point on I decided to save as much money as possible, because I knew that June would be an expensive month!

When I saw Jack Pilersky at work, I asked him what he and his wife thought of Jo Ann. He said they liked her very much, and that his wife had enjoyed their conversation about fashion and New York, where they had also lived at one time. Several of my other coworkers asked about my vacation, and I told them the big news that Jo Ann and I had set our wedding date.

On Friday, I went to the club, which was always the highlight of my week. Eric and Felix asked me about our New Year's Eve celebration, and told me how nice Jo Ann was. They congratulated me about our forthcoming wedding.

Then, I watched a volleyball game from the balcony in the gym. After the game the players came upstairs to have a drink, and the restaurant became very lively. I was pleased, because the restaurant was a very important source of revenue in keeping the club solvent.

Except for Friday nights, it was hard for me to fill my weekends, and I didn't want to always impose on the Diviseks. I had to find an outlet to take up my time. So, because Jo Ann had written that she needed more space in my apartment for her clothes, I decided to make some furniture. I looked for ideas, and in a magazine I saw a Swedish-type bedroom set, with a chest of drawers, a bureau, and a chiffonier with many drawers. I decided to make them after-hours at Recordak.

One thing that bothered me about making the furniture was that I had to stay so late at work, sometimes close to midnight. When I used the elevator to go down, there was frequently a man sleeping in it, obviously someone homeless or drunk. That worried me since the building was dark and empty. I began to use the steps instead of the elevator, but the situation was the same, because often some man was there also. I didn't report it, but became more cautious. Finally I finished my project and took the pieces to my apartment. In total there were twenty-four new drawers, hopefully enough space for Jo Ann.

Jo Ann and I were exchanging letters, and often I also called her. One night she told me that she'd made arrangements with Reverend Stefl at the Jan Hus Church for our June 8 wedding. She said that I needed to send a blood test certificate to the church. She also mentioned that she was extremely busy with the preparations: her wedding gown, and dresses for the flower girl, maid of honor, and bridesmaids. In a joking way, Jo Ann said I was lucky to be so far away and not involved in all those details.

I still reserved every Friday evening to go to the Club. During my next visit, I spoke to the president, Joe Malek, about contacting the soldiers at Fort Ord in Monterey to do a Czech program in the gym. I also told him that there was a Radio Free Europe station in New Hampshire, whose chief broadcaster was Jara Kohout, formerly an outstanding comedian in Czechoslovakia. I suggested that we contact him to present a program. Joe thought it was an excellent idea and suggested that we have the soldiers from Fort Ord do their program at the same time.

Despite my club activities, and occasional visits with the Diviseks, Mr. Schadek, and Bob, my weekends were long and lonely. On Sundays, I usually wrote to my brothers and sisters in Czechoslovakia. Occasionally, I also sent them packages of clothes that were given to me by my coworkers.

I discovered in downtown San Francisco a post office that was open twenty-four hours a day. I went there late at night with my packages. It cost eighteen dollars to send a parcel to Czechoslovakia, and since I was a postage-stamp collector, I decided to place many small-denomination stamps on the top, on the sides, and all the way around the packages. Then I wrote to my relatives and asked them to return the stamps to me in their letters. But most of the stamps came back very heavily canceled and were useless as collector's items.

I decided to take care of that. I noticed one postal clerk smoking a cigar, and asked him which nights he worked. From then on, I took my parcels to the post office on one of those nights. I would give the clerk a couple of cigars, and ask him to be kind enough to cancel the stamps very lightly, because they were for a stamp collector. It worked beautifully. He so carefully canceled all the stamps that they were returned to me looking just the way I wanted.

On Thursday, March 28, I phoned Jo Ann to wish her a happy birthday. She wished me the same, since mine was on March 30. I told her I missed her and gave her news about the Diviseks and my other friends she had met.

When I arrived at the club the next night, Joe Malek gave me some welcome news. He said that the choral director at Fort Ord had informed him they would be happy to present a Czech recital for us. We arranged the date and hoped that by then, we would also hear from Jara Kohout.

Because there were not many shows performed at the club, the hall was almost always used just as a gym. We decided to make the hall more presentable, and many club members worked many evenings to paint, clean, and decorate it. By now, Joe had received a favorable answer from Jara Kohout, so we would be able to combine the two performances.

Finally, the day came: a Sunday afternoon. Twenty-five soldiers arrived by bus from Fort Ord. Jara Kohout arrived in his own car with a friend who was a pianist. Neither the soldiers nor Kohout wanted to be paid, but we served them a traditional Czech meal, of viennerschnitzel, potato salad, beer, coffee, and kolace. The performers expressed their enjoyment of the lunch by applauding and thanking the ladies who did the cooking.

The hall was packed. Many people stood because we didn't have enough chairs; frankly, we didn't expect such a large audience. Joe Malek introduced the military chorus.

The choral director announced that the first song would be the Czechoslovakian national anthem—which was a combination of Czech and Slovak parts, sung in both languages. It went very well, and the group received a loud applause. This was followed by three lively Czech songs. Considering the fact these soldiers were non-Czechs, I was very impressed they had mastered the lyrics so well.

The next part of the program was the comedian Jara Kohout, who had escaped from the Communists and established a Radio Free Europe station in New Hampshire. Now he traveled all over the U.S.A. performing at Sokol clubs, and any donations he received went to Radio Free Europe.

When Joe announced him, Kohout received a long ovation. His first song was a favorite, "The Rabbit Paw," which was well-known throughout Czechoslovakia. The song ("Zajeci Pacicka," in Czech) tells a story that anyone possessing a rabbit paw would never have bad luck, because the paw is magic. It also advises a husband to keep a paw in his hand; this way, all the girls would love him, and his wife would never find out. Kohout's song—and his very presence—were so welcome that he received deafening applause.

After the performance, he came to the restaurant upstairs and thanked the organizing committee for continuing Czech culture here in the United States. Kohout said that he admired the spirit and activities of all the Sokol Clubs, and was proud to be a part of it.

The entire event was a huge success. Although admission was free, we received many generous donations that helped cover the expenses and maintain the club. We decided at our next meeting that we would send a donation to Radio Free Europe, since it informed Americans about Communist oppression in Czechoslovakia.

When I arrived at the club a week later, several members congratulated me on the successful program and suggested that we should do similar events more often. But now I was extremely busy painting and cleaning the apartment. There were only a few weeks left before my flight to New York.

Jo Ann phoned to say she had made an invitation list of sixty-five relatives and friends, including my sponsors, the Zacks. The reception would be at the Blue Sokol Hall in New York. She had booked a five-piece Czech band, and one of the musicians was her brother Jerry, who played the drums.

I told Jo Ann I intended to buy a new Chevrolet station wagon that I had seen priced at $3,400. I liked the car very much, but I knew I couldn't drive it to New York, because I didn't have enough vacation days; we planned to take our honeymoon trip cross-country after the wedding.

Between visits to the club, the Diviseks occasionally asked me to visit. I told them all about the wedding arrangements, including the fact that Jo Ann was planning to rent a tuxedo for the bridegroom—me!

Just to reassure myself about Jo Ann, I asked Fred and Ann if they thought I had made the right decision—to transplant a glamour girl from New York City to the West. It was on my mind constantly, and I felt the need to talk about it with someone who would understand. I couldn't find better friends than the Diviseks to put my mind at ease. They agreed I was doing the right thing, because my job was here. Ann told me they both liked Jo Ann very much, and couldn't wait until she came to San Francisco.

Because I knew my aunt and uncle, the Zacks, would be at the wedding, I wrote to ask them if they would lend me $500, explaining that I didn't have enough money to both buy a car and pay for the honeymoon. I also had to buy a few new clothes, and purchase my plane ticket.

A few days later, I received a letter from my aunt, who promised that they would bring the money to the wedding. I felt relieved, since I certainly didn't want to ask Jo Ann to loan me any money.

About a week before my trip, Jo Ann sent me an ad from a New York newspaper showing the same station wagon I wanted to buy. It was a bank repossession, and priced at $1,975. This was fine, but I was worried it would be sold before I got to New York. Well, I just had to cross my fingers it would still be there—but that seemed too good to be true.

CHAPTER 38

PRE-WEDDING TIME

FINALLY, THE TIME HAD COME FOR ME TO FLY TO NEW YORK. THE DAY BEFORE, I went to the Bank of America and got a bank check for $2,000. I also withdrew $200 in cash.

The next morning I took a United flight rather than TWA, since they had treated Jo Ann so unfairly with the reimbursement for her damaged luggage. Less than nine hours later we landed safely in New York, and I thought of Jack Pilersky. He would have lost a dollar had I taken out flight insurance in his name.

I took a taxi to the same hotel in which I had stayed during my first visit. I phoned Jo Ann, who asked me to come to her apartment. On the way I stopped at a florist shop and bought her a bouquet of gladiolas, her favorite flowers. It was good to see her, and I gave her a big hug and kiss. Over drinks Jo Ann told me about the nice good-bye party her coworkers at Bergdorf Goodman had given her. They had presented her with a beautiful gift: a gold disc on a chain, with inlaid rubies and marcasites on one side and her engraved initials, JAS, on the other.

We decided to go look at the second-hand station wagon the next day and hoped it still would be there. I told her I had enough money to pay cash for it, and perhaps we could haggle a little over the price.

I picked up Jo Ann at 8:30 the next morning, and we took the subway. The name of the dealer was Trylon Station Wagon Exchange on Queens

Boulevard. We entered the yard which was full of hundreds of station wagons—no cars, no trucks. And there was my dream Chevrolet, as advertised. Jo Ann advised me not to appear too interested, and we walked around and inspected many others. Then we returned to my dream car to take a closer look.

The car was clean inside and out, but the floor was scratched very badly behind the third row of seats, as if someone had been carrying heavy or rough objects in it. I looked at the odometer, and it read only 10,000 miles.

Soon a salesman approached us. I asked him if that was the wagon advertised and he said it was, at a price of $1,975. As Jo Ann and I had prearranged, I offered him $1,700 cash. He said the price was firm because the wagon belonged to the bank, so he couldn't reduce it by even $10. It was a repossessed wagon, and the bank got the full amount.

Well, my plan hadn't worked this time, but I agreed to buy it anyway. I said I would pay for it by check. He looked at the check and said, "Bank of America, $2,000. Sorry, I cannot accept a check for this amount. You'll have to give me cash. You can go to a nearby bank and cash the check."

I couldn't believe what I heard. The Bank of America was recognized as the largest bank in America, and he wouldn't accept its check! Well, there was nothing we could do, so we went to a bank the salesman had suggested. But when I presented the check to the teller, she told me she had to ask her supervisor. The supervisor returned with her and informed me that the only place I could cash it would be at the bank at the New York Stock Exchange on Wall Street. Since Jo Ann had a lot of last-minute details to take care of, I would have to go to the New York Stock Exchange alone.

We went to the subway station and traveled part of the way together; then I continued on to Wall Street. When I entered the huge bank, I couldn't believe its incredibly beautiful decor. I presented the check to the teller, and she said she couldn't cash it.

I had enough of this, and demanded to see the president of the bank. She pointed out his office, and I knocked at the door. In the office was a well-dressed man who asked what he could do for me. I told him of my difficulty in cashing my check. He requested some identification, and I showed him my California driver's license. He looked at it, took a small slip of paper, wrote O.K. on it, signed it, and sent me back to the teller. Finally, I cashed the check.

Now I was a bit nervous about carrying all that money in my billfold. I looked around to see if anyone was watching, and walked quickly out of the luxurious bank, half-ran to the subway station, and looked back to make sure I wasn't being followed.

I took the subway, then again half-ran to the Trylon Station Wagon Exchange. The same salesman saw me and was happy to learn that I had cashed the check. He asked me for my name and address and began to fill out a pink form.

When he finished, he told me there was a state tax, and the total amount would be $2,054. I wasn't too happy to learn that, but I gave him all the cash from the bank and paid him the extra $54. He counted the money and asked me to wait while a mechanic checked and serviced the car.

Finally the salesman told me to go to the service garage, where the car was waiting. He handed me the completed pink form, which showed the amount of the sale as $2,054. He signed it, but I couldn't read his signature, so he told me his name was Messner.

I went to the service garage and found the car washed, with a carpet covering the scratches on the floor. An attendant gave me the keys, and I left for 72nd Street, following the directions that Jo Ann had given me. I'd been so flustered that only after reaching her apartment did I realize that the back row of seats was missing. I sheepishly told Jo Ann about the seats, and that the car had cost more than we'd expected because I had to pay a tax.

When she saw the bill of sale, Jo Ann hit the roof. She said he should have itemized the bill to show the amount of the tax; otherwise, I would have to pay tax on the entire amount of $2,054. Jo Ann asked if I was hungry, but I hesitated, upset about the trick Messner had pulled. She said, "Would you like me to make you a bacon, lettuce, and tomato sandwich? Then we'll go back to that dealer. Because you have an accent, he took advantage of you and cheated you."

I was anxious to taste Jo Ann's sandwich, since she had never prepared any food for me. I didn't say anything, but I loved watching her as she assembled the ingredients. I was imagining how it would be in the future to finally have someone take care of my meals. I will never forget that feeling—and the sandwich was delicious!

After lunch, we were off to nail that crook. There was Mr. Messner in his office. Jo Ann immediately showed her temper and asked, "What kind of business is this?" She showed Mr. Messner the bill of sale. "Why did you include the tax with the price of the car? Now George will have to pay an extra tax because he's from out of state. And where is the missing third row of seats?" Then she said, "George, please give me two dimes—one to call the police and one to call my lawyer, Mr. Rosenberg." This was quite a bombshell for Mr. Messner. His face was red as a beet and he protested, "Wait a minute, Miss, don't get excited, there must be some misunderstanding." Jo Ann replied quickly, "Oh, yes, some misunderstanding. You noticed George's accent, so you thought he was a greenhorn from Europe and cheated him." She continued, "You better rip up that paper and make out a new one, itemized, or I shall report you to the police right now."

I guess Mr. Messner miscalculated this time. He took another form, but before he began to fill it out, he said he had to phone his partner. "John, did you remove the seats from the 1956 Chevy station wagon?" The reply was slow but undoubtedly "yes." Mr. Messner looked at me and asked, "Would you like to sell the seats? I will pay you $25 for each one." That made Jo Ann even more furious. She said heatedly, "You had better get those seats back here, and quickly." He told John to get the seats ready, then finished the new bill of sale, without a word of apology.

He instructed us to go to pick up the seats, but when we stopped in front of the garage, they weren't ready. John had put them away on the second floor, and had to get them down for us. When the missing seats at last appeared, I opened the tailgate and made him install them. Even then, he didn't apologize, because he was another crook like Messner. There was no good-bye from either of them as we drove off.

Then we were off on a happier errand: to pick up the wedding rings. The ring she bought for me cost $17 and fit perfectly. The ring I bought for Jo Ann was platinum to match her engagement ring and cost over $100.

Then we went to the same Czech restaurant where we had eaten on my first trip to New York. Jo Ann introduced me to Mr. Jinoch, the manager, who had known her for many years. He congratulated us and brought us wine for a toast.

I didn't know if it was customary in the United States, as it was in Czechoslovakia, that the groom wasn't supposed to see his bride on the day prior to the wedding. Jo Ann said we should keep that tradition, so I had the next day "off." I gave her a hug and kiss and said I would see her in the Jan Hus Church on Saturday at 11:30 A.M.

On Friday, my last day to be single, I decided to do a lot of walking to break in my new shoes. I also sent postcards to my sisters and brothers, and told each of them how much I wished they could be here in New York for my wedding.

CHAPTER 39

WEDDING TIME

FINALLY THAT HISTORIC DAY OF MY LIFE ARRIVED: JUNE 8, 1957. THE WEATHER was inclement, with a few sprinkles here and there. I walked to the church, where many guests were gathering. Since I was dressed as a bridegroom, some of them introduced themselves to me—uncles, aunts, cousins, and friends of Jo Ann's. I asked one of the cousins to take movies with my camera. Unfortunately, when I had the film developed later, only one part was good—outside of the church, when the guests threw rice at us for good luck.

To my great surprise, the church was filled. There were eight bridesmaids and a flower girl, and Jerry, my future brother-in-law, was best man. The organ played, "Here comes the bride," and I felt a lump in my throat as Jo Ann and her father came down the aisle. This was a very emotional moment. We stood in front of the altar as Reverend Stefl began the ceremony. He talked for a few minutes, reminiscing about the early years when he had often visited the Sytar family and watched Jo Ann and Jerry growing up. He stressed their good behavior, and Jerry's return from the war as a hero. It was all quite moving.

After this brief talk, Reverend Stefl asked us to repeat the marriage vows, and we placed rings on each other's fingers. Then he pronounced us man and wife and we kissed. As we left the church, a friend of Jo Ann's sang the lovely "Ave Maria."

Now my single days were over. In something of a daze, I took Jo

Ann's arm and we were off to our reception at the Blue Sokol Hall.

The hall was rather small and narrow, allowing only seven people to sit at the head table: the bride, groom, the bride's parents, the best man, the maid of honor, and the flower girl. I was a little uncomfortable that the Zacks were not seated with us, but I didn't say anything since it was "the bride's day."

I went to talk to my aunt and uncle, and they expressed a certain degree of disappointment about their seating arrangement. I explained that I had nothing to do with it and told them that if I had spoken to Jo Ann before, I certainly would have insisted that they be next to me at the head table.

During our discussion, my uncle said he had brought the requested loan of $500. He requested that Jo Ann come to their table, because both of us must sign a note. It was all right with me, but Jo Ann was surprised and asked me why she had to sign the note. I told her what my uncle had said: that if something happened to me, my wife would be responsible for the loan. Jo Ann agreed, we both signed, and my uncle gave me the envelope. I didn't even count it, since I knew it must already have been counted numerous times. My previous experience with the Zacks had shown me they were very careful with their money.

I thanked my uncle and assured him I would repay the loan with interest as soon as possible. Jo Ann left after signing the note, but I stayed to visit with the Zacks a bit to show my respect and appreciation for their help. They had given me the sponsorship required by the Immigration and Naturalization Service, and that I could never forget.

The meal was chicken with all the trimmings, and there was an open bar. Everyone was having an enjoyable time, and the hall was humming with conversations in both Czech and English. After we finished lunch, Jo Ann asked me to accompany her so that she could introduce me to everyone. I was asked many questions: where I was living, how we met, and when I had come to the United States. I didn't mind answering, but I knew I would never remember all the names of the people to whom I was introduced.

When we ended our tour at my aunt and uncle's table, they asked Jo

Ann why she had chosen such a small hall for so many people, and also why there wasn't good parking. Uncle said he was given a parking ticket and had to pay a $5 fine. I could sense that this didn't set very well with Jo Ann.

Very late in the afternoon, the band started to play—first very softly, just to maintain a nice atmosphere. Since I have perfect pitch and could play several instruments, I knew they were very fine musicians. This promised to be an enjoyable night.

It didn't take long before the bandleader announced that the first dance was for the bride and bridegroom. Then they started a polka, a lively dance I love very much. After a few rounds, I gestured at the guests to join us. Almost instantly, the hall was full of dancing couples. Just as was customary in Czechoslovakia, the band played three songs, and then paused to give the dancers a chance to change partners.

After a few dances, the bandleader announced that there would be the cutting of the cake by Jo Ann and me. The cake was beautiful, and Jo Ann told me she had paid the baker an extra five dollars to use only butter. She said she had attended numerous weddings, and the cakes without butter were not tasty. Sure enough, the cake was excellent.

As soon as the cake was cut, I asked the bandleader if I could say a few words. I wanted to do something for my aunt and uncle. I introduced them and thanked them for being my sponsors and helping me come to the U.S.A. I stressed the fact that without them I would never have had a chance to live in America. I asked the guests to join me in applause.

Then I pulled a little box out of my pocket in which there was a necklace I had bought for Jo Ann in San Francisco. It matched the jade and gold earrings I had bought when she was there for a visit. When I presented it to her, everyone applauded. Then the dancing continued.

Everyone seemed to be having a great evening, and with the drinking and dancing the mood got better and better. I talked to several of Jo Ann's relatives, and they told me they hadn't had such a good time in ages. I also danced with some of her friends to become better acquainted.

After a few hours, my aunt and uncle wished me happiness and asked me to write them from San Francisco. I thanked them again and said good night. Jo Ann had gone to change her clothes, and when she returned, I explained that the Zacks couldn't wait for her and had left. She said that she didn't like their urgency about signing the note for the loan, because it suggested they didn't trust us. I asked Jo Ann to remember that they had worked hard for their money and were from "the old school," so we should forget the incident and not let it spoil our day.

Jo Ann cheered up when I told her that many of her relatives had said how much they were enjoying the reception. The musicians had been paid to play for five hours, but now we saw a couple of men passing a hat to collect money for the musicians to stay longer. The bandleader announced the group would play until one o'clock in the morning, and they began another lively polka.

Shortly after eleven, Louella Ochs, the maid of honor, said that she would like to leave but had no transportation. Jo Ann was going to call and order a taxi, but I offered to drive Louella home. When I walked around the back of my car, I noticed a sign on the trunk, "JUST MARRIED," written on a tablecloth. I told Louella to take a look. She laughed and thought it was very funny that she was replacing the bride. I drove to her apartment, thanked Louella for her contribution to the wedding, and wished her good luck.

When I returned to the hall, the festive mood was still in full swing. However, Jo Ann and I decided to leave. We had a reservation at the Barbizon Plaza Hotel that night, and at the Roosevelt Hotel the following night. The Sytars were going to sleep in Jo Ann's apartment, and we told them we would be in Staffordville two days later.

On Monday, we arrived at the Sytars' home. We chatted about the wedding, the relatives they hadn't seen for a long time, and the reception. I listened patiently, but after a while, I excused myself and walked down to the lake. I was still trying to get used to the fact that I was a married man.

CHAPTER 40

POST-WEDDING TIME

WE HAD ARRANGED TO LEAVE FOR SAN FRANCISCO THE NEXT MORNING, because I had only ten days vacation time left. This gave us eight days to travel across the U.S.A. for our honeymoon trip—including a visit to Niagara Falls.

Now that I was married, I had to become accustomed to calling Jo Ann's mother "Mati" in Czech—but I called her father "Dad" in English. Both parents liked it. In spite of the fact they only spoke Czech at home, Jo Ann called her mother "Mom," and her father "Pop." The entire family was very close, as my own family had been in Czechoslovakia.

In the morning "Mati" prepared a tasty breakfast. Then, when we finished eating, she surprised me. She said she was happy to have me as another son, but I had to promise her that I would bring Jo Ann back East after one year. With tears in her eyes, she handed me a piece of paper on which she had written that statement in English. She asked me to sign it! I looked at the paper, startled. But because I didn't want to make the separation any harder I signed it, not having any idea what would lie ahead.

Now it was time to leave. This was the most difficult good-bye I had ever experienced in my life. None of our eyes were dry; it was as if we were at a funeral. We gave each other hugs and kisses, and walked slowly out to the car. Jo Ann and I waved-and left. This was the beginning of our new life.

It took a long time for Jo Ann to calm down, but after a while she felt better, and we concentrated on the trip. I gave Jo Ann the map, and put her in charge of navigating the route to Rochester, New York-where I wanted to see the headquarters of the Eastman Kodak, the parent company of my employer, the Recordak Corporation.

As we were approaching San Francisco eight days later, Jo Ann burst into tears. I understood, and told her to cry and let out the sadness of leaving her family.

Before we reached our apartment, I stopped at a florist shop and bought her a dozen beautiful roses. Then, at our front door, I took Jo Ann in my arms and carried her across the threshold. I gave her a big hug and kiss and said, "Welcome."

Jo Ann liked the city of San Francisco, she loved the Diviseks, and enjoyed our Fridays at the Sokol Club. But after a time, Mrs. Sytar started to write to her how much she missed her daughter. This guilt-inducing correspondence escalated until even Jo Ann's father wrote that if we didn't move to Connecticut, her mother would die of a broken heart.

Finally Jo Ann told me that we had to go. She said I could always find a job, but perhaps never a wife like her. She added that if I loved her enough, I would agree to live in the East.

I kept my promise—my signature on the paper—and we returned to Staffordville to make her mother happy.

I found a position at Linatex Corporation and worked there for two years. My next job was at Combustion Engineering in Windsor, Connecticut, where I worked for twenty-five years until my retirement in 1985.

Jo Ann's father died in 1966 at the age of 81, her brother died in 1977 at the age of 53, her mother died in 1984 at the age of 89. I lost Jo Ann to a heart attack in 1992. She was seventy years old. We had no children.

My quest for freedom has taken me from Czechoslovakia, to Germany, Australia and finally to the U.S.A. My life has been touched by many. People take freedom for granted. Life would change drastically should they lose it—fortunately, my dream has been fulfilled.